MORAL, CHARACTER, and CIVIC EDUCATION in the Elementary School

Edited by
JACQUES S. BENNINGA

Foreword by Kevin Ryan

TEACHERS
COLLEGE
PRESS

Teachers College, Columbia University
New York and London

Published by Teachers College Press, 1234 Amsterdam Avenue
New York, NY 10027

The following material is reprinted by permission:

Quotations in Chapter 1 from:
Schools of Tomorrow by John and Evelyn Dewey. Copyright, 1915,
by E. P. Dutton & Co., Inc., renewed 1943 by John Dewey and Evelyn
Dewey. Reprinted by permission of the publisher, E. P. Dutton,
a division of Penguin Books USA Inc.

Values in the Classroom by C. B. Volkmor, A. L. Pasanella, and L. B.
Raths. Copyright, 1977, C. B. Volkmor. Reprinted by permission of
author.

Library of Congress Cataloging-in-Publication Data

Moral, character, and civic education in the elementary school /
    edited by Jacques S. Benninga.
        p.   cm.
    Includes bibliographical references and index.
    ISBN 0-8077-3056-4 (alk. paper) : $43.95. — ISBN 0-8077-3055-6
(pbk. : alk. paper) : $22.95
        1. Moral education—United States.   2. Civics—Study and teaching
(Elementary)—United States.   I. Benninga, Jacques S.
LC311.M55 1991
372.83'2044—dc20
                                                    90-43424
                                                    CIP

Printed on acid-free paper

Manufactured in the United States of America

96 95 94 93 92 91 90   8 7 6 5 4 3 2 1

To Suzanne

Contents

Part V: Epilogue

Foreword

TOWARD the end of the 1970s, I helped organize a conference on moral education at the Ohio State University. At the time, the topic was not particularly fashionable. The bloom of the value-free 1960s that had lit up the values clarification movement was fading fast. A punishing review of the research on values clarification and cognitive developmental moral education, written by Alan Lockwood, had recently been published. And, while it dampened the enthusiasm for cognitive developmental moral education, it was a dagger in the heart of the values clarification movement. But still the issues of introducing the young to the moral life and to their moral responsibilities persisted and school teachers and administrators from across the Midwest came to the conference, hungry for directions and suggestions on what to do in their classrooms.

Lawrence Kohlberg came at my invitation. In the past, I had been critical of his theory and his suggestions for applying his work in schools. I thought his stages of moral development to be arbitrary and simplistic, his focus overly cerebral, and his suggestions for schooling impractical. I was particularly concerned by what I saw as the growing hegemony (at least, in university circles) of Kohlberg's view of what schools needed to do to help students attain moral maturity. And I repeated my complaints at the conference. In turn, Kohlberg chided me for what he saw to be my overemphasis on moral socialization, my focus on behavior, and the burden I placed on teachers—insisting as I had that they be moral exemplars and moral leaders. Kohlberg was, as usual, wonderfully open and accepting of criticism. For my part, as I recall it, I was pleased that, at least, he took me seriously!

After the conference we had dinner together and talked about the plight of children and the resistance of public schools to address the moral education of students in a serious and sustained way. But while we lamented the fact that schools were doing little in a conscious way to address these issues, we agreed that the moral education community, that is, the scholars and teacher educators who took the moral development of children as their domain of study and professional work, were not ready. We were saying, in effect, that if America's political leaders and elementary and secondary educators turned to the moral education community for guidance about how to put together specific programs to form character and to aid in the development of ethical reasoning skills, they would continue to be discouraged. The arena of moral education was a battlefield of antagonistic theories, strident dialogue, and competing instructional suggestions and practices. It was a good meal, but a depressing conversation.

In the dozen years since that event, the landscape has changed. For one thing, Lawrence Kohlberg is no longer with us. For another, many of his earlier ideas were modified or redirected. In addition, though, the crisis of our young, particularly of our urban poor, has deepened, and there is growing recognition that many American children, the children of the rich *and* the poor, are coming into adult life lacking a moral compass and the moral habits to regulate their own lives and to contribute to their communities. Public opinion polls attest to the deep concern of parents and of the general public about the conditions of youth and their recognition that schools do and schools should play an important role (along with the home and the church) in helping the nation's young achieve moral maturity. Political leaders from the left and the right are calling the schools back to deeper and more conscientious involvement in the moral lives of their students. And while the public demand seriously outstrips the moral education community's supply (or attempts to satisfy that demand), it seems to this observer that the situation is a good deal more promising than it was 12 years ago. This volume is testimony to my optimism.

In 1988 Jacques Benninga, the editor of and contributor to this volume, wrote a short piece for the *Kappan* in which he showed how the two strands of moral education could be woven together and how the war between the developmentalists, such as Piaget, Kohlberg, and Damon, and the traditionalists, such as Bennett and Wynne, could be negotiated and how each approach could contribute to the actual ground level work of moral education in schools. As such, the article was an ambitious declaration of what might be possible.

At about the same time, the American Moral Education Association, which had long been the seeming captive of Lawrence Kohlberg and his followers, held its annual conference in Chicago and made as its theme a dialogue between cognitive developmental moral educators and some of us who advocate a focus on character formation through more direct and external approaches. The conference was, by traditional standards, a great success (which means that participants, in general, went to the sessions, that there was no bloodshed, and that a book emanated from it).

And there were other encouraging signs. Many of us realized that one can beat a dead theory for just so long, and, lo and behold, values clarification bashing subsided. Also, the Department of Education's Office of Educational Research and Improvement (OERI), which had largely ignored the moral and ethical aspects of schooling, decided to hold a small conference to identify a research agenda in this field. Plans were drawn up for a Department of Education National Center for Civic and Character Education. And while the plans have yet to come to fruition, the very fact that moral education and character education were being discussed in these circles indicated both public support and confidence that a theoretical foundation for this work had evolved to the point where further research and curricular development would be efficacious.

It would appear, then, that moral education and character development have moved into a new stage. This new stage is characterized by a lowered tone among competing theoreticians and a greater willingness to learn from one another. Part of this new openness may have come from the triumph of sweet reason, but certainly it has been aided by the experimental moral and character education programs in public schools, programs such as that in the Clovis Public Schools (described in this volume) and the San Ramon Public Schools. These collaborative efforts between theoreticians and practicing educators have eschewed the typical one-right-way approach to what turns out to be complex human problems. Instead these projects have taken a very catholic approach, drawing on developmental theory here, social learning theory there, and feeding in the successful practice and craft wisdom of teachers and administrators. The results are much needed existence proofs.

In this fine book, Jacques Benninga has fulfilled the promise of his earlier article. He has brought together competing points of view and cast them in a light that shows how they can coexist and, indeed, reinforce one another. He has selected successful practitioners and given them a platform to make their work better known to others. But more than this, Benninga's book gives direction and hope to all of us—parents, educators, policy makers—that schools can have a significant impact on the moral lives of children.

Kevin Ryan
Professor of Education
Center for the Advancement
of Ethics and Character
Boston University

Acknowledgments

THIS book has been in the making for several years and many people influenced my thinking as the project took shape. I am grateful to Robert Howard, Suzanne Benninga, Richard Sparks, and Steven Lempel for their willingness to discuss particular ideas about content and authors, and I am particularly grateful to Professors Edward A. Wynne and Thomas Lickona, both of whom have become friends through this project and both of whom have provided support, conceptual as well as moral, when most needed.

I thank the California State University, Fresno, for furnishing me with a summer grant to complete the initial editing of the manuscript; Carolyn Pope Edwards who made suggestions as to the book's organization; and Kevin Ryan for his encouragement and support. My students at CSUF added unwittingly to the final text by providing feedback and commentary on the various chapters. I hope they learned from the experience. The staff of Teachers College Press have been most supportive. Sarah Biondello fought for this book and made its publication possible and Karen Altman's copyediting was excellent. The input of Brian Ellerbeck, my editor at TCP, and our long, critical cross-country analyses of certain issues added depth to the book. Brian painstakingly edited each chapter and improved the manuscript as it progressed, and I am grateful to him for it.

I owe a professional and personal debt to each of these people.

Introduction

CHAPTER ONE

Moral and Character Education in the Elementary School: An Introduction

JACQUES S. BENNINGA

ALL elementary schools offer students a formal curriculum, which includes instruction in various subjects and extracurricular activities. But in many of these schools, an informal, unwritten curriculum exists as well, focusing broadly on socializing students and preparing them for citizenship. That such a "hidden curriculum" exists was made clear more than 20 years ago by Robert Dreeben (1968), who stated that

> schools, through their structural arrangements and the behavior patterns of teachers, provide pupils with certain experiences largely unavailable in other social settings, and that these experiences, by virtue of their peculiar characteristics, represent conditions conducive to the acquisition of norms. (p. 84)

On a surface level, schools teach "norms" by insisting that students sit in their assigned seats, turn in their homework, finish their lunch, participate in class by raising their hands, behave courteously, dress neatly, and so forth. On a deeper level, children acquire norms through example and attitude assimilation. As the result of societal changes, norms that once were part of the hidden curriculum are today becoming part of planned school experiences as our society matures and becomes more committed to the concept of equal opportunity for all students. Thus schools throughout the southern states have become racially integrated as the result of the 1954

Supreme Court decision in Kansas, and handicapped children now have available to them a free, appropriate public education as the result of the 1975 Education for All Handicapped Children Act of Congress. In addition, today's schools have responded to other urgent issues, such as child abuse, sexual abuse, and the dangers of drugs.

According to Gutmann's (1987) definition, moral education is a conscious effort shared by parents, society, and professional educators to help "shape the character of less well educated people" (p. 19). That topics like sex and drug abuse, however veiled, are included in the elementary school curriculum is evidence that schools, in addition to parents, do indeed serve a moral educational function, even though specific *outcomes* are not always evident (e.g., what *do* we expect as the result of a sex education curriculum?). Increasingly, however, districts and schools are designing moral or character education programs as part of their formal curricula. They now have a public point of view; they take a public stand. Some of those important views and programs are considered in this book, because although their overall goal (to produce thinking citizens for a democratic society) is remarkably similar, their methodology is not. The purpose of this book, then, is to shed light on current methods of teaching moral and character development and to provide students and practitioners alike with examples of the possibilities that exist. To foster a fuller understanding of the issues, we begin our discussion with a bit of perspective.

A Debate

The founders of our democratic society and the formulators of its schools certainly believed that one of the central purposes of education was to provide training in citizenship and related responsibilities; for as Jefferson put it, "If a nation expects to be ignorant and free in a state of civilization, it expects what never was and never will be" (Padover, 1965, p. 74). Thus Jefferson, in his endorsement of a system of public schools, hoped that establishing such a system would elevate citizens to the moral status necessary to ensure good government (Wagoner, 1976). This theme, the education of the population for citizenship, is continued throughout major writings on American education. It was a central focus in the work of Horace Mann (Curti, 1959) and Henry Bernard (Brubacher, 1931) in the 19th century and permeated the progressive ideas of John Dewey (1974) as well as the essentialist ideas of William Bagley (1938), Arthur Bestor (1955), Max

Rafferty (1962), and the report, *A Nation at Risk* (1983), in the 20th century.

Today, more than ever before and perhaps as a result of the rising rate of juvenile crime, teenage pregnancy, drug use, and suicide, society expects help from the schools in instructing its youth in moral and civic ideals. What these ideals are, however, has never been a simple task to define. Edward Wynne (1982) lists America's central values as "persistence, tact, self-reliance, generosity and loyalty" (p. 1). Other authors include "hard work, social cooperation, delayed gratification and savings, order and patience, success in life through doing well in school, rational and scientific thought and achievement, and success" (Jensen & Knight, 1981, p. 86). Individual school boards around the country have attempted to define subsequent community values. For example, Salt Lake City has developed a Code of Ethics for teachers (Thomas & Lewy, 1982); Minneapolis schools have adopted an overall code of behavior for students, which includes a dress code banning punk or breaker clothes (Associated Press, 1985); and Fresno, California, has adopted nine values and character traits to be upheld by students and adults alike (Micek, 1987). These modern-day examples can trace their roots to continuing public concern over what has often been seen as a lack of quality academic and moral instruction (see, e.g., Bagley, 1938; Scott & Hill, 1954; and recent reports on education, such as Goodlad, 1984).

The problem for classroom teachers and school principals, then, is not to define the values to which students should adhere (school boards, relying on parents and community standards, have this responsibility in most cases) but rather to decide how to teach these values honestly and realistically. The question of *how* becomes for them more important than the question of *whether*, and the debate is as current as the problems facing today's society. Take, for example, the issue of AIDS.

The AIDS epidemic has killed more than 80,000 Americans in the past 10 years, and the Surgeon General has recommended that all children receive "AIDS education." Again teachers are asked to be agents of social change, in some cases by educating children with the disease and in all cases by educating children about it. The tough question thus becomes, What should young elementary school children know about AIDS, and what is the rationale behind giving them this information?

Young children have internalized a startling amount of misinformation about the disease. They worry, for example, that kissing a mother who works in a hospital or helping a friend who receives a cut might cause them to get the disease (Verniero, 1986). Direct instruction focused on how the disease is acquired and transmitted is indeed necessary to alleviate their fears.

The moral questions, however, go deeper. How should the school respond in an attempt to influence students' future behavior? Two broad approaches to this problem can be defined. Although both seek to educate with the goal of prevention, one advocates a direct approach to values whereas the other encourages more open-ended discussion, with decisions left to the students themselves (Benninga & Richardson, 1988). Which one to pick?

Teaching directly about AIDS means emphasizing established value standards set by adults to be transmitted to children. Such an approach is clear and purposeful. A prime example has been presented by the U.S. Department of Education in its publication *AIDS and the Education of Our Children* (Bennett, 1987). This booklet, a guide for parents and teachers, suggests four principles of AIDS education.

1. Help children develop clear standards of right and wrong.
2. Set a good example.
3. Help children resist social pressures to engage in dangerous activities.
4. Instruct children about AIDS. (pp. 9–17)

Some specific advice in the booklet tells parents and teachers that "children who firmly hold to the principles of appropriate moral and social conduct are less likely to act in ways that would place them at risk of becoming infected with AIDS. The most important determinant of children's actions is their understanding of right and wrong." Thus children should be taught "the importance of self-discipline and personal responsibility" (Bennett, 1987, p. 9), and concerned adults must help children counteract the negative peer influences "to engage in promiscuous sex and drug use" (Bennett, 1987, p. 13). The booklet further recommends that parents and teachers should teach children about AIDS, and that personal responsibility and restraint must be integral parts of this educational effort. The message of such instruction is clear—there are correct and incorrect behaviors, and, in the case of AIDS, the consequences of incorrect behaviors can be irreversible.

Advocates of the less direct approach to moral education about AIDS, on the other hand, advise that only through participation and discussion can students apply principles of autonomy and self-reliance. Rather than being unilaterally handed down by adults, these principles must involve students in personal decision making to be truly instructive. The goal of this approach, however, is the same as that of the direct approach, namely, the prevention of AIDS.

In many elementary school classrooms, however, children have little opportunity to discuss these very sensitive issues. Yet many educators agree that discussion is helpful to alleviate the confusion, distress, and fear that do exist in the minds of children and that incorporating information about AIDS in the normal program of health education is useful in helping children make their own decisions about their later behavior. A curriculum of this type would begin with "a little basic biology [related to living things and include] some basic information about communicable diseases and wellness. AIDS can be defined for young children as a very serious disease that some people get, a disease that's hard to get but that can be passed from one person to another" (Schall & Harbaugh, 1987, p. 27). By the middle elementary school grades, these educators suggest, children may be ready for specific AIDS lessons. According to the Sex Information and Education Council of the United States (SIECUS), because of the change of puberty, "preteens are very curious about sexual behaviors and need to be given accurate and basic information about what is meant by sexual intercourse, homosexuality, oral and anal sex" (Planned Parenthood, 1986). "It's better to be too early than too late," observes Joan Haskin, health administrator for San Francisco schools. "Kids need to know these things early, before they're involved in all the heavy emotion puberty brings" (Schall & Harbaugh, 1987, p. 27). Knowledge of the facts thus provides a basis for personal judgments about alternative behaviors.

As we can see by the conflict represented in the example above, advocates of both approaches share a common goal—the prevention of AIDS through education. Yet their procedures are distinctly different. Advocates of the direct approach to AIDS education call for adherence to a strict code of conduct necessary to maintain an orderly society and ensure the well-being of its citizens. For them the simple messages of "Say NO to sex before marriage" and "Say NO to drugs" serve society well, result in higher standards of morality and virtue, and will eliminate AIDS in the process.

Advocates of the indirect approach criticize this methodology. They argue that adolescents "clearly practice behaviors that put them at risk for AIDS: one-half of the boys and one-third of the girls in the nation's high schools have had sexual intercourse, starting on average at age 16 . . . [and] about 200,000 teenagers have used IV drugs"

(Schram, 1987, p. 7). These rates are on the increase, and the response to these statistics should not be reiteration of an unattainable moral standard but rather a realistic approach, focused on helping adolescents make personal decisions based on clearly articulated personal values.

A variety of educational programs about AIDS are either under way or in the development process. Which of these programs should be used in schools depends on our making a moral choice. Do we attempt to influence our children's value orientation through a directed program advocating restraint and higher moral standards? Or do we educate them to cope and adapt by providing a variety of alternatives and letting them make their own informed choices?

This dilemma is a recurring theme in American education, and reasonable people disagree over which approach is best suited to achieve the desired goal. During the early part of this century, contrasting methodological approaches were defined and subsequently implemented and refined that addressed this debate head-on. Their differences revolved around two central questions: (1) Should moral education be taught as a separate part of the curriculum (Pietig, 1983); and (2) should the values to be emphasized be those developed by adults and transmitted *to* the students directly, or should they be developed *with* the students through discourse and discussion? Stated another way, the ongoing methodological debate can be defined as an interaction between the product desired as a result of moral or character education and the process used in achieving that product (Benninga, 1988). This interaction is diagrammed in Table 1.1.

Changing Behavior—The Direct Approach

Teaching moral education directly can mean either devoting a specified time to emphasizing desired values or character traits or integrating these values or traits throughout the curriculum. This instruction can involve presenting concepts through examples or definitions, class discussions, and role-playing or through rewarding students for proper behavior (Jensen & Knight, 1981).

The McGuffey Readers (1920), used during the early part of the 20th century, offer an example of this direct approach. These readers presented stories and poems to teach academics as well as moral conduct and character building. The following poem from the fourth reader in the McGuffey series is illustrative and its lesson clearly is

Table 1.1 Products and Processes in Moral Character Education

		PRODUCT OF MORAL/CHARACTER EDUCATION	
		RELATIVISTIC THINKING	DEFINED THINKING
Educational Processes	CHANGING BEHAVIOR/ DIRECT INSTRUCTION		• Developing character traits • Instilling proper habits
	ENHANCING JUDGMENT/ INDIRECT INSTRUCTION	• Clarification of individual values	• Emphasizing democratic values • Stimulating higher stage thinking

designed to change behaviors of children; that is, one has to work for what one wants.

LAZY NED

"T'is royal fun," cried Lazy Ned,
"To coast upon my fine, new sled,
    And beat the other boys;
But then, I can not bear to climb
The tiresome hill, for every time
    It more and more annoys."

So, while his schoolmates glided by,
And gladly tugged uphill, to try
    Another merry race,
Too indolent to share their plays,
Ned was compelled to stand and gaze,
    While shivering in his place.

Thus, he would never take the pains
To seek the prize that labor gains,
    Until the time had passed;
For, all his life, he dreaded still
The silly bugbear of *uphill,*
    And died a dunce at last.

            (pp. 38–39)

The direct approach is advocated by many educators today. To them, standards should be clearly defined. For example, in an article on the problem of drugs on college campuses, Secretary of Education William Bennett (1986a) suggested that, "If a college is really interested in teaching its students a clear lesson in moral responsibility, it should tell the truth about drugs in a straightforward way. This summer our college presidents should send every student a letter saying that they will not tolerate drugs on campus—period. The letter should then spell out precisely what the college's policy will be toward students who use drugs" (p. 5, Sec. 2). Bennett concluded that "being simple and straightforward about . . . moral responsibility is not the same as being simplistic and unsophisticated" (p. 5, Sec. 2). For elementary schools, Bennett suggested that "every school should have a discipline code, making clear to children and to parents what the school expects of them. Then it should enforce that code" (1986b, p. 56).

This direct approach to teaching morality has been labeled Conservative Moralism by political philosopher Amy Gutmann (1987). The aim of the conservative moralist "is to teach children to behave morally. It is not the process but the result of moral education—moral behavior, not moral reasoning—that matters" (p. 57). The methodology used by these educators is not indoctrination but rather inculcation of democratic character through the moral example of teachers, peers, and other school personnel. This approach to moral education is still the most widely used methodology for teaching morality in American schools and is represented here in Part III by William Bennett, Edward Wynne, Richard Sparks, and JoAnne Martin-Reynolds and Bill J. Reynolds.

Enhancing Judgment—The Indirect Approaches

Other approaches to moral and character education are less direct and seek to help students define their own and others' values as well as the moral perspectives in themselves and others that support those values. The two approaches most illustrative are known as values clarification and cognitive moral education.

Values Clarification

The values clarification approach aims at helping students clarify "what their lives are for, what is worth working for" (Raths, Harmin, & Simon, 1966, p. 7). Students are presented with dilemmas and asked, individually and/or in small groups, to respond. It is expected that this procedure will help students define their own values and make them aware of others' values as well. Students proceed through a series of seven steps to clarify their values; these include prizing one's beliefs and behavior (steps 1 and 2), choosing one's beliefs and behavior (steps 3, 4, and 5), and acting on one's beliefs (steps 6 and 7) (Raths, Harmin & Simon, 1966).

Take, for example, the following selection from *Values in the Classroom* (Volkmor, Pasanella, & Raths, 1977). Students are asked to select from among 10 people 6 who will be admitted to a fallout shelter during World War III.

Suppose you are a government decision maker in Washington, D.C., when World War III breaks out.

A fallout shelter under your administration in a remote Montana highland contains only enough space, air, food and water for six people for three months, but ten people wish to be admitted.

The ten have agreed by radio contact that for the survival of the human race you must decide which six of them shall be saved. You have exactly thirty minutes to make up your mind before Washington goes up in smoke. These are your choices:

1. A 16-year-old girl of questionable I.Q., a high school dropout, pregnant.
2. A policeman with a gun (which cannot be taken from him), thrown off the force recently for brutality.
3. A clergyman, 75.
4. A woman physician, 36, known to be a confirmed racist.
5. A male violinist, 46, who served seven years for pushing narcotics.
6. A 20-year-old black militant, no special skills.
7. A former prostitute, female, 39.
8. An architect, a male homosexual.
9. A 26-year-old law student.
10. The law student's 25-year-old wife who spent the last nine months in a mental hospital, still heavily sedated. They refuse to be separated. (p. 1)

Through their participation in such an activity, students are taught a process of valuing that is value-free. There are no "better answers," and any response using the framework of the seven steps is as acceptable as any other. Clarification of values is thus left up to the individual student.

Critics of this approach claim that because of its controversial content, values clarification often offends community standards (Eger, 1981; Bennett, 1986b). They also believe that because of its relativistic process, it undermines accepted values (Ravitch, 1985), does not induce a search for consensus, does not stress truth and right behavior, and does not distinguish between morality as a generalizable system of norms and morality as a system based on personal preference or whim (Oser, 1986). Today even the proponents of this approach are in retreat (Harmin, 1988).

Dewey and Democratic Values

There are more reasoned indirect approaches to moral and character education than that of values clarification. Like the supporters of values clarification, advocates of these more reasoned approaches challenge the methodology of direct moral instruction. But unlike values clarification, their approaches do not attempt to be value-free; they assert the validity of values such as democracy and justice. In a system based on checks and balances, free speech, and protection of individual rights, they argue, Should standards be imposed *on* children in schools, or should standards of behavior come *from* the students through environments and exercises that stimulate higher levels of thinking? They question whether, if standards are imposed, children can ever fully integrate, fully understand, the rights and responsibilities of fruitful participatory citizenship. They believe that only through participation and discussion can students apply the rules and principles of cooperation, trust, community, autonomy, and self-reliance.

John Dewey, who believed that institutions (including schools) were either democratic from top to bottom or not democratic at all, addressed himself to these issues. He advocated *community* in the schools, a shared effort and participation by pupils in the planning process, without turning over to them the responsibility of curriculum making and without questioning the need for responsibility and authority in the administration of the school (Wingo, 1974). As early as 1897 Dewey spoke to this in his *My Pedagogic Creed*:

> I believe that the moral education centers on the school as a mode of social life, that the best and deepest moral training is precisely that which one gets through having to enter into proper relations with others in a unity of work and thought. The present educational systems, so far as they destroy or neglect this unity, render it difficult or impossible to get any genuine, regular moral training. (1988, p. 403)

Years later, Dewey and his daughter described experimental schools and systems in the United States to underscore this theme. One chapter in their book describes the public schools of Gary, Indiana, a city "made up principally of laborers in the steel mills and . . . 60 percent foreign born . . ." (Dewey & Dewey, 1962, p. 142). Students in Gary, in addition to their usual academic curriculum, were responsible for one hour daily of "application" time, which could be spent doing work for the school building.

> Thus an older pupil, studying stenography and typewriting or bookkeeping, might go to the school office and do an hour of real work,

helping one of the clerks. The boys in the fifth grade put in this time in tending the school storeroom. They take entire charge of the school supplies, check up all the material sent in by the board and distribute it through the building to the teachers and janitors. The records of the pupils in the different shops are kept by other pupils in their application time. Pupils also run a post office for the building, and the writer saw a sixth grade boy delivering salary checks and collecting receipts for them through the building.

The school lunchroom is conducted by the cooking department . . . student waiters serve the food they have cooked—real lunches to their fellow students, who pay a student cashier. The girls do all the menu planning and buying for the lunchroom and keep the accounts. They have to pay expenses and serve menus that come up to the standard set by the chemistry department, where they have analyzed food and made tables of comparative values. The result is steaming hot food, nourishing and well cooked, sold very cheaply.

Children who do this kind of work are not only learning arithmetic and bookkeeping, they are learning as well responsibility and reliability. They get an appreciation of what their school means, and are made wide awake to its welfare; they learn that they are the real school, identical with its interests.

Pupils who have made the furniture and the cement walks with their own hands, and who know how much it cost, are slow to destroy walks or furniture, nor are they going to be very easily fooled as to the value they get in service and improvements when they themselves become taxpayers. (pp. 146–147)

Thus, by involving students in the very fundamental processes of school life, the school environment fostered the values of hard work, cooperation, responsibility, and caring—values fundamental to informed participation in the larger democratic society. Modern-day examples, based on these ideas and those of Lawrence Kohlberg, described below, can be found in Part II of this book.

Kohlberg and Higher Stage Thinking

By extending Dewey's approach, Lawrence Kohlberg has greatly influenced the development of a cognitive-developmental theory of moral education. From 1958 until his death in 1987, Kohlberg conducted research on children's moral reasoning (1981, 1984), which resulted in a definition of six successive stages of moral reasoning and judgment, each with an underlying conception of justice and each more adequate than the preceding one for resolving justice problems (see Chapter 3 by Howard for a full description of Kohlberg's stage theory). Coupling the results of his research with Dewey's notion of the social nature of education, and with the philosophical construct of *duty* as described by Immanuel Kant and other formalist moral philosophers, Kohlberg and his colleagues have provided ideas for educators who desire to establish an environment consistent with students' emerging moral maturity.

Dewey's influence has been noted, but no description of influences on Kohlberg is complete without reference to Kant. Kant wrote about the duties and obligations of moral people. According to him, judgments about whether behavior is morally right depend on the reasoning behind the behavior; the consequences of that behavior are secondary. Truly moral actions, therefore, must be performed from motives of duty—from an obligation to act. But how can we know if our actions are truly moral in this sense? Kant's answer to this is that people are rational beings, that good people act in accordance with this rationality, and that reason must be something universally agreed upon. Thus if we followed this universally agreed upon reason, all good people would arrive at the same conclusions when faced with moral decisions. From this line of thinking emerged the famous Kantian categorical imperative—one should act in such a way that one could wish the outcome of one's action to become a universal law of human conduct (Hospers, 1961). In other words, Kant is saying that whenever we act voluntarily (e.g., helping a less fortunate classmate), we always act on a rule that can be formulated (e.g., one should help others in need). These rules become moral rules if and only if one would be willing to see his or her rule acted on consistently by everyone who is in a similar situation, even if he or she turned out to be on the receiving end (Frankena, 1963, p. 25). Thus not helping a classmate in need because he or she is not well liked would be a violation of the rule just created.

In applying these ideas to education, Kohlberg stated that as individuals move upward through his stages of more adequate moral thinking, the moral perspectives they become cognitively capable of integrating become increasingly broader. Thus whereas younger children, dominated by moral thinking at the lower stages, evaluate their own actions only as to the effects on themselves, students at the higher stages become increasingly better at taking the perspective of others. Their thinking becomes more reversible; that is, they become better able to put their thinking into the perspective of how others may think about the same issues and to relate others' thinking to their own. Therefore they become more cognitively capable of "trading places" with the perspectives of others. This increasingly elaborated cognitive ability to understand others leads to more adequate decisions and can be enhanced by what Kohlberg (1981) called exercises in "moral musical chairs" (p. 199), where decisions are made only after a consideration of all pertinent points of view. Thus when presented with dilemmas calling for a moral solution, students at successive stages of moral judgment evaluate possible solutions more objectively, creating more sophisticated universal rules to guide their own behavior. Through experiences of this kind, students can be aided to become more morally mature.

Hence, its critics notwithstanding, Kohlberg's theory of moral judgment is not relativistic or morally neutral. In fact, it clearly delineates higher order thinking and behavior as better (more adequate) than thinking at the lower stages, and it postulates that higher order thinking can be stimulated through focused discussions of moral issues and dilemmas found both in academic content (e.g., good literature and history) and in naturally occurring classroom interactions (see Chapter 4, Part II). In this sense, the *process* for moral education advocated by the Kohlbergians is not altogether different from that used by advocates of values clarification, but the *product* (more adequate moral thinking) certainly is.

Gutmann (1987) calls this indirect approach to moral education Liberal Moralism (p. 59), stating that its aim is the creation in children of *moral autonomy*, the respect for moral principles rather than established moral authority. This approach is fully described in Part II by Robert Howard, Thomas Lickona, Ethel Sadowsky, and Robert Weintraub.

Organization of the Book

The purpose of *Moral, Character, and Civic Education in the Elementary School*, then, is to explore these and other options for moral education. Although major attention is devoted to the two broad approaches outlined above, other curricular efforts are also described, all of which attempt to help students grow into informed citizens capable of shaping the future of democracy. We have come far since Noah Webster admonished his contemporaries in the 18th century that "the only practical method to reform mankind is to begin with children, to banish, if possible, from their company every low-bred, drunken, immoral character" (Webster, 1790/1965, p. 63).

Society is too complex for this simplistic solution, but we are not ready either to present children with *all* the possible options that may be available (e.g., racism, sexism, persecution) and allow them to choose freely from among them. Society as we know it would not benefit from our efforts. The answer for the public schools lies somewhere in between.

Thus our process of rational exploration begins with a discussion of children's thinking. Larry Nucci (Chapter 2) furthers the discussion presented here by distinguishing between children's conceptions of morality and social values and relating those types of thinking to educational programs.

Parts II and III, respectively, explore in depth the indirect and direct approaches. Part II begins with an overview of the cognitive-developmental theory of Lawrence Kohlberg by Robert Howard (Chapter 3) and connects that theory to primary education. In Chapter 4, Thomas Lickona gives teachers a rationale and specific strategies consistent with Kohlberg's theory. Chapters 5 and 6, by Ethel Sadowsky and Robert Weintraub, respectively, describe elementary school programs that are now implementing that theory.

Part III addresses the direct, morally conservative, approach to moral education. William Bennett (Chapter 7) makes a plea for character education and offers a rationale for it. In Chapter 8, Edward Wynne applies this rationale at the elementary school level and provides specific strategies for character education in relation to a school's academic program. Chapters 9 and 10, by JoAnne Martin-Reynolds and Bill Reynolds and by Richard Sparks, describe school programs, both rural and urban, as they relate to the formation of character.

Part IV contains four chapters that address various curricular programs related to enhancing democratic values in our youth. Chapters 11 and 12 by Alita Letwin and Carolyn Pereira describe national curriculum projects with an emphasis on making American law understandable to children. Letwin outlines the programs of the Law in a Free Society Project and Pereira the work of the Constitutional Rights Foundation. Next, James Fox, Mary McEvoy, and Robert Day (Chapter 13) describe a newly developed program to enhance the socialization skills of children receiving special education, and Robert Valett (Chapter 14) tells how and why peace education is a legitimate curricular focus for the elementary school. Finally, in Chapter 15 I attempt to synthesize the various perspectives and programs presented, delineating some common ground; then I describe a program, with evaluation instruments, for use by districts seeking ways to acknowledge schools that offer worthy programs in moral or character education. With this background, school officials and teachers will have available to them philosophically consistent choices as they begin or refine efforts to offer students more meaningful programs.

References

Associated Press. (1985, March 29). Students protest dress codes. *Fresno Bee,* p. A9.

Bagley, W. C. (1938). An essentialist platform for the advancement of American education. *Educational Administration and Supervision, 24,* 241–256.

Bennett, W. J. (1986a, July 15). Drugs and college don't, shouldn't mix. *Los Angeles Times,* part 2, p. 5.

Bennett, W. J. (1986b). *First lessons: A report on elementary education in America.* Washington, DC: U.S. Government Printing Office.

Bennett, W. J. (1987). *AIDS and the education of our children.* Washington, DC: U.S. Department of Education.

Benninga, J. S. (1988). An emerging synthesis in moral education. *Phi Delta Kappan, 69*(6), 415–418.

Benninga, J. S., & Richardson, V. (1988). Young children and AIDS instruction: Practical and moral questions about education. *Ethics in Education, 7*(4), 4–6.

Bestor, A. E. (1955). *The restoration of learning.* New York: Knopf.

Brubacher, J. S. (1931). *Henry Bernard on education.* New York: McGraw Hill.

Curti, M. (1959). *The social ideas of American educators.* Totowa, NJ: Littlefield, Adams.

Dewey, J. (1974). *The school and society.* Chicago: University of Chicago Press.

Dewey, J. (1988). My pedagogic creed. In K. Ryan & J. M. Cooper (Eds.), *Kaleidoscope: Readings in education* (5th ed., pp. 401–407). Boston: Houghton Mifflin.

Dewey, J., & Dewey, E. (1962). *Schools of tomorrow.* New York: E. P. Dutton.

Dreeben, R. (1968). *On what is learned in school.* Reading, MA: Addison-Wesley.

Eger, M. (1981). The conflict in moral education: An informal case study. *The Public Interest, 63,* 62–80.

Frankena, W. K. (1963). *Ethics.* Englewood Cliffs, NJ: Prentice-Hall.

Goodlad, J. (1984). *A place called school.* New York: McGraw Hill.

Gutmann, A. (1987). *Democratic education.* Princeton, NJ: Princeton University Press.

Harmin, M. (1988). Value clarity, high morality: Let's go for both. *Educational Leadership, 45,* 24–27.

Hospers, J. (1961). *Human conduct: An introduction to the problems of ethics.* New York: Harcourt, Brace, and World.

Jensen, L. C., & Knight, R. S. (1981). *Moral education: Historical perspectives.* Lanham, MD: University Press of America.

Kohlberg, L. (1981). *The philosophy of moral development: Moral stages and the idea of justice.* New York: Harper and Row.

Kohlberg, L. (1984). *The psychology of moral development: The nature and validity of moral stages.* New York: Harper and Row.

Micek, P. (1987). Values education in Fresno Unified Schools. Unpublished monograph. Fresno, CA.

McGuffey's Fourth Eclective Reader. (1920). New York: H. H. Vail.

National Commission on Excellence in Education. (1983). *A nation at risk.* Washington, DC: U.S. Government Printing Office.

Oser, F. K. (1986). Moral education and values education: The discourse perspective. In M. C. Wittrock (Ed.), *Handbook of research on teaching* (3rd ed., pp. 917–941). New York: Macmillan.

Padover, S. K. (1965). *Thomas Jefferson and the foundations of American freedom.* Princeton, NJ: D. Van Nostrand.

Pietig, J. (1983). Values and morality in early 20th century elementary schools: A perspective. *Social Education, 47,* 262–265.

Planned Parenthood. (1986). Age guidelines for talking to children about AIDS. [Adapted from the pamphlet, *How to talk to your children about AIDS*]. Washington, DC: Sex Information and Education Council of the United States.

Rafferty, M. (1962). *Suffer, little children.* New York: Signet.

Raths, L. E., Harmin, M., & Simon, S. B. (1966). *Values and teaching.* Columbus, OH: Charles E. Merrill.

Ravitch, D. (1985). *The schools we deserve: Reflections on the educational crises of our times.* New York: Basic Books.

Schall, J., & Harbaugh, M. (1987, September). Teaching children about AIDS. *Instructor.*

Schram, N. R. (1987, December 15). What teens don't know can kill. *Los Angeles Times,* part 2, p. 7.

Scott, C. W., & Hill, C. M. (Eds.). (1954). *Public education under criticism.* New York: Prentice-Hall.

Thomas, M. D., & Lewy, R. (1982). Education and moral conduct: Rediscovering America. In E. A. Wynne (Ed.), *Character policy: An emerging issue* (pp. 23–28). Washington, DC: University Press of America.

Volkmor, C. B., Pasanella, A. L., & Raths, L. E. (1977). *Values in the classroom.* Columbus, OH: Charles E. Merrill.

Verniero, J. C. (1986, December). Teaching children about AIDS. *Education Digest.*

Wagoner, J. L. (1976). *Thomas Jefferson and the education of a new nation.* Bloomington, IN: Phi Delta Kappa Educational Foundation.

Webster, N. (1965). On the education of youth in America. In F. Rudolph (Ed.), *Essays on education in the early republic* (pp. 43–77). Cambridge, MA: Harvard University Press. (Original work published 1790)

Wingo, G. M. (1974). *Philosophies of education: An introduction.* Lexington, MA: D. C. Heath.

Wynne, E. A. (Ed.). (1982). *Character policy: An emerging issue.* Washington, DC: University Press of America.

CHAPTER TWO

Doing Justice to Morality in Contemporary Values Education

LARRY P. NUCCI

THE resurgence of interest in moral education stimulated by proponents of traditional values reopens a basic question. Is it possible to define a set of moral values that can serve as the basis for education in a pluralistic society? At the level of public discourse, people seem to disagree about what constitutes morality. Furthermore, the intrusion into moral education by religiously affiliated groups such as the self-described Moral Majority has raised new questions regarding whether public schools can teach morality without also promoting religion. In such a context it would come as little surprise if, despite all the hoopla and edited books on the subject, schools and teachers should choose to keep moral education at arms length.

My purpose in this chapter is to contribute to the clarification of these issues and to offer public schools a basis upon which to begin to construct defensible programs of moral education. It is my view that much of the current public disagreement about morality is not about what is moral but about what is "proper." Recent research in the area of social development indicates great consistency in the ways in which children and adults identify matters of morality (Turiel, 1983). This overall agreement becomes apparent when one distinguishes individuals' conceptions of morality from other forms of social values such as societal convention.

In other places I have presented research on the teaching implications of this distinction between morality and other social values (Nucci, 1989). My focus here, however, is not so much on educational practice as on the aims of values education in light of what we now know about children's social development. In this context we will take up the issue of the relation between morality and religious rules, and consider the relation between morality and such controversial aspects of personal behavior as sexuality and drug use.

Distinguishing Between Morality and Convention

To begin consideration of these issues, we turn to the distinction between matters of morality and societal convention. Children in any society need to learn to conform to a number of social rules if they are to become participants in the culture, a point frequently made by traditional educators (Ryan, 1989) and something we will return to later in this chapter. Among the rules that children in our society are expected to learn are such things as that certain classes of adults (e.g., teachers and doctors) are addressed by their titles and that males and females use separate restroom facilities. These are examples of social conventions. Conventions are the agreed-upon uniformities in social behavior determined by the social system in which they are formed (Turiel, 1983). Conventions are arbitrary because there is nothing inherently right or wrong about the actions they define; for example, children could just as easily refer to their teachers by first names. Through accepted usage, however, these standards serve to coordinate the interactions of individuals within social systems by providing them with a set of expectations regarding appropriate behavior. In turn, the matrix of social conventions and customs is an element in the structuring and maintenance of the general social order. Thus social conventions are based on underlying conceptions of social organization.

The moral domain refers to concepts of justice, human welfare, and derivative rights. In contrast with conventions, moral considerations are not arbitrary but stem from factors intrinsic to actions: consequences such as harm to others. Although moral prescriptions (i.e., "It is wrong to hurt others") are an aspect of social organization, they are determined by factors inherent in social relationships as opposed to a particular form of social, cultural, or religious structure (Nucci, 1985; Turiel, 1983; Turiel, Nucci, & Smetana, 1988).

This distinction between morality and convention is nicely illustrated by the following example (collected during the research for Nucci, Turiel, & Encarnacion-Gawrych, 1983) and taken from an interview with a 4-year-old girl regarding her perceptions of spontaneously occurring transgressions at her preschool (Turiel, 1983, p. 49).

> MORAL ISSUE: *Did you see what happened?* Yes. They were playing and John hit him too hard. *Is that something you are supposed to do or not supposed to do?* Not so hard to hurt. *Is there a rule about that?* Yes. *What is the rule?* You're not to hit hard. *What if there were no rule about hitting hard, would it be all right to do then?* No. *Why not?* Because he could get hurt and start to cry.
>
> CONVENTIONAL ISSUE: *Did you see what just happened?* Yes. They were noisy. *Is that something you are supposed to or not supposed to do?* Not do. *Is there a rule about that?* Yes. We have to be quiet. *What if there were no rule, would it be all right to do then?* Yes. *Why?* Because there is no rule.

Research on the Moral-Conventional Distinction

Although similar distinctions between morality and convention can be found in philosophy (Lewis, 1969; Dworkin, 1978) and sociology (Gerth & Mills, 1970), they have not generally been made in values education. Traditional values educators such as Wynne (Chapter 8) hold that moral values are established by society. They treat all values including morality as matters of custom and convention to be inculcated in children as a part of what they refer to as character education. The kind of distinction drawn here is also at variance with accounts (Piaget, 1932; Kohlberg, 1984) that have had the greatest impact on developmental approaches to moral education, such as the ones outlined by Howard and Lickona (Chapters 3 & 4). Proponents of the earlier views hold that only at the highest stages of moral development can morality (justice) be differentiated from and displace convention as the basis for moral judgments. Over the past 15 years, however, more than 30 published accounts have reported research demonstrating that morality and convention are differentiated at very early ages and constitute distinct conceptual and developmental domains. These studies have been recently summarized in Turiel, Killen, and Helwig (1987).

Four major forms of evidence have been offered in support of the moral-conventional distinction. First, interview studies have reported that subjects as young as 2½ years differentiate between moral and conventional issues. [See Smetana & Braeges (1987) for research on the youngest subjects.] These studies have found that subjects view moral transgressions (e.g., hitting and hurting, stealing personal property, slander) as wrong irrespective of the presence of governing rules, whereas conventional acts (children's addressing teachers by first names, women's wearing pants, adults' engaging in premarital sex) are viewed as wrong only if they are in violation of an existing standard. We saw an example of this sort in the excerpt from the interview with the 4-year-old girl presented earlier. Interview studies have also found that individuals view conventional standards as alterable but moral prescriptions as universal and unchangeable.

The second form of evidence comes from observational studies of children's and adolescents' social interactions in family, school, and playground contexts (see Nucci, 1985; Smetana, 1989; Turiel et al., 1987). These studies have reported that the forms of social interactions in the context of moral events differ qualitatively from interactions in the context of conventions. It was found that children's and adults' responses to events in the moral domain focus on features intrinsic to the acts (e.g., the harm or justice created), whereas responses in the context of conventions focus on aspects of the social order. The general pattern of results reported in the interview and observational studies has been replicated with subjects in other cultures (Hong Kong—Song, Smetana, & Kim, 1987; Indonesia—Carey & Ford, 1983; Nigeria—Hollos, Leis, & Turiel, 1986; U.S. Virgin Islands—Nucci et al., 1983), indicating that the distinction between morality and convention is not confined to subjects reared in Western societies.

The third piece of evidence comes from developmental studies examining age-related changes in children's moral and conventional judgments. These studies have reported that concepts in the moral and conventional domains follow distinct developmental patterns. The sequence of changes observed in the moral domain indicates that as children develop, they form increased understandings of benevolence, equality, and reciprocity (Damon, 1977, 1980; Enright, Franklin, & Manheim, 1980; Irwin & Moore, 1971; Lapsley, 1982). In the conventional domain development entails transformations in the child's underlying conceptions of social organization and moves toward an understanding of convention as a basis of social systems and as important for coordinating social interactions (Turiel, 1983).

Although very young children have an intuitive grasp that actions such as hitting and stealing are prima facie wrong, theirs is a rather primitive notion of justice and the rights of others. For example, although young children view it as wrong to keep all of the classroom toys to oneself and not share any of them with other children (Smetana, 1981), preschoolers think it is quite all right to keep all of the favored toys to oneself as long as one shares the remainder (Damon, 1977, 1980). With development, the 4-year-old's premise—that one should satisfy one's own wishes before considering the needs of others—is replaced by the idea that distributive decisions should be based on strict equality or reciprocity—everybody should get an equal share. This strict reciprocity is replaced in turn by a recognition that there can be multiple valid claims to justice by different individuals and that persons with special needs, the poor or the handicapped, deserve special consideration (Damon, 1977, 1980; Enright et al., 1980).

As with morality, young children have an intuitive grasp of societal conventions and by age 6 have considerable knowledge of what society expects in the way of appropriate behavior. However, the societal functions of conventions are usually quite complex, and even when children have learned what is "expected," they do not fully understand the reasons why such behaviors are considered reasonable and right. Conceptions of social convention progress through seven developmental levels (Turiel, 1983). Development follows an oscillating pattern between periods affirming the importance of convention and phases negating it. This oscillation indicates the difficulty children have in accounting for the function of arbitrary social norms and illustrates the slow process of reflection and construction that precedes the older adolescent's understanding of convention as important to maintaining the social system.

The fourth piece of evidence in support of the distinct domains hypothesis was provided by an intervention study (Nucci & Weber, in press) examining whether educational practices that differentially address the development of moral and conventional concepts will be more effective in promoting their development than practices that treat these forms of social knowledge as the same. In the study, eighth-grade students engaged in small-group discussions and wrote essays regarding moral and social conventional issues that were drawn from their course materials. Students were assigned to one of three conditions. In the first, the convention-only condition, students were directed in their small-group discussions and essays to treat all issues as if they were matters of convention. Emphasis was on the norms involved and their function in structuring society and maintaining social order. In the second, the moral-only condition, students were directed to treat all issues as if they were matters of morality and were asked to consider their justice and welfare implications. In the third, the domain-differentiated condition, the focus of discussions and essays was concordant with the domain of the issues being studied. That is, moral issues were discussed in moral terms, and conventional issues were discussed in terms of normative regulation and social order.

At the end of the 7-week instructional period subjects were assessed for moral development level by means of the Defining Issues Test "P" score (Rest, 1979). Findings were that students in the moral-only and in the domain-differentiated conditions had significantly higher moral development scores than those in the convention-only condition. With regard to development in the conventional domain, the outcome was the inverse. Students in the convention-only and in the domain-differentiated conditions demonstrated significantly higher levels of development in the conventional domain than did those in the moral-only condition. If it were the case that normative/moral issues formed a single conceptual system, then raising students' level of understanding in one area (e.g., convention) should have resulted in a corresponding increase in their conceptual level in the other (i.e., morality). If, on the other hand, morality and convention form different conceptual systems, then one would expect the results obtained in this study.

Domain Overlap

At this point the thoughtful reader is likely to be puzzled by what appears to be a contradiction between the data and theory just summarized and the reader's own knowledge of issues that seem to overlap our definitions of morality and convention. For example, most Americans have stood in line waiting to buy movie tickets. This behavior is clearly a social convention in that one can well imagine an alternative arrangement that would meet the same purpose. On the other hand, anyone who has lined up only to have someone cut in recognizes that queueing, by establishing turn taking, serves the moral function of distributive justice.

Early critics of the domain model (Rest, 1983) argued that such instances of overlap falsified the claim that morality and convention constitute distinct areas of knowledge. Those criticisms, however, reflected an incomplete understanding of the model. The existence of analytically distinct structures of social knowledge does not preclude their conjoining or coordinating in reasoning about social events (Turiel et al., 1987). In such cases understanding the issue is a function of the person's level of development in each domain, his or her awareness of the social norms involved, and the manner in which the individual coordinates (or fails to coordinate) both the moral and conventional features considered.

The picture of social reasoning that emerges from the distinct domains view indicates that we cannot take a global approach to values education. Indeed our current understanding of the domain nature of social knowledge is consistent with reinterpretation of earlier global theories of social development, such as Kohlberg's stages of moral development (see Figure 3.1), as an approximation of the age-related changes in the development of domain coordinations. Because Kohlberg (1984) assumed that moral development entails the progressive differentiation of moral (justice) from nonmoral (conventional) considerations in moral decision making, he assessed moral development by asking individuals to resolve dilemmas in which someone's personal needs were in conflict with social norms or the law. The resulting stage descriptions of individuals' reasoning about such multidimensional issues thus reflect developmental changes in concepts of both morality and convention. For example, Stage 4 (conventional) moral reasoning as described in the Kohlberg system reflects the emergence in middle to late adolescence of understandings in the *conventional* domain that social norms are constituent elements of social systems. Although these age-typical integrations are captured by Kohlberg's stage descriptions, they do not represent the full range of socio-moral decision-making patterns that individuals present. For example, recent research conducted by the Kohlberg group (Kohlberg, 1984) shows that individuals at all points in development may respond to Kohlberg's moral dilemmas by reasoning from a perspective of either rules and authority or justice and human welfare. From my point of view, such within-stage variation can be accounted for only by recognizing that the Kohlberg tasks generate reasoning employing knowledge from more than one conceptual system.

Morality and Religion

If even young children differentiate between actions in the moral and conventional domains and reason differently about the two, then moral or values education should reflect this distinction. One obvious implication is that we may now be able to identify in a nonarbitrary way the core values that would comprise the focus of moral education. Perhaps the most controversial aspect of such a claim is whether morality can be defined independent of religious values. The current request by fundamentalists to put God and prayer back into the classroom derives from an enduring belief shared by a broad spectrum of religious people that morality and religion are inseparable (Barth, 1957; Bonhoeffer, 1955). The constitutional issues this request raises for moral education have already been alluded to and are beyond the scope of this chapter. What we can bring to the public debate are our findings from research with devout Christian and Jewish children that address whether children's concepts of morality are independent of religion (Nucci, 1985, 1989).

Moral and Conventional Values as Seen by Christian Fundamentalists

Subjects in our first study with Christian fundamentalists were 64 Amish and Conservative Mennonite children, ages 10 to 17, from rural northern Indiana (Nucci, 1985). These children were notable for strictly adhering to biblical commands and disavowing any church hierarchy empowered to intercede between scriptural rules and their own actions. Among the strictures they followed was one prohibiting use of either radio or television in the home.

Each child was individually interviewed regarding four moral issues: hitting, stealing, slandering, and damaging another's property; and six nonmoral issues akin to matters of social convention: day of worship, work on the Sabbath, women's head coverings, baptism, interfaith marriage, and women as preachers. Adolescents over the age of 14 were also interviewed regarding a seventh nonmoral issue: premarital sex between consenting adults. It should be pointed out that nonmoral religious prescriptions are not, strictly speaking, social conventions, because they are derived presumably from scripture and are not considered by the devout to be the products of social consensus. Thus understanding subjects' reasoning about such issues required us to generate questions that would probe the relationships among conceptions of religious authority, God's word, religious rules, and the nature of moral versus nonmoral areas of behavior.

In the study, subjects were asked to make several judgments, three of which I will discuss here. First, Would it be all right for the congregation and its authorities to remove or alter the various religious rules, and, if so, would it then be all right for Christians to engage in formerly prohibited actions once the rules were gone? Second, Would it be wrong for members of another religion to engage in these behaviors if the other religion had no rules or standards regarding them? Third, Suppose Jesus (God) had not given us a law about (some particular act); would it be all right for a Christian to do the act in that case?

Briefly, findings from the study were as follows. With respect to questions about removing or altering religious rules, many more subjects on average objected to removing rules governing moral actions (98%) than to those regulating nonmoral (65%) actions. Thus it appears that subjects differentiated between moral and nonmoral religious prescriptions. An examination of individual items, however, revealed that on some specific nonmoral items, such as the prohibition against work on Sunday, nearly as many subjects (91%) objected to removing that religious rule as objected to eliminating rules governing moral actions. Their primary reason for objecting to the alteration of prohibitions regulating nonmoral religious behavior was that the given rule was commanded by God. That is, these fundamentalist subjects engaged in a literal reading of the Bible and treated statements such as Paul's admonishments that women wear head coverings (I Cor. 11) as direct commands from God. From their perspective, earthly beings have no authority in such matters.

With respect to relativity questions (i.e., questions about other religions), considerably fewer (25%) of the subjects felt it was wrong for members of other religions to engage in actions contrary to nonmoral Mennonite religious rules than to engage in actions such as slander, which constitute moral transgressions (94%). The primary reasons subjects gave for saying that it was all right for others to engage in acts counter to Mennonite rules governing nonmoral acts (e.g., women's wearing head coverings) were that such nonmoral religious rules were a function of particular religious systems or that others were ignorant of God's laws. In contrast with this relative tolerance regarding nonmoral issues, these subjects viewed it as wrong for members of other religions to engage in moral transgressions. Their primary reason for viewing actions such as hitting and stealing as universally wrong was that they resulted in harm or injustice to others.

Our clearest findings came in response to questions regarding the propriety of given actions if God had made no rule governing the act. On average only 1% of subjects said it would be wrong to engage in the nonmoral (conventional) actions (e.g., not wearing head coverings, working on the Sabbath, engaging in premarital sex) in this case. In contrast, 85% said it would continue to be wrong to engage in actions involving moral transgressions (e.g., stealing, slander). That such actions entail harmful or unjust consequences for others was the reason each child gave for this position.

In sum, the results of our interviews with Amish/Mennonite subjects indicate that the majority of religiously devout children make conceptual distinctions between those behavioral norms that are particular to their religion and those moral acts that have an intrinsic effect on the rights or well-being of others, Christians and non-Christians alike. That the overwhelming majority of children regarded these latter acts as unacceptable even in the absence of a prohibition from God indicates that morality, at least for these Christians, is independent of religious prescription.

Moral and Conventional Values as Seen by Conservative and Orthodox Jews

The study with Christian fundamentalists was followed up by an interview study with 64 conservative and 32 orthodox Jewish children ages 10 to 17 from the Chicago metropolitan area. The subjects all attended private religious schools. All of the orthodox children followed Jewish dietary laws, dress customs, and holiday rituals. Many of the conservative children followed these same traditional practices.

As in the study with the Christian children, subjects were interviewed regarding moral issues: stealing, hitting, slander, property damage; and a series of nonmoral issues: day of worship, work on the Sabbath, circumcision, men's wearing head coverings (Kippah), interfaith marriage, dietary laws, premarital sex between consenting adults. Although there were some differences in children's responses between the two groups (conservative children tended to be more flexible regarding the alterability of nonmoral religious rules), the general pattern was similar. Thus I will discuss the findings with these subjects together.

With respect to whether it would be right for religious authorities to remove or alter the various rules in question, our Jewish subjects were even more reluctant than the fundamentalist Christians to consider nonmoral (conventional) rules as alterable by human beings. About 75% of subjects overall felt that such rules could not be changed by religious authorities, essentially because they were presumed to be God-given. The only exception to this pattern was the prohibition against women's studying the Torah, which was seen as alterable by two thirds of orthodox children and three quarters of conservative. As with the Amish, the overwhelming majority of Jewish subjects (90%) indicated that rules governing moral transgressions could not be altered because the acts resulted in harm or injustice.

Unlike the Amish, few of the Jewish subjects universalized non-moral rules of their religion. That is, over 90% on average felt it was all right for members of another religion to engage in actions such as working on the Sabbath if their religion did not regulate such behavior. On the other hand, like the Amish, the great majority of our Jewish subjects (90%) felt it would be wrong for members of another religion to engage in moral transgressions whether their religion regulated the behavior or not. Again these subjects argued that such moral transgressions are wrong because of the harm or injustice they cause.

Finally, like the Christian subjects, virtually all of the Jewish subjects felt it would be all right for Jews to engage in nonmoral (conventional) acts such as premarital sex and interfaith marriage if God had not established a rule regulating the behavior. On the other hand, and again like our Christian subjects, the overwhelming majority of Jewish children stated that it would be wrong to engage in moral transgressions such as hitting or stealing whether or not God had established a rule or commandment regarding the behavior. As with the Christians, the Jewish children gave justice and welfare reasons for their responses.

Morality and God's Commands

The evidence reviewed so far indicates that both Christian and Jewish children differentiate between moral and nonmoral religious rules. What is more, it appears that children's treatment of moral issues as obligatory and universal is independent of religious prescription, including the commands of God. This latter finding was investigated more thoroughly through an additional set of questions posed to our Jewish subjects and to 64 Calvinist Protestant children ages 10 to 17. We asked the children how they know that what God commands is the right thing to do, and whether God's commands can make morally right an act, such as stealing from another, that children treat as a moral transgression. Our questions were informed by philosophical (Nielsen, 1973) and theological (Ramsey, 1966; Bultman, 1966) speculation originating in Socrates' dialogue with Euthyphro. Put simply, these philosophical and theological arguments presume that in order to evaluate whether the commands of God are moral, a person must invoke criteria for the good that are independent of God's word. In Nielsen's treatment of this issue, the case is made that in order for God's command to be moral, it must at least be the case that God is good. From this premise, Nielsen argues that Judeo-Christian conceptions of God presuppose prior, independent conceptions of goodness that serve as criteria for differentiating God from Satan or from other preternatural forces.

These philosophical treatments are consistent with our notion of domain coordination (Turiel et al., 1987). In this case the child's responses to our questions reflect the subject's coordination of independent domains of theological and moral understandings. What we found in our studies (Nucci, 1985; Nucci & Turiel, 1989) was that the majority of children at all ages and from both religious groups rejected the notion that God's command would make it right for a person to steal. At ages 10 to 11 and 12 to 13 years, more than 65% of subjects responded in this way, whereas more than 80% of subjects at ages 14 to 15 and 16 to 17 years gave such responses. The following excerpt from an 11-year-old conservative Jewish boy illustrates the children's answers to our questions.

> *Question.* How do we know that what is written in the Torah is really the right thing to do? *Answer.* He doesn't harm us, do bad for us. We believe in God. We think God wrote the Torah, and we think God likes us if we do those things and we think we are giving presents to God, by praying, and by following his rules. *Question.* Okay, But how can we be sure that what God is telling us is really the right thing? *Answer.* We've tried it. We've tried every rule in the Torah and we know. *Question.* Let's suppose that God had written in the Torah that Jews should steal, would it then be right for Jews to steal? *Answer.* No. *Question.* Why not? *Answer.* Even if God says it, we know he can't mean it, because we know it is a very bad thing to steal. We know he can't mean it. Maybe it's a test, but we just know he can't mean it. *Question.* Why wouldn't God mean it? *Answer.* Because we think of God as very good—absolutely perfect person. *Question.* And because He's perfect, He wouldn't say to steal? Why not? *Answer.* Well—because we people are not perfect, but we still understand. We are not dumb either. We still understand that stealing is a bad thing.

What we discovered through these interviews is that children's conceptions of morality cannot be accounted for in terms of a simple adherence to God's word. Instead children attempt to coordinate their notions of God with what they *know to be morally right.* Indeed, one young Calvinist said to our interviewer (tongue-in-cheek), "If God said to steal, and the Devil said, 'Don't steal,' we would worship the Devil."

Summary of Findings on Morality and Religion

Taken as a whole, the findings from our studies with religious children indicate that children's moral understandings are independent of specific religious rules and that morality is conceptually distinct from one's religious concepts. In addition, morality for the secular child as well as for the devoutly religious focuses on the same set of fundamental interpersonal issues: those pertaining to justice and compassion. For the public schools, this means that there can be moral education compatible with and yet independent from religious doctrine. Such moral education would focus on developing children's conceptions of justice, fairness, and concern for the welfare of others.

Morality and Personal Behavior: Sexuality and Drug Use

Just as our research has informed our understandings of the relationship between morality and religious doctrine, it also has important implications for assumptions regarding other aspects of moral and social values curricula. In essence, this research indicates that we need to rethink whether many of the areas of personal behavior often the subject of moral education are in fact conceptualized by children as moral issues. The domain approach provides a basis for conducting such an analysis and permits us to identify the moral and non-moral elements of issues that entail domain overlap. From our perspective such an analysis not only enables us to define the parameters of moral education but allows us to construct values education curricula concordant with the natural epistemology of the learner (Nucci, 1982). To illustrate, we turn to an examination of two controversial issues considered by some to be content for moral education: drug use and sexual behavior.

The traditional inclusion of behaviors such as drug use or sexuality as matters of morality stems from theories that equate morality with self-control over appetitive drives or urges (esp. Freud, 1905/ 1962, 1930/1961). Thus the notion of moral or character education is sometimes equated with the development of impulse control and delay of gratification (Wynne, 1989). From this perspective, a child's selfishness or aggressive behavior is seen as having the same status as the child's or adolescent's indulgence in such self-gratifying activities as drug use or masturbation. In treating such behaviors as morally equivalent, no distinction is made between actions that have consequences for the welfare of others and those that primarily affect the self. To be sure, some aspects of drug use, and particularly of sexual behavior, have implications for others' welfare and the general social order. We will take up these societal and truly moral aspects of drug use and sexuality later. What I wish to stress at this point, however, is that for some philosophers and educators, drug use and sexuality have "moral" meaning simply by virtue of their appetitive nature.

Children and adolescents, however, conceptualize aspects of their behavior that primarily affect the self as "personal" and outside the bounds of societal regulation or moral obligation (Nucci, 1981). Among the areas of behavior viewed by American children and adolescents as personal are one's choice of recreational activities, selection of friends and associates, the content of one's diary, and choices pertaining to one's body (e.g., hair length) (Nucci & Herman, 1982; Smetana, 1982). When reasoning about personal issues, children emphasize the personal choice or preferences of the actor and aspects of prudence such as the personal costs and benefits associated with the act (Tisak & Turiel, 1984). More detailed analyses have indicated that reasoning about personal issues is related to conceptions of self, personal autonomy, and identity (Nucci, 1977; Smetana, 1982, 1988).

Morality and Drug Use

Children's and adolescents' conceptions of the personal, moral, and conventional aspects of drug usage have been the subject of several recent studies (Berndt & Park, 1986; Killen, Leviton, & Cahill, 1989; Nucci, Guerra, & Lee, 1989). Each of them found that older elementary and high school students view drug use as an essentially "personal" matter to be evaluated in terms of costs and benefits to the user rather than an issue of interpersonal morality or social convention. For example, Nucci et al. (1989) found that less than 20% of non-drug-using adolescents in their study viewed regular use of cocaine as wrong because of the harm it might cause to others. Not surprisingly, they also found that fewer than 10% of non-drug-using subjects included school or church as a legitimate source of authority with respect to drug use. These findings reflect the subjects' assumptions that the primary consequences of drug use fall upon the user rather than others. Killen and her colleagues (1989) pressed this issue by asking whether one had the right to engage in self-harm if the action also had negative consequences for others. Although, on average, 75% of their adolescent sample thought it all right to engage in self-harm, only 70% of 10th-grade subjects felt one had the right to engage in self-harm if the act had a negative impact on others.

Though subjects in each of these studies viewed drug use as a matter of personal choice rather than morality or normative regulation, they did not necessarily take a laissez faire attitude toward it. Instead, the majority of subjects, including those most heavily involved in drug use, took into account the potential harm to the self when evaluating whether it would be wrong or all right to use drugs (Nucci et al., 1989). In this regard it is interesting that adolescents in the Nucci, Guerra, and Lee study rated cigarette smoking as more dangerous than occasionally using either alcohol or marijuana. One might add that the one area of drug use to have shown a marked decline among Americans over the past generation has been cigarette smoking. This decline can be directly attributed to a generation-long effort to heighten public awareness of the health risks associated with smoking.

The findings from this set of studies imply that drug education programs will fare much better by focusing on the personal consequences of drug use than by moralizing about such behavior. The extent that one can connect drug use to morality will be a function of the degree to which one can induce children and adolescents to consider how their personal drug use might have meaningful consequences for the welfare of others. Although inclusion of such a moral component could well be a part of a comprehensive approach to drug education (Berkowitz, Guerra, & Nucci, in press), it would be a far cry from viewing drug use as evidence of a weakness in moral character (Wynne, 1989).

Morality and Sexual Behavior

Our analysis of drug use illustrates that we cannot simply reduce our concerns regarding all serious forms of children's and adolescents' behavior to issues of morality and moral education. Much of what we hope children will develop in the way of values, whether in the arts or in polite conduct, is constructed in other domains of the child's psyche. In some instances, as in the case of sexual conduct, issues are so complex that they draw from a number of areas of social and interpersonal understanding (Turiel, 1989). Here again, however, we are in error if we reduce the values elements to morality. As we saw in our interviews with devout Christian and Jewish children, even a behavior as heavily condemned as premarital intercourse was not treated as an inherently moral issue. The moral aspect of sexuality, as in any other area of interpersonal conduct, has to do with issues of fairness, caring, and human welfare. To the extent that moral education may be integrated into sex education, it would be in these often overlooked aspects of intimate conduct.

Conclusion

As Americans we live in a pluralistic society in a period of rapid technological and social change. The philosopher Alasdair MacIntyre (1982), reflecting not just on the contemporary American scene but on modern society more generally, has characterized this current historical period as one of moral discord. Perhaps because of the apparent air of moral uncertainty, the great majority of American parents expect schools to contribute to the moral development of children (Gallup, 1976). What we have seen in this chapter is that current research on children's social development affords us a way to define the content and aims of moral education in terms of a set of universal and prescriptive considerations. The research indicates that morality is centered on concerns for justice and human welfare that are available even to young children. Those findings provide a basis for moral education that is both nonindoctrinative and nonrelativistic.

The research also makes clear that values education should not be reduced solely to concerns for moral development. A substantial and integral part of students' social values is within other areas of social knowledge, particularly the domain of social convention. Understanding the necessary social organizational function of convention equips the student to understand his or her own sociocultural system as well as to interpret and interact with the social systems of others. Concepts of convention, rather than being a subset of morality, provide the necessary knowledge base for cultural tolerance and a critical perspective on one's society.

The multifaceted nature of social values also means that attempts to generate educational programs likely to contribute to the development of "good" people will have to draw from many sources and disciplines. The need to go beyond simplistic and one-dimensional programs of moral development or character formation has been recognized recently by developmentalists (Turiel, 1989) and members of the character education camp (Ryan, 1987). To provide values education that is concordant with the nature of children's social knowledge, systems will have to extend beyond the domain of morality. It is only by recognizing this that we can do justice to morality in values education.

References

Barth, K. (1957). *The doctrine of God: Church dogmatics: Vol. 1, part 2.* Edinburgh: T. & T. Clark.

Berkowitz, M., Guerra, N., Nucci, L. (in press). Sociomoral development and drug and alcohol abuse. In J. Gewirtz & W. Kurtines (Eds.), *Handbook of moral behavior and development: Vol. I.* Hillsdale, NJ: Erlbaum.

Berndt, T., & Park, K. (1986). *Children's reasoning about morality, convention, personal issues and drug use.* Unpublished manuscript, Purdue University, Lafayette, IN.

Bonhoeffer, D. (1955). *Ethics.* New York: Macmillan.

Bultman, R. (1966). Reply to D. Heinz-Horst Schrey. In C. W. Kegley (Ed.), *The theology of Rudolf Bultman* (pp. 279–280). New York: Harper and Row.

Carey, N., & Ford, M. (1983, August). *Domains of social and self-regulation: An Indonesian study.* Paper presented at the annual meeting of the American Psychological Association, Los Angeles.

Damon, W. (1977). *The social world of the child.* San Francisco: Jossey-Bass.

Damon, W. (1980). Patterns of change in children's social reasoning: A two-year longitudinal study. *Child Development, 51,* 1010–1017.

Dworkin, R. (1978). *Taking rights seriously.* Cambridge, MA: Harvard University Press.

Enright, R., Franklin, L., & Manheim, L. (1980). On children's distributive justice reasoning: A standardized and objective scale. *Developmental Psychology, 16,* 193–202.

Freud, S. (1961). *Civilization and its discontents.* New York: Norton. (Original work published 1930)

Freud, S. (1962). *Three essays on the theory of sexuality.* New York: Avon. (Original work published 1905)

Gallup, G. (1976). Eighth annual Gallup Poll of public attitudes toward the public schools. *Phi Delta Kappan, 58,* 37–50.

Gerth, W. W., & Mills, C. W. (1970). *From Max Weber: Essays in sociology.* London: Routledge & Kegan Paul.

Hollos, M., Leis, P., & Turiel, E. (1986). Social reasoning in Ijo children and adolescents. *Journal of Cross-Cultural Psychology, 17,* 352–376.

Irwin, D., & Moore, S. (1971). The young child's understanding of social justice. *Developmental Psychology, 5,* 406–410.

Killen, M., Leviton, M., & Cahill, J. (1989). *Social reasoning regarding drug use in adolescence.* Unpublished manuscript, Wesleyan University, Middletown, CT.

Kohlberg, L. (1984). *Essays on moral development, Vol. 2: The psychology of moral development.* San Francisco: Harper and Row.

Lapsley, D. (1982). *The development of retributive justice in children.* Unpublished doctoral dissertation, University of Wisconsin, Madison, WI.

Lewis, D. (1969). *Convention: A philosophical study.* Cambridge, MA: Harvard University Press.

MacIntyre, A. (1982). *After virtue.* Notre Dame, IN: University of Notre Dame Press.

Nielsen, K. (1973). *Ethics without God.* Buffalo, NY: Prometheus Books.

Nucci, L. (1977). *Social development: Personal, conventional, and moral concepts.* Unpublished doctoral dissertation, University of California, Santa Cruz.

Nucci, L. (1981). Conceptions of personal issues: A domain distinct from moral or societal concepts. *Child Development, 52,* 114–121.

Nucci, L. (1982). Conceptual development in the moral and conventional domains: Implications for values education. *Review of Educational Research, 49,* 93–122.

Nucci, L. (1985). Children's conceptions of morality, societal convention, and religious prescription, In C. Harding (Ed.), *Moral dilemmas: Philosophical and psychological reconsiderations of the development of moral reasoning* (pp. 137–174). Chicago: Precedent Press.

Nucci, L. (1989). Challenging conventional wisdom about morality: The domain approach to values education. In L. Nucci (Ed.), *Moral development and character education: A dialogue* (pp. 183–203). Berkeley: McCutchan.

Nucci, L., Guerra, N., & Lee, J. (1989, April). *Adolescent judgments of the personal, prudential, and normative aspects of drug usage.* Paper presented at the biennial meetings of the Society for Research in Child Development, Kansas City, MO.

Nucci, L., & Herman, S. (1982). Behavioral disordered children's conceptions of moral, conventional, and personal issues. *Journal of Abnormal Child Psychology, 10,* 411–426.

Nucci, L., & Turiel, E. (1989, April). *God's word, religious rules and their relation to Christian and Jewish children's concept of morality.* Paper presented at the biennial meetings of the Society for Research in Child Development, Kansas City, MO.

Nucci, L., Turiel, E., & Encarnacion-Gawrych, G. (1983). Children's social interactions and social concepts: Analyses of morality and convention in the Virgin Islands. *Journal of Cross-Cultural Psychology, 14,* 469–487.

Nucci, L., & Weber, E. (in press). The domain approach to values education: From theory to practice. In W. Kurtines & J. Gewirtz (Eds.), *Handbook of moral behavior and development* (Vol. 3). Hillsdale, NJ: Erlbaum.

Piaget, J. (1932). *The moral judgment of the child.* Glencoe, IL: Free Press.

Ramsey, I. T. (1966). Moral judgment and God's commands. In I. T. Ramsey (Ed.), *Christian ethics and contemporary philosophy* (pp. 152–171). London: SCM Publishing Co.

Rest, J. (1979). *Revised manual for the defining issues test.* Minneapolis: Moral Research Projects.

Rest, J. (1983). Morality. In J. Flavell & E. Markman (Eds.), *Handbook of child psychology Vol. III: Cognitive development* (pp. 556–629). New York: Wiley.

Ryan, K. (1987). The moral education of teachers. In K. Ryan & G. F. McLean (Eds.), *Character development in schools and beyond* (pp. 358–379). New York: Praeger.

Ryan, K. (1989). In defense of character education. In L. Nucci (Ed.), *Moral development and character education: A dialogue* (pp. 358–379). Berkeley: McCutchan.

Smetana, J. (1981). Preschool children's conceptions of moral and social rules. *Developmental Psychology, 52,* 1333–1336.

Smetana, J. (1982). *Concepts of self and morality: Women's reasoning about abortion.* New York: Praeger.

Smetana, J. (1988). Adolescents' and parents' conceptions of parental authority. *Child Development, 59,* 321–335.

Smetana, J. (1989). Toddlers' social interactions in the context of moral and conventional transgressions in the home. *Developmental Psychology, 25,* 499–508.

Smetana, J., & Braeges, J. L. (1987). *The development of toddlers' moral and conventional judgments and their relation to language development.* Paper presented at the biennial meetings of the Society for Research in Child Development, Baltimore, MD.

Song, M., Smetana, J., & Kim, S. (1987). Korean children's conceptions of moral and conventional transgressions. *Developmental Psychology, 23,* 577–582.

Tisak, M., & Turiel, E. (1984). Children's conceptions of moral and prudential rules. *Child Development, 55,* 1030–1039.

Turiel, E. (1983). *The development of social knowledge: Morality and convention.* Cambridge, MA: Cambridge University Press.

Turiel, E. (1989). Multifaceted social reasoning and educating for character, culture, and development. In L. Nucci (Ed.), *Moral development and character education: A dialogue* (pp. 161–182). Berkeley: McCutchan.

Turiel, E., Killen, M., & Helwig, C. (1987). Morality: Its structure, functions, and vagaries. In J. Kagan & S. Lamb (Eds.), *The emergence of morality in young children* (pp. 155–243). Chicago: University of Chicago Press.

Turiel, E., Nucci, L., & Smetana, J. (1988). A cross-cultural comparison about what? A critique of Nisan's (1987) study of morality and convention. *Developmental Psychology, 24,* 140–143.

Wynne, E. (1989). Transmitting traditional values in contemporary schools. In L. Nucci (Ed.), *Moral development and character education: A dialogue* (pp. 19–36). Berkeley: McCutchan.

The Developmental or Indirect Approach to Moral Education

The four chapters in Part II present what has been called the indirect or developmental approach to moral education. As delineated by Robert Howard in Chapter 3, children, as they mature, pass sequentially through different stages of development, and the aim of education is to promote and support this development. Toward this end, children are encouraged to discuss moral dilemmas they encounter in the school curriculum or in problematic classroom situations. Thus students actually practice discussing moral problems at the appropriate level in the same manner as moral philosophers do at higher levels. In this way their thinking is constantly challenged and, as a consequence, their reflective abilities mature.

Because moral or social problems occur in a variety of settings, moral education experiences must find multiple forums. Many of these are presented in this section. After a discussion of Kohlberg's theory of moral development and education, especially regarding his "just community" concept as applied at the high school level, Howard discusses the application of that theory at the elementary school level. He then provides a personal example of how discussion can help students grow.

In Chapter 4 Thomas Lickona discusses classroom practices designed to promote a moral community based on fairness, caring, and democratic participation. This end is brought about in classrooms that promote the self-worth of students through cooperative learning, moral reflection, and participatory decision making. Lickona suggests that these four classroom processes can be expanded to the entire school.

The final two chapters elaborate on Lickona's last thoughts. Ethel Sadowsky (Chapter 5) describes her K–8 school and the distinct approaches she has developed there to promote democracy and citizenship in the children. She documents through example how the classroom teachers and children discuss and develop rules jointly; how classes at different grade levels share experiences and care for each other, all the time focusing on academic content; and how the school uses the Town Meeting model to discuss and resolve schoolwide issues. All of these approaches emphasize inquiry, cooperation, and divergent thinking and, taken together, lead to social understanding, a sense of community within the school, and moral growth.

In Chapter 6, Robert Weintraub takes the Town Meeting model described in the previous chapter one step further. In a useful and comprehensive manner, Weintraub describes how, as the new principal of a school with strong academic program, he worked with his staff and his students in creating a democratic governance structure. Over the course of one school year the students had representation as a House of Representatives to the faculty's Senate, and together they tackled and resolved fundamental problems related to lunchroom schedules, skateboards, and the school's writing center, learning much about democracy in the process.

As a whole, these chapters give a theoretical and practical rationale for student participation, at developmentally appropriate levels, in issues directly affecting their school life. Adults in these schools know children's limits and allow maximum growth within those limits. As a consequence, children and adults work together effectively in solving problems of concern to each other while maintaining a proper respect for their respective roles.

CHAPTER THREE

Lawrence Kohlberg's Influence on Moral Education in Elementary Schools

ROBERT W. HOWARD

In 1974 Lawrence Kohlberg—supported by Kennedy, Danforth, Ford, and the W. T. Grant Foundations—created the Center for Moral Development and Education at the Harvard Graduate School of Education. "The Third Floor," its location in Larsen Hall, became the short-hand reference for the institution. Kohlberg (1981, 1984, in press), the major figure in moral development and education for three decades, was director of the center until his death in January 1987. Soon after that the center, regrettably, ceased to exist. Although we can no longer draw upon Kohlberg's intellectual insights or the institutional resources of the center, his theory of moral development and his approach to moral education continue to guide educators in countless classrooms and schools.

Kohlberg's theory of moral development claims that individuals, as they mature, pass sequentially through qualitatively different stages of development (see Figure 3.1). He argues that humans are intrinsically philosophers. That is, individuals, irrespective of their ages, ask philosophical questions such as, How ought I to live? and What is the right action to take, and how do I know it to be right? What differentiates mature from immature moral reasoning is not the questions posed, nor the simple answers, but the reasons behind them. Kohlberg devoted over 30 years to the study of what these underlying reasons are, what their internal logic or "structure" is, and how those structures change over time.

In Kohlberg's view, the aim of education in general, and of moral education in particular, is to promote and support development (1981). The aim of moral education is to encourage individuals to become autonomous, moral agents. They should make decisions about what is right and wrong based on moral principles (e.g., respect and caring for persons) rather than on selfish or peer-influenced motivations. In training the next generation of world leaders, we want to encourage the development of Mahatma Ghandis and Janusz Korczaks (Frost, 1983; Kohlberg, 1981) rather than Idi Amins or Adolf Eichmanns.

According to Kohlberg, moral reasoning develops through a sequence of six stages. Moral education consists of promoting change or development through these stages as an individual *interacts* with his or her environment and makes sense of those experiences. Even at low stages people are able to make claims about what is right and wrong, but Kohlberg holds that people at higher stages of moral development are more likely to act in accordance with their moral judgments.

For Kohlberg, psychological development of the individual is the primary aim of education and is promoted by engaging in discussions of moral issues and dilemmas—both hypothetical and real—within a supportive, caring, and just community. Participating in these discussions helps students to recognize and to understand the perspectives of others and to have their own reasoning supported at some times and challenged at others.

In this chapter we will discuss moral education in the classroom setting, in alternative "schools-within-schools" programs, and in whole school programs.

The Moral and Psychological Foundations of Kohlberg's Moral Education

In the development of his moral and educational *philosophy*, Kohlberg was greatly influenced by Socrates, Kant, Dewey, and Rawls. His *psychology* was influenced by James Mark Baldwin and Jean Piaget. Like many philosophers and psychologists of his generation, Kohlberg was also deeply affected by World War II and the Holocaust and was motivated to understand moral reasoning, moral action, and the imperfect and perilous relationship between the two. Kohlberg was too young to have served in the military during World War II, but as a merchant marine he did participate in the transportation of Jewish refugees into what was then Palestine. Kohlberg's (1948) first published article, "Bed for Bananas," was his description of those experiences. The title referred to the beds used by the refugees, but which to any suspicious authority were described by sailors as beds to carry bunches of bananas. After his experiences in the merchant marine, Kohlberg returned to the United States and began his research into the psychology of moral reasoning. Although he initially designed his study to replicate Piaget's (1965) research with a U.S. population, Kohlberg soon noticed psychological phenomena and patterns he felt Piaget's analysis had not captured. Kohlberg recognized structural similarities among the reasoning of different individuals. These similarities became Kohlberg's widely cited "stages" of moral growth. Because Kohlberg [as well as Dewey (1963, 1966)] found the psychological development of the individual to be the paramount aim of education, he became involved in researching the ways in which schools can promote moral reasoning. His research and its application are discussed below.

Kohlberg's Theory of Moral Development

Kohlberg argued that moral reasoning develops through the stages he defined experimentally (see Figure 3.1). He argued that these stages are:

1. Universal—that they hold true across cultures, race, gender, etc.
2. Hierarchical—that individuals grow in stepwise progress, never skipping a stage or regressing, except under trauma
3. "Structured wholes"—that, except during transition, individuals are "in" one stage or another

In other words, individuals do not jump back and forth between stages of reasoning depending on the dilemma, day, or barometric pressure. Kohlberg's theory makes bold claims about the nature of moral reasoning and its development. His boldness attracts both supporters and challengers. A full discussion of these arguments is beyond the scope of this chapter. Kohlberg provides a scholarly synopsis of the positions of his challengers and his response in *The Psychology of Moral Development: The Nature and Validity of Moral Stages* (1984, chaps. 3 & 4).

To come to understand the structure of an individual's moral thought, Kohlberg presented his research subjects with a series of

Continued on page 49

Figure 3.1   Kohlberg's Stages of Moral Development

Level A: Preconventional Level

Stage 1: The Stage of Punishment and Obedience

Content.   Right is literal obedience to rules and authority, avoiding punishment, and not doing physical harm.

1. What is right is to avoid breaking rules, to obey for obedience's sake, and to avoid doing physical damage to people and property.
2. The reasons for doing right are avoidance of punishment and the superior power of authorities.

Social Perspective.   This stage takes an egocentric view. A person at this stage doesn't consider the interest of others or recognize they differ from actor's, and doesn't relate two points of view. Actions are judged in terms of physical consequences rather than in terms of psychological interests of others. Authority's perspective is confused with one's own.

Stage 2: The Stage of Individual Instrumental Purpose
and Exchange

Content.   Right is serving one's own or other's needs and making fair deals in terms of concrete exchange.

1. What is right is following rules when it is to someone's immediate interest. Right is acting to meet one's own interests and needs and letting others do the same. Right is also what is fair; that is, what is an equal exchange, a deal, an agreement.
2. The reason for doing right is to serve one's own needs or interests in a world where one must recognize that other people have their interests, too.

Social Perspective.   This stage takes a concrete individualistic perspective. A person at this stage separates his or her own interests and points of view from those of authorities and others. He or she is aware everybody has individual interests to pursue and these conflict, so that right is relative (in the concrete individualistic sense). The person integrates or relates conflicting individual interests to one another through instrumental exchange of services, through instrumental need for the other and the other's goodwill, or through fairness giving each person the same amount.

Figure 3.1 (*continued*)

Level B: Conventional Level

Stage 3: The Stage of Mutual Interpersonal Expectations,
Relationships, and Conformity

Content. Right is playing a good (nice) role, being concerned about
other people and their feelings, keeping loyalty and trust with partners, and
being motivated to follow rules and expectations.

1. What is right is living up to what is expected by people close to one or what
   people generally expect of one another in such roles as son, sister, friend,
   and so on. "Being good" is important and means having good motives,
   showing concern about others. It also means keeping mutual relationships, maintaining trust, loyalty, respect, and gratitude.
2. Reasons for doing right are needing to be good in one's own eyes and those
   of others, caring for others, and because if one puts oneself in the other
   person's place one would want good behavior from the self (Golden Rule).

Social Perspective. This stage takes the perspective of the individual in
relationship to other individuals. A person at this stage is aware of shared
feelings, agreements, and expectations, which take primacy over individual
interests. The person relates points of view through the "concrete Golden
Rule," putting oneself in the other person's shoes. He or she does not consider
generalized "system" perspective.

Stage 4: The Stage of Social System and Conscience Maintenance

Content. Right is doing one's duty in society, upholding the social
order, and maintaining the welfare of society or the group.

1. What is right is fulfilling the actual duties to which one has agreed. Laws
   are to be upheld except in extreme cases where they conflict with other
   fixed social duties and rights. Right is also contributing to society, the
   group, or institution.
2. The reasons for doing right are to keep the institution going as whole, self-
   respect or conscience as meeting one's defined obligations, or the consequences: "What if everyone did it?"

Social Perspective. This stage differentiates a societal point of view
from interpersonal agreement or motives. A person at this stage takes the
viewpoint of the system, which defines roles and rules. He or she considers
individual relations in terms of place in the system.

Figure 3.1 *(continued)*

Level B/C: Transitional Level

Stage 4½: This Level is Postconventional but not yet Principled

Content of Transition. At Stage 4½, choice is personal and subjective. It is based on emotions, conscience is seen as arbitrary and relative, as are ideas such as "duty" and "morally right."

Transitional Social Perspective. At this stage, the perspective is that of an individual standing outside of society and considering himself or herself making decisions without a generalized commitment or contract with society. One can pick and choose obligations, which are defined by particular societies, but one has no principles for such choice.

Level C: Postconventional and Principled Level

Moral decisions are generated from rights, values, or principles that are (or could be) agreeable to all individuals composing or creating a society designed to have fair and beneficial practices.

Stage 5: The Stage of Prior Rights and Social Contract or Utility

Content. Right is upholding the basic rights, values, and legal contracts of a society, even when they conflict with concrete rules and laws of the group.

1. What is right is being aware of the fact that people hold a variety of values and opinions, that most values and rules are relative to one's group. These "relative" rules should usually be upheld, however, in the interest of impartiality and because they are the social contract. Some nonrelative values and rights such as life and liberty, however, must be upheld in any society and regardless of majority opinion.
2. Reasons for doing right are, in general, feeling obligated to obey the law because one has made a social contract to make and abide by laws for the good of all and to protect their own rights and the rights of others. Family friendship, trust, and work obligations are also commitments or contracts freely entered into and entail respect for the rights of others. One is concerned that laws and duties be based on the rational calculation of overall utility: "the greatest good for the greatest number."

Social Perspective. This stage takes a prior-to-society perspective—that of a rational individual aware of values and rights prior to social attachments and contracts. The person integrates perspectives by formal mechanisms of

Figure 3.1   (*continued*)

agreement, contract, objective impartiality, and due process. He or she considers the moral point of view and the legal point of view, recognizes they conflict, and finds it difficult to integrate them.

Stage 6: The Stage of Universal Ethical Principles

Content. This stage assumes guidance by universal ethical principles that all humanity should follow.

1. Regarding what is right, Stage 6 is guided by universal ethical principles. Particular laws or social agreements are usually valid because they rest on such principles. When laws violate these principles, one acts in accordance with the principle. Principles are usually universal principles of justice, the equality of human rights, and respect for the dignity of human beings as individuals. These are not merely values that are recognized but are also principles used to generate particular decisions.
2. The reason for doing right is that, as a rational person, one has seen the validity of principles and has become committed to them.

Social Perspective. This stage takes the perspective of a moral point of view from which social arrangements derive or on which they are grounded. The perspective is that of any rational individual recognizing the nature of morality or the basic moral premise of respect for other persons as ends, not means.

hypothetical dilemmas. The most famous of these is the "Heinz" dilemma, where Heinz, whose wife is dying from a rare cancer, is faced with a decision of whether to steal a drug that might save her. Although the druggist invented the drug, he refuses to sell it to Heinz or to issue him credit, despite being able to realize a fivefold profit with the money that Heinz has raised. Subjects are asked both what Heinz should do and, more importantly, the reasons why.

At any stage of development, individuals can argue that Heinz should or should not steal the drug, but their reasons for their choice change at different stages. (Kohlberg did argue, however, that at higher stages of reasoning there is greater agreement about what constitutes the morally correct action.) Beginning in the 1950s, Kohlberg asked three groups of male adolescents to respond intermittently over a 30-year period to the same moral dilemmas.

Transition Between Stages

According to Kohlberg, each stage is a balanced, self-contained view of the moral world. Individuals develop from one stage to another when they come to recognize the limitations and inadequacies of their moral understanding. This recognition can be achieved by confronting moral issues and dilemmas, actual or hypothetical. Moral reasoning is also facilitated by having moral discussions with others, particularly others who, because they are at higher stages, can expose the individual to more complex moral structures.

Discussing moral dilemmas involves a balance between supporting and challenging students' reasoning. This balance is not always easy to maintain. I recall one incident in my own classroom when I pushed too hard. A sixth grader, Amy, came up to me before class one morning. She had been pondering the discussion of the previous day and told me, quite pleased with herself, "I know how to decide what is right and wrong." Curious, I asked her how. "You should do what God wants you to do." In previous weeks we had discussed Shiite Muslims and the Islamic revolution in Iran. Seeking to challenge (read *promote*) Amy's reasoning, I seized what I thought was a golden opportunity. "That's interesting," I responded, "but you are a Christian. How do you know what God wants you to do? After all, Ayatollah Khomeini is a Muslim, and his views of what God wants might be different from yours." In the next few seconds, Amy let me know that I had missed an opportunity to be supportive and had challenged her reasoning when it was too fragile. "Why? Why? Why? All you ever ask me is why!" She then turned and walked to her seat as the bell rang. Although not ready to deal with those issues at that time, Amy was to raise these questions on her own several years later.

Kohlberg-Inspired Programs in Moral Education

Two major prescriptions for educators follow from Kohlberg's theory of moral development. The first is that because students—as well as their teachers—are moral philosophers, the moral development of students can be promoted by engaging them in moral dialogues and discussions with their peers and educators. These discussions can and should be integrated into a school's or a teacher's existing curricula. Specific curricula have been and can be created to emphasize and to focus on the moral issues that exist within particular subjects, such as history or geography, or can be raised for examination through a more interdisciplinary approach (Garrod, 1989; Garrod & Staines, 1984; Lockwood & Harris, 1985; Parr, 1982; Timm & Timm, 1983).

Of course, the most powerful moral issues in an individual's life are the ones that affect him or her personally, and these issues should also be part of the classroom and of school life. This concept brings us to Kohlberg's second major prescription: Students and teachers should participate in making the decisions that have an impact on them, and their participation should be made possible through a democratic, "just community" approach to education (Power, Higgins, & Kohlberg, 1988; Reimer, Paolitto, & Hersh, 1983).

In his approach to moral education, Kohlberg placed explicit emphasis on the process of making moral choices. Kohlberg did not believe virtues could be taught didactically but rather that both the concept of justice as well as the individual's understanding of it were constructed through experiences with the moral world.

Rather than focusing on a list of virtues to be transmitted to students, Kohlberg argued that virtue and justice are synonymous and that the "teaching of virtue [justice] is the asking of questions and pointing of the way, not the giving of answers. Moral education is the leading of men upward, not the putting into the mind of knowledge that was not there before" (1970, p. 58).

This approach is in contrast to others that emphasize the transmission of specific actions, beliefs, and/or values or the natural development of innate values. Kohlberg disdainfully refers to the former as the "bag of virtues" approach to moral education and rejects the latter as "romantic." The former approach recommends selecting virtues (e.g., the Boy Scout Oath) and transmitting them to children and adolescents. The latter views the child as innately disposed to the good and dictates a tightly constrained role for educators. For Kohlberg, moral development and education are neither matters of transmitting values nor the natural unfolding of moral goodness. Moral knowledge, Kohlberg asserts, is a construction made by each individual as a result of experience in the moral world and a reflection upon that experience. Kohlberg also argues that it is not possible to divorce moral action from moral reasoning. For example, stealing might be wrong in most cases but might be morally justified in such extreme cases as that of Heinz.

Kohlberg's giving philosophical and psychological primacy to justice has been challenged by both philosophers (e.g., Noddings, 1984) and psychologists. Among the arguments made against Kohlberg is that he errs in the claim that virtue and justice are synonymous. They argue for what they see as a broader view of both morality and moral reasoning. One of Kohlberg's best-known challengers, Carol Gilligan (Gilligan, 1982; Gilligan, Ward, Taylor, & Bardige, 1989), argues that Kohlberg's equation of morality and justice as well as his methodology (i.e., selecting an all-male, Caucasian sample upon which he based his theory) ignores aspects of the moral domain (namely, *care* and *responsibility*), aspects that she feels are more likely to be articulated by women.

This issue is a large one that raises several philosophical and empirical questions [Baumrind, 1986; Rest, 1989; Sichel, 1988; *Social Research* (entire issue), 1983; Walker, 1986]. I believe that justice and care "orientations" to moral reasoning are compatible and are captured by the structures of Kohlberg's stages.

A full discussion of this position must be articulated in detail elsewhere, but let us consider the issue of compatibility by examining the moral reasoning prescribed by Kohlberg and that prescribed by Noddings. In describing moral reasoning at the sixth and highest of his stages, as applied to the Heinz dilemma, Kohlberg (1984) argues that one type of Stage 6 reasoning is what Kohlberg colloquially calls "moral musical chairs." He writes:

> "Moral musical chairs": [is] a second order application of the Golden Rule. Not only is Heinz to take the point of view of the dying person, of the druggist, and of himself, but in doing so each person (druggist, Heinz, dying person) is expected to take the point of view of the other in putting forward his claim and so modifying it. (pp. 636–637)

> [The moral agent at] Stage 6, in addition to [considering] the principle of equality, uses the principle of equity or fairness. At this stage equity does not include reference to special rewards for talent, merit, or achievement. These are largely seen as resulting from differences in genes or in educational and social opportunities which are morally arbitrary, or to unequal distribution by society. However, Stage 6 equity does include recognition of differential need, that is, the need to consider the position of the least advantaged. Where distribution of scarce basic goods must be unequal (e.g., issues of who should live in "life-boat" dilemmas) a lottery approach is preferred to favoring the strong or the more socially useful. (p. 638)

In other words, to solve the Heinz dilemma at Stage 6, the moral reasoner should take the perspective of each individual affected by the dilemma and give special (equity) consideration to the plight of the "least-advantaged" or the person most "at-risk." Kohlberg argues that if each individual in the Heinz dilemma would reason in this manner, the dilemma would be resolved by communication and deliberation because the druggist would realize an obligation to be cooperative. Failing that, Kohlberg argues, Heinz is morally justified in stealing the drug.

This idea of moral musical chairs is not cited by Noddings (1984) in the following example, but I believe the reader will readily see the compatibility of the approach with the "care orientation" to moral judgment:

> In a very common—and sometimes deceptively simple—dilemma, we fall into conflict over the needs or wants of two different persons for whom we care. Consider Ms. Brown, who has promised to attend the symphony with her husband, and then their child comes down with an illness. Sometimes the decision is easy: the child is obviously too ill to leave, or the child is hardly ill at all and happily engaged in some activity. But often the dilemma is real, and we struggle with it. There is fever and, while there is no clear danger, the child keeps asking, "Mother, *must* you go?" The solution to this sort of conflict cannot be codified. Slogans such as "Put your husband (child) first!" are quite useless. There are times when he must come first; there are times when he cannot.
>
> Is this problem a "moral" problem? In the important sense that it involves the needs and wants of others in relation or in conflict with our own, it certainly is and, without doubt, it is a problem of caring. When Ms. Brown looks at her husband and listens to him, she adds thinking to feeling; she, too, hates to miss the evening and "waste the tickets." She sees disappointment in his eyes and wants to respond to that. There is no probability calculus that will solve this problem for her. After analysis and argument, and perhaps a period of watchfulness to see if the child's anxiety eases, she has to decide. When she decides, if she cares, she decides not by formula, nor by a process of strict "rational decision making." There is . . . a turning point. She turns away from the abstract formulation of the problem and looks again at the persons for whom she cares. Perhaps her child is still anxious and irritable, she receives his pain clearly. Perhaps her husband is merely annoyed, not hurt; perhaps, at some deeper level, he too wants only support for his best self. If she sees this, having received both persons, she decides to stay with the child. If the child is sound asleep one-half hour after the decision—and we all know how likely this is—her decision is not thereby proved wrong, for this is not the sort of decision that can properly be labeled "right" or "wrong" according to outcome. It is right or

wrong according to how faithfully it was rooted in caring—that is, in a genuine response to the perceived needs of the others. (pp. 52–53)

At the core of each approach the moral reasoner has the imperative to understand the world from the perspective of others, then to make a choice that gives special consideration to the person who is most "at-risk" or "least advantaged." Noddings declines to formulate this as a principle; but I feel that in fact it functions as such. In the Heinz dilemma as in that of the sick child, "moral musical chairs" and an appeal to caring lead to the same conclusions. Although characterized differently—as "perspective-taking" as opposed to "receiving the other"—I believe the underlying prescriptive process to be inherently compatible if not identical.

Just Community Approaches to Moral Education

Kohlberg's initial approach to moral education focused on research using hypothetical moral dilemmas in the classroom to stimulate moral discussion and thought, emphasizing the power of moral discourse to promote development (Berkowitz, 1981, 1985; Blatt & Kohlberg, 1975; Damon & Killen, 1982; Leming, 1981). Kohlberg and his colleagues were disheartened to find that many successful programs—judged in terms of promoting the moral reasoning of students—were short-lived. Both teachers and students found the experience too hypothetical and removed from their day-to-day life in school, home, and community.

Influenced by his observation of collective education on an Israeli kibbutz, Kohlberg broadened his approach to moral education, shifting away from the individual student and his or her moral deliberation over a hypothetical dilemma to focus on the interactions between individuals in the social group.

Although psychological development remained the aim of education, Kohlberg came to conclude, "The unit of effectiveness of education is not the individual but the group" (Power, Higgins, & Kohlberg, 1988, p. 48). Since moral development is a construction, and is the result of one's interaction with one's environment, it follows that some environments are more conducive to moral growth than others. Kohlberg argues for the creation of "just communities" in schools, correctional institutions, and workplaces to promote the moral development of both the individual and the community. Creating a *community* that would address moral issues that arose naturally out of social interaction within the group became the educational prescription:

> The key to the just community is that we . . . do more than teach about democratic citizenship. . . . Instead of relying on club sport and various extracurricular activities to promote student relationships of friendship and care, we have tried to build community throughout the entire school day.
>
> While democracy and community are familiar notions for most readers, high schools organized as direct participatory democracies (parents, students, staff members each have one vote) and explicitly dedicated to a communitarian or *Gemeinschaft* ideal are rarely if ever encountered in this country. (Power et al., 1988, pp. 1–2)

Each of these school projects is a school-within-a-school, an alternative program in a public high school, that involves roughly 100 students. They operate by a system of participatory democracy where each student and faculty member has one vote in setting and enforcing community rules. The just community operates through three institutions; advisor groups, community meetings, and discipline committee. Each student is assigned to an advisory group that meets weekly with a faculty advisor. The purpose of this group is twofold: first, to create a sense of community by providing members with an opportunity to get to know each other and, second, to provide an opportunity to discuss in a small group school issues that will be raised in the larger community meeting that includes all members of the group in a direct democracy.

In the weekly community meeting, school rules and expectations dealing with issues of lying, stealing, drug use, attendance, and expulsion are discussed and democratically adopted. Explicit emphasis in these programs is placed on the community's operating by consensus rather than by majority rule in order to encourage full moral examination of the issue under discussion and to prevent the "tyranny of the majority."

Students join in the community program both by participating in the just community institutions and by signing up for courses taught by the just community teachers. Because students are usually required or desire to take courses unavailable in the community program, they will return to the host school for a portion of the day.

Kohlberg and his colleagues argue that the moral dimensions of the community can be measured by monitoring the norms that are proposed and enforced by the community. As the community develops, the norms will reflect a higher stage of moral content and they will be more "collective," that is, subscribed to by a greater percentage of the community. This claim is critical in determining the essentially moral character of school climate. For example, a norm may be advanced in its degree of collectivity and its phase of enforcement yet represent a pernicious value. In *Oliver Twist*, for example, Fagan's band had a collective, well-enforced norm of stealing. Hence the moral stage of the norm is important and differentiates just communities from Fagan's Den of Thieves.

With his colleagues at Harvard's Center for Moral Education, Kohlberg created and researched such just community programs at the Cluster School in Cambridge and at the Scarsdale Alternative School in Westchester County, New York. There have been and still are many programs heavily influenced by Kohlberg's approach. Several of Kohlberg's former colleagues are continuing with a project that he initiated in 1985 to create just communities at the Bronx High School of Science and Theodore Roosevelt High School in the Bronx, New York. This project has grown to include Martin Luther King, Jr. High School in Manhattan.

Moral Education Programs in Elementary Schools

Kohlberg's Center for Moral Education had far more experience on the high school than on the elementary level. However, many educators who have been influenced, directly or indirectly, by Kohlberg have created impressive moral education programs at the elementary level. Three programs demonstrate the range of Kohlbergian moral education from whole-school level to individual curriculum changes.

1. The just community program at Grace and St. Peter's School in Baltimore, Maryland (Karp, 1989), which created at the elementary level the weekly community meeting and fairness committee that exist in just community programs in the high school
2. The Classroom Councils developed by Paul Sain in Salt Lake City, Utah (Sain, 1981)
3. The values education program at The Fay School in Southborough, Massachusetts

At Fay, Pliny Norcross and his colleagues have developed a program that does not attempt to influence school policy or enforcement but does engage students in weekly moral discussions of school, community, and national issues (Wheeler, 1986).

In the Salt Lake City program, Sain has organized all of the fifth- and sixth-grade classes in his school into a cooperative community. If the class members involved in a dispute cannot resolve their problems without outside help, the conflict is taken to four classroom representatives for mediation and resolution. In cases where a student in Classroom A has a disagreement with a student in Classroom B, treaties developed between/among classes allow for the student who is charged with violating a school rule to be sent to another room's class council for a resolution of the problem. Before any conflict resolution is dealt with by the council, the class deals with what they call "good complaints," which are compliments given by one member of the class to another for some prosocial behavior. Teachers in the classroom councils have veto power, but their veto can be overridden by appeal to student-based Appeals Council. This Appeals Council is made up of the four classroom representatives and an alternate who serves as the Appeals Judge.

Moral Education in the Elementary Classroom: A Personal Perspective

A more comprehensive perspective on applying Kohlberg's theory may become clearer if I relate some experiences from my own classroom. Before attending Harvard (to study under Kohlberg), I was an elementary school teacher, and I have been a consultant in elementary and secondary schools for the past 5 years. I am a firm believer in a school- or systemwide commitment to democratic education; however, from both personal experience and observation, I know that individual teachers can make a difference. Concomitantly, they cannot legitimately claim moral impotence: One can and should act alone, if necessary. As David Purpel and Kevin Ryan indicated in the subtitle of their book (1976), moral education inherently "comes with the territory"; that is, teaching is inherently a moral endeavor, and educators have an obligation to consider both moral issues and the moral implications of their teaching methods. It is not a question of *whether* we will engage in moral education but rather a question of *how*.

During my teaching experience, I never found a critical mass of support among my colleagues to set up a schoolwide program of democracy or cooperative moral education. As a result, my attempts, some of which are described below, were limited to my own students in my own classroom.

Discussing Moral Dilemmas in the Classroom

In my classrooms (white and Latino fifth and sixth graders from working-class neighborhoods), I used the daily newspaper and weekly class meetings as the two central sources of moral dilemmas. Those from the newspaper were ones that I was trying to resolve in my own mind. In the meeting, I tried to emphasize that when it comes to moral decision making, we are "all in it together."

Typically we used the first minutes of class for our morning class meeting and for these discussions. The time was flexible—sometimes as short as 5 minutes but occasionally much longer—and anyone in the class could raise an issue or a topic to be discussed. For example, one student brought in a list of the ten most admired men and women in the nation. We used the list as the basis for an interesting discussion of the criteria used by respondents to the survey. The most admired men tended to be political leaders or sports figures; the women were more likely to be the wives of prominent men. Sometimes we listened to Tom Lehrer records and then discussed the moral issues that he raised about such topics as pollution, racial discrimination, nuclear proliferation, and disarmament. During local or national elections, we frequently discussed the issues of the campaigns and the progress or demise of candidates.

The Singer Family: A Case Study in Moral Dilemmas for Class Discussion

As a teacher of fifth and sixth graders in Salt Lake City, Utah, during the 1970s, I found that one of the most powerful series of dilemmas discussed in my classroom revolved around a Utah farmer, John Singer. He had decided to remove his children from public school and teach them at home, and his activities were widely publicized in print and broadcast media. Singer, who was born in Germany and was often cited as having been a member of the Nazi Youth, lived in rural Utah with his wife and five children. He had what most people would consider unusual religious and political views, including beliefs in racial segregation and racial inequality. Ogden Kraut (1988) describes the motivation behind Singer's need to educate his children himself:

John and Vickie Singer valued [their] rights and freedoms. They had studied [their] scriptures, the Constitution, and the teaching of the Founding Fathers of the LDS [Mormon] Church [from which they had been excommunicated because of their views and practices] and the American nation. They were also familiar with U.S. Supreme Court Justice William Brennan's 1963 statement:

> Attendance at the public school has never been compulsory; parents remain morally and constitutionally free to choose the academic environment in which they wish their children to be educated.

Therefore, in 1973 they felt justified, in fact duty bound, to take their children out of public schools to protect them from the vices and corruptions so prevalent there, and provide them with a better education at home—just as many other concerned American families were doing. (p. 10)

Between March 1973 and January 1979, when he was killed by law-enforcement officers attempting to carry out the orders of the court to arrest him, John Singer took his children out of school and taught them at home. He refused to allow the state to test his children's academic progress, and he refused to attend court proceedings against him because he feared that he would lose custody of his children. The court found Singer guilty of child neglect for his refusal to send his children to school and sentenced him to 60 days in jail and a fine. Later, while still married to his first wife Vickie, he married a second wife and welcomed her children into his home. (These actions were against their father's wishes, leading to additional legal problems for Singer.) He also began carrying a weapon with him on his farm. In January 1979, while Singer was walking to collect his mail, he was confronted by officers who had been circling his home on snowmobiles for several days in their attempt to enforce the orders of the court. It became a showdown: After allegedly drawing a weapon in a threatening manner, Singer was shot and killed.

As the Singer family story unfolded, the issues were chronicled in the media, and students in my classroom discussed both the factual and the moral aspects of each development in turn. The extent and nature of the coverage as well as Singer's manipulation of the press presented additional moral discussion topics. The issues that we addressed included the following:

• Do/Should parents have a right to keep their children out of school and teach them at home?

- Does/Should *what* the parents intend to teach have any bearing on *whether* they should be allowed to teach their children at home?
- Does/Should the state have any role in monitoring or supervising the academic progress of the children?
- Under what circumstances, if any, does a person have the right or moral obligation to disobey a law?
- If a person feels an obligation to disobey a state's law, does that person have any obligation to accept the state's punishment or can he or she morally attempt to avoid punishment?
- Does/Should a person's belief in commandments from a god have any bearing on social policy? Should John Singer's religious beliefs be treated differently from the religious beliefs of others (e.g., Jehovah's Witnesses' refusing to participate in the Pledge of Allegiance)?
- Does/Should a man have the right to marry more than one woman at the same time (polygamy)? Does/Should a woman have the right to marry more than one man at the same time (polyandry)? What is the case in other cultures? Is it possible for one action to be morally right in one culture and morally wrong in another?
- Should Mrs. Black (Singer's second wife) or her first husband have custody of their children? On what grounds?
- How should law-enforcement officials carry out their orders? Is violence justified in carrying out orders? Were there other alternatives to the ones used in this case? If so, were any morally preferable?

Given the wide coverage in the media, Singer's violent death had a predictable effect on the populace of Utah. On the morning following his death, he was the topic of conversation across the state, and given our class's history of interest in the case, it was the first item that we discussed. Students offered their opinions about why the officers' shooting of Singer was or was not justified. Their responses illustrated a range of moral reasoning from Stage 1 to Stage 3. Students at Stage 1 argued out of concrete self-interest that the officers were right to shoot, that a policeman has to punish people because it is his job. Students at Stage 2 argued "an eye for an eye, a tooth for a tooth": Because Singer had pulled a gun, the officers were justified to reciprocate. Stage 3 responses took in the consequences for the wider community, arguing that this shooting would act as an example to prevent others from disobeying the law. On the other hand, there were also many student responses at different stages arguing that the officers were not justified in shooting. These disagreements made for a lively classroom discussion that challenged students' justifications for their answers. Kohlberg believes that such discussions expose students to levels of moral reasoning higher than their own and promote moral development. Once they hear it, students prefer moral reasoning at a stage higher than their own, even though they cannot generate it spontaneously.

On that particular morning, my students and I were witness to what was for us a dramatic example of how we—children/young adolescents and adults—were trying to make sense of our moral world. From my comments and questions during discussions of current events, my students did not find it unusual to see me grappling with a moral issue. Although they may have attributed my struggles to nothing more than a lack of intelligence or common sense on my part, they soon found that such struggles are universal. On the morning after Singer's death, the principal of the school, a man not typically unsure about his decisions or publicly given to moral deliberation, quietly took a seat in the classroom and sat for an hour listening to the discussion. Although he volunteered little about his own position, he listened attentively to the students and thanked us at the end of the hour for letting him sit in on the discussion. His obvious interest had a powerful impact on the students.

The Weekly Class Meeting

Each Thursday afternoon, we held the class meeting. At this meeting, our classroom rules were created and enforced. I had certain "Big Rules" that were nonnegotiable and not subject to the will of the class. These rules, including "We will treat others as we would like to be treated," "People are safe in this classroom," "Property is safe in this classroom," and "People are treated with respect in this classroom," were distributed to and signed by both students and parents at registration on the first day of school. My aim was to create a sense of self-government and both individual and group responsibility through the creation of a "social contract" made up of these Big Rules and voluntarily entered into by both students and parents.

The existence of the Big Rules in combination with the social contract that the students and parents had entered into gave me the opportunity to exercise a veto if the students wanted to create a class rule or establish a punishment that I felt violated the Big Rules.

Although I never had to exercise my veto power, I wanted to avoid a predicament like the following. A colleague, who was an elementary school teacher and an educational consultant, had been helping teachers in his district to conduct class meetings. One of the teachers with whom he was working came to understand democratic procedures but failed to understand her role as a moral leader in the classroom or to have Big Rules that would allow her to—and dictate that she should—intervene. (Kohlberg argued that teachers should exercise moral leadership by advocating their own positions and arguing for the good of the community.) A student in her class was guilty of spitting on another student. In the class meeting, the students democratically decided that the "appropriate" punishment would be for the guilty student to stand in a circle made up of his fellow classmates and have each class member spit upon the offender in turn. Because such a punishment would have violated the Big Rules of my classroom, I would have argued against it in class meeting. Had it come to a vote and won, I would have vetoed it on the grounds that the punishment failed to treat the student with respect and dignity.

During our class meetings, students and I negotiated other class rules and procedures and discussed disputes. For example, seating was one class procedure that was created in the class meeting. After a long discussion of other alternatives, we decided to conduct a seating lottery at the end of each Thursday's class meeting. The seating lottery allowed students a random and fair chance of sitting next to their friends. It also meant that if a student had to sit next to someone other than a best friend, it would be for only a week. The random nature of the procedure also helped break down "cliques."

A student drew slips of paper out of a ballot box to determine the "agenda" for the class meeting. For most of the year, the box was used as the repository for questions, issues, or disputes that students or I wanted to raise in the class meeting. During local and national election campaigns, the ballot box was used in mock elections to give students a "voice." The papers could be either signed or anonymous. As each paper was read, we asked if we should discuss the matter. (In some cases, disputes between students, originally thought to be important enough to discuss in the class meeting, had already been resolved by the time of the meeting. In those cases, we simply moved on to the next sheet of paper drawn from the box.)

During one class meeting, a slip of paper was pulled from the box that read: "We thought that in this class people were safe." There was no name or further explanation. After a moment or two of silence, three girls started expressing their displeasure with me. Earlier in the week, the class had taken a tour of historical buildings near the school. A member of the State Historical Society had been our guide.

At one point, we had walked around a mansion undergoing renovation. A chain-link fence had been installed around the grounds to prevent unauthorized entry. One of my students, short and thin in stature, wondered whether he could squeeze through the gate and into the property. Unhappy with his decision, I walked over to Michael and pulled him out of the gate when he was about half-through. While the rest of the class continued the tour of the mansion, I spent a few minutes with Michael discussing "appropriate and inappropriate" behavior.

The girls who had written the note were not close friends of Michael; however, they had interpreted my actions as an attack on Michael and accused me of hypocritically breaking the Big Rule that people are safe in the classroom. With Michael's permission, he and I discussed with the class what had happened during the field trip, and the class clarified the distinction between a physical restraint and an attack. We would not have had this opportunity without a class meeting where students felt free to call their own, their peers', and my actions into question. I did not always fare as well when challenged about hypocrisy and, hence, taught myself and my students about fallibility in moral judgment and moral action.

In this section I have attempted to demonstrate through personal experience the opportunities to discuss moral issues through current events and classroom meetings. Moral issues can range from trivial to formidable. The goal is to create an environment and community where students are encouraged to enter moral discussions with both peers and adults.

Although I lack formal evaluation measures, the strengths of this approach are evident in the accomplishments I witnessed during the course of each year. The major weakness of the classroom democracy is that it is limited to the individual classroom. Ideally, democratic classrooms can function within a larger democratic program or democratic school (Howard & Kenny, in press). Students in my classroom improved the ability to negotiate and to solve interpersonal disputes; increased their awareness of the well-being of other students; came to appeal readily to moral and democratic principles in advocating their positions on issues; gained an awareness of issues in the school and the wider community; and increased their knowledge of governmental institutions and how they functioned. My experience has replicated that of other educators in both elementary and secondary classrooms in urban, suburban, and rural environments (e.g., Arbuthnot, 1988; Kreisberg, 1988; Sain, 1981; Shaheen, 1986, 1988).

Conclusion

According to Kohlberg, the core of moral education is the practice of engaging students in reasoning about moral issues within a supportive environment. This is equally true whether one is teaching at the nursery school or in a doctoral level program. This chapter has focused on moral education in the elementary school. Whatever the age of the students, the educator must create a supportive environment that helps students to clarify their moral reasoning and actions through discussion and that challenges them to understand the perspective of others—whether it be in the classroom, in the wider community, in literature, or in history.

Although for Kohlberg development of the individual is the aim of education, this aim is not incompatible with the good of the community. In fact, both Kohlberg and I argue, they are inexorably linked. Kohlberg's just community emphasizes that moral reasoning arises in social contexts and is both influenced by and has an impact on the collective. The goal of moral education in classrooms and schools is to create the environments and experiences that will promote moral development. As a result of such an environment and a collaborative attempt by students and educators to examine ethical issues and engage in both moral communication and actions, students will have the ideal educational conditions for growth. Such moral education will be beneficial to the individual student, his or her peers, the local community, the nation, and ultimately the whole of humanity.

ACKNOWLEDGEMENT.   I would like to acknowledge and thank Mayra Besosa, Susan deGersdorff, Cheryl Howard, Vera Michalchik, and Sue Paxman for their critical comments and editorial suggestions on an earlier draft of this chapter.

References

Arbuthnot, C. (1988). Primary forum. *Democracy and Education, 3*(1), 27–30.
Baumrind, D. (1986). Sex differences in moral reasoning: Response to Walker's (1984) conclusion that there are none. *Child Development, 57,* 511–521.
Berkowitz, M. (1981). A critical appraisal of the educational and psychological perspectives on moral discussion. *Journal of Educational Thought, 15,* 20–33.

Berkowitz, M. (1985). The role of discussion in moral education. In M. Berkowitz & F. Oser (Eds.), *Moral education: Theory and application* (pp. 197–218). Hillsdale, NJ: Erlbaum.

Blatt, M., & Kohlberg, L. (1975). The effects of classroom moral discussion upon children's level of moral judgment. *Journal of Moral Education, 4,* 129–161.

Damon, W., & Killen, M. (1982). Peer interaction and the process of change in children's moral reasoning. *Merrill-Palmer Quarterly, 28,* 347–368.

Dewey, J. (1963). *Experience and education.* New York: Free Press.

Dewey, J. (1966). *Democracy and education.* New York: Free Press.

Frost, S. (1983). Janus Korczak: Friend of children. *Moral Education Forum, 8*(1), 4–22.

Garrod, A. (1989). Promoting moral development through a high school English curriculum. *The Alberta Journal of Educational Research, 35*(1), 61–79.

Garrod, A., & Staines, D. (1984). *Illuminations: The days of our youth.* Toronto: Gage.

Gilligan, C. F. (1982). *In a different voice: Psychological theory and women's development.* Cambridge, MA: Harvard University Press.

Gilligan, C. F., Ward, J. V., Taylor, J. M., with B. Bardige (Eds.) (1989). *Mapping the moral domain.* Cambridge, MA: Center for the Study of Gender, Education and Human Development, Harvard Graduate School of Education.

Howard, R., & Kenny, R. (in press). Education for democracy: Promoting citizenship and critical reasoning through school governance. In A. Garrod (Ed.), *Learning for a lifetime: Moral Education in perspective and practice.*

Karp, A. (1989, April 12). Ethics in the eighties: Putting value on values. *Baltimore Sun,* Section E, p. 1.

Kohlberg, L. (1948). Bed for bananas. *Menorah Journal, IIIVI*(4), 285–399.

Kohlberg, L. (1970). Education for justice: A modern statement of the Platonic view. In N. F. Sizer & T. R. Sizer (Eds.), *Moral education: Five lectures* (pp. 57–83). Cambridge, MA: Harvard University Press.

Kohlberg, L. (1981). *The philosophy of moral development: Moral stages and the idea of justice.* New York: Harper and Row.

Kohlberg, L. (1984). *The psychology of moral development: The nature and validity of moral stages.* New York: Harper and Row.

Kohlberg, L. (Ed.) (in press). *Ethical stages and the life cycle.* New York: Harper and Row.

Kraut, O. (1988). The Singer/Swapp siege: Revelation or retaliation? *Sunstone, 12*(6), 10–17.

Kreisberg, S. (1988). Creating a democratic classroom: One teacher's story. *Democracy and Education, 3*(2), 13–20.

Leming, J. (1981). Curriculum effectiveness in moral/values education: A review of research. *Journal of Moral Education, 10,* 147–164.

Lockwood, A., & Harris, D. (1985). *Reasoning with democratic values: Ethical problems in United States history: Vols. I and II.* New York: Teachers College Press.

Noddings, N. (1984). *Caring: A feminine approach to ethics and moral education.* Berkeley: University of California Press.

Parr, S. R. (1982). *The moral of the story: Literature, values, and American education.* New York: Teachers College Press.

Piaget, J. (1965). *The moral judgment of the child.* New York: Free Press.

Power, C., Higgins, A., & Kohlberg, L. (1988). *Lawrence Kohlberg's approach to moral education.* New York: Columbia University Press.

Purpel, D., & Ryan, K. (1976). *Moral education . . . it comes with the territory.* Berkeley: McCutchan.

Reimer, J., Paolitto, D., & Hersh, R. (1983). *Promoting moral growth: From Piaget to Kohlberg.* New York: Longman.

Rest, J. (1989). With the benefit of hindsight. *The Journal of Moral Education, 18*(2), 61–79.

Sain, P. (1981). *A democratic management system emphasizing social growth and development as a content area.* Unpublished master's project, Westminster College, Salt Lake City, UT.

Shaheen, J. (1986). Steppingstones toward citizenship: Little children speak up for fairness. *Moral Education Forum, 11*(2), 1–16.

Shaheen, J. (1988). Democratic discipline, discipline lives. *Democracy and Education, 3*(2), 1–8.

Sichel, B. A. (1988). *Moral education: Character, community and ideals.* Philadelphia: Temple University Press.

Social Research, Fall, 1983.

Timm, J. S., & Timm, H. S. (1983). *Athena's mirror: Moral reasoning in poetry, short story and drama.* Schenectady, NY: Character Research Press.

Walker, L. J. (1986). Sex differences in moral reasoning: A critical review. *Child Development, 55,* 677–691.

Wheeler, D. (1986, December 14). Teaching values. *Newswest,* p. 29.

CHAPTER FOUR

An Integrated Approach to Character Development in the Elementary School Classroom

THOMAS LICKONA

THE current debate in moral education—between those who stress moral thinking and those who stress moral experience or action—goes all the way back to Plato and Aristotle. Plato said that if a person really "knew" the good, he would *be* good. Aristotle disagreed, arguing that we become just by the practice of just actions, virtuous by doing virtuous deeds. From Plato came moral education programs with an emphasis on improving thinking; from Aristotle, moral education with an emphasis on practicing right behavior.

To do an adequate job of moral education, however, one has to combine Aristotle and Plato. By itself, the Aristotelian emphasis runs the risk of producing outward conformity without inner conviction or understanding. By itself, the Platonic emphasis runs the risk of producing moral reasoning that does not carry over into moral action.

For the last two decades, in my own work with teachers I have sought to develop an integrated approach to moral education, one that brings together the Platonic and Aristotelian agendas. This integrated approach aims to develop the three interrelated aspects of character: thinking, action, and the moral affect that serves as a motivational bridge between knowing what is right and actually doing it.

Character Development Goals

Within an integrated approach to character development, these broad goals are appropriate for the elementary years:

1. To promote development away from egocentrism toward more consistent relations of cooperation and mutual respect
2. To lay the foundations of good character, defined as habits of moral thinking, moral feeling, and moral action (so that children come to judge what is right, care deeply about it, and act accordingly)
3. To develop, in the classroom and school, a moral community based on fairness, caring, and democratic participation—both as a moral good in itself and as a support system for the character development of each individual

A classroom dedicated to these broad goals would seek to develop in each child the following specific qualities:

1. A self-respect that derives feelings of worth not only from achievement but also from prosocial behavior toward others
2. Social perspective taking ("How do others think and feel?")
3. Moral reasoning ("What is the right thing to do?")
4. Empathy, defined as the tendency to identify with and care about the welfare of others
5. The skills and attitudes needed for cooperative participation in human communities
6. Stable dispositions to respond to situations in moral ways—manifested in observable patterns (character traits) of kindness, honesty, responsibility, and a generalized respect for others

An integrated approach to character development is consistent with a Piagetian constructivist view of children as collaborators in their own development. It urges the teacher to view the child as a moral thinker, to try to see things from the child's viewpoint, and to recruit the child as a partner in creating a just and caring community in the classroom. But it also argues that the teacher must be a moral leader—must play a deliberate and central role in orchestrating the processes of moral education. And this educational model assumes that to achieve the goals for children listed above, children will need lots of practice at being moral persons: many opportunities to solve problems, act upon their best moral reasoning, be in social roles that give them real social responsibilities, and otherwise participate in a moral community. This last assertion reflects the Aristotelian idea that virtue must be practiced, not merely known.

Classroom Processes

The character development goals of an integrated approach may be pursued through four classroom processes:

1. Building self-worth and moral community
2. Cooperative learning
3. Moral reflection
4. Participatory decision making

Taken together, these four processes embrace both the formal academic curriculum and the "human curriculum" (the roles, rules, and relationships) that make up the intellectual and social-moral life of the classroom. The four processes should also be understood as overlapping, because any one process, done well, frequently involves the others at the same time. To flesh out the four processes, three questions need to be addressed: What is meant by a given process? Why is that process important for character development? How does a teacher do it?

Building Self-Worth and Moral Community

To build self-worth in the elementary school years is, first of all, to foster the sense of competence that is at the core of the child's self-concept. Second, it means to teach children to value themselves, to have the kind of self-respect that will enable them to stand up for their rights and command respect from others.

To build moral community in the classroom means to create a group that extends to others the same respect one has for oneself. A half-century ago, John Dewey (quoted in Archambault, 1964) argued that "much of present education fails [as moral training] because it neglects this fundamental principle of school as a form of community life" (p. 431).

A moral community in the classroom exists when three conditions are created: Children know each other; they respect and care about each other; and they feel membership in, and accountability to, the group. When teachers create this kind of moral community in the classroom, they simultaneously foster the self-worth of each individual member. Let me briefly illustrate each of these three aspects of classroom community.

Helping Students Know Each Other. It is easier for children to value other people and feel an attachment to them if they know something about them. The long-range goal of character development, of course, is to produce people who have a principled, universalized respect for others, those they do not know as well as those they do. But at earlier stages of moral growth, students' best moral selves will be called forth and developed by the bonds of personal relations.

Building those bonds begins on the first day of school. For example: On day one, two teachers who team-teach in a combined third and fourth grade pair their students with someone they do not already know and give them about 10 minutes to complete a sheet titled "Partners." This sheet is divided into two columns: "Ways We Are Different" and "Ways We Are Alike." It includes questions (e.g., "What are two things you like to do?" "What are two things you're good at?") that students can use to explore their similarities and differences. Then the teachers ask students to draw their chairs into a circle and tell, as partners, one way they discovered they are similar and one way they are different. The groundwork is thereby laid for developing a classroom community that values individuality and diversity as well as unity.

Helping Children Respect and Care about Each Other. When students know something about each other, it is easier for a teacher to develop the second aspect of moral community: respecting and caring about each other. There are many ways to do that; one is to help children develop habits of affirming each other.

For example, one fifth-grade teacher does "appreciation time." Every other day, she invites her students to "tell something that someone else did that you appreciated." On one such occasion, one girl said: "I'd like to appreciate Julie for giving me some paper when I forgot mine. All I did was tell Donna that I forgot my paper, and there was Julie standing there offering me some of hers." A boy said: "I'd like to appreciate Stan for helping me remember everything I needed to do to finish my project." This activity, and others like it, fosters children's self-worth through public peer affirmation and serves at the same time to develop group norms of helpfulness and caring.

Helping Children Develop Membership In, and Accountability To, the Group. Several things contribute to this third aspect of community: The class has high cohesion, a strong sense of group identity; each individual student feels that he or she is a valued member of the group; individuals feel accountable to the group; and there is an ethic of interdependence in that the group feels a measure of responsibility for the welfare of each member.

Teachers can develop class cohesion through class traditions (such as opening the day with a class meeting) and symbols (a class name, a class banner, a class T-shirt) that make group unity visible and concrete. Teachers can help each child feel like a valued member of the group by ensuring that each has a "classroom helper" job, offering all the children a chance to be in the limelight (e.g., "Student of the Week") and giving public recognition to all the ways that individual children contribute to the life of the classroom. Teachers can develop children's accountability to the group by encouraging them to take the group's perspective and consider how their personal behavior affects the functioning of the class as a whole. This accountability is formalized through the group's participation in creating and implementing classroom rules and in solving interpersonal conflicts when those arise.

Finally, teachers can invite the group to show concern for the welfare of all its members. A first-grade teacher, for example, found she could foster this ethic of collective responsibility by posing the following question at class meeting: "Who has a problem you would like others to help you solve?" She reports that children listened and participated much better during these discussions than they did during traditional "show and tell" and became skilled at helping each other solve a variety of practical problems (ranging from conflicts over playground equipment to what to do about a quarrelsome sibling at home). Other teachers, even at the preschool level, report similar success with this peer-assisted problem solving. Being invited to help solve a classmate's problem appears to tap into and further develop even young children's capacity for empathy and prosocial behavior.

All of these are ways of implementing the first and most fundamental process of character development: fostering the self-worth of the child by developing the child's membership in the moral community of the classroom.

Cooperative Learning

Classroom community will be "thin" if students come together occasionally to share thoughts but spend the rest of the day working individually on academics. The second process of character development, cooperative learning, is based on the premise that students must work together as well as talk together.

Fifty years ago, Piaget (1965) argued that the school's determination to "shut the child up in work that is strictly individual" was "contrary to the most obvious requirements of intellectual and moral development" (p. 405). One does not learn cooperative morality, Piaget said, by working alone.

As an example of the power of cooperative learning, consider the following account from a sixth-grade teacher in Montreal, Quebec. At the start of the school year, the class was plagued by racial conflict. Black students and white students insulted and physically assaulted each other during recess and after school. "There was so much hate between them," the teacher said, "that I thought the class would have to be split up."

The school psychologist observed the class and recommended that the teacher set up cooperative learning groups. He suggested putting together the children who had the most trouble getting along, giving them joint assignments and projects. He advised that the groups meet for at least part of every day and that the teacher monitor them closely. Most important, he said, was to stick with the groups even if they didn't seem to be working in the beginning.

The teacher took this advice. She had the students work together—usually in threes and fours—in all subjects for part of every day. They worked on math projects in groups, researched social studies projects in groups, practiced reading to each other in groups, and so on. "I assigned each group an observer," the teacher explained. "The observer's job was to notice and later comment on the kind of communication group members were using."

"It took them 2 months to make this really work," the teacher said, "but they finally got it together. What's more, their test scores went up." One day, as these students were working in their groups, another teacher stopped by who had seen them in September when they were at each other's throats. She said she found it hard to believe it was the same class.

How does cooperative learning help children develop morally? It does so by giving them an opportunity and a reason to:

1. Get to know and learn to work with others who are different from themselves, as illustrated by the story of the Montreal sixth-graders

2. Take the viewpoints of co-workers, because cooperative learning provides a social structure in which perspective taking is a necessary and naturally occurring feature of social interaction
3. Make fair decisions about the division of labor and the resolution of conflicts that arise in the course of group work
4. Learn that it is a decent thing to help others
5. Raise these cooperative attitudes and skills to the level of habit through the regular practice in prosocial interaction that cooperative learning provides.

Elsewhere (Lickona, 1990) I have described ten forms of cooperative classroom work: learning partners; cluster group seating; student team learning; jigsaw learning; team testing; small-group projects; team research; team competition; extending cooperative learning throughout the academic curriculum; and whole-class projects. The research on the academic and social-moral benefits of these approaches is now considerable (see, e.g., Johnson & Johnson, 1984; Slavin et al., 1985).

Social observers often decry me-first individualism among young people and their lack of concern for the common good. If we wish to strengthen ethical cooperation within society, we should strive to make it a character trait of children as they live and work in the small society of the classroom.

Moral Reflection

The third process crucial to character development is moral reflection. "Reflection" is intended to cover a wide range of intellectual activity: reading, thinking, and writing; discussion or debate about moral matters; straightforward explanations by the teacher (e.g., of why it is wrong to take someone's property or make fun of a retarded child); and firsthand inquiry and experience (e.g., studying and caring for plants, animals, and the environment) that increase children's awareness of the complex ecosystem to which they belong and for which they must care.

Of all the processes of character development, moral reflection is aimed most directly at developing the cognitive, rational aspects of character. At the same time, however, this more self-consciously rational aspect of character education should be carried out in such a way as to foster a union of cognition and affect—so that children come to feel deeply about what they think and value. That union is important, because it is when moral values have affective importance that the person holding those values is most likely to act upon them.

Good literature is one excellent resource for raising moral issues in a way that engages both mind and affect. One fifth-grade teacher (Frey, 1983), as part of a unit on the Middle Ages, reads her students Barbara Leonie Picard's novel, *One Is One* (1965). The protagonist, a boy reared to regard knighthood as the only admirable life for a man, finds himself drawn instead to the peace of the monastery and the beauty of art. Mocked by his brothers, however, he reluctantly becomes a knight. But appalled by the brutality of battle and the horrible aftermath of war, he finally returns to the monastery to become a creative artist. The book, says the teacher, makes a deep impact on her fifth graders. It stirs discussion of the difference between physical and moral courage—and the difficulty of moral choices.

Sometimes the life of the classroom provides a ready-made moral dilemma that fully engages children. A teacher can develop an "ethical eye" that spots these important opportunities for moral reflection and debate. One second-grade teacher saw just such an opportunity during a science project that had the class incubating 20 chicken eggs. She had suggested to the class that they might wish to open an egg each week to monitor the embryonic development. Later that day, in his reading group, 7-year-old Nathaniel confided to his teacher: "Mrs. Williams, I've been thinking about this for a long time—it's just too *cruel* to open an egg and kill the chick inside!" Mrs. Williams listened without comment and said she would bring it up for discussion with the whole class.

When she did, there was some agreement that Nat's point was worth thought. But many children said they were curious to see what the embryo looked like. Nat replied that being curious wasn't a good enough reason for killing a chick. "How would you like it," he said, "if somebody opened your sac when you were developing because they were curious to see what you looked like?" Anyway, he argued, the library must have pictures of chick embryos; that would be a better way of finding out what they looked like. But, countered some of the children, they wanted to see the *real* chick. "Is it alive?" became a question. Some said it isn't alive until it hatches; others said it's alive now, and it *is* a chicken.

Mrs. Williams asked the children to think about the issue overnight, and they would reach a decision the next morning. By that time, a majority of the children had come to feel that Nat's objection should be honored; they should not open the eggs.

The potential moral learnings here are many: that all life, even that of a chick embryo, is to be taken seriously; that just wanting to do something is not a good enough reason for doing it; that when a member of the group has strong feelings about something, he or she has a right to express them and others an obligation to listen; and, if possible, a conflict should be solved in a way that tries to meet the needs of all parties (the class did, in fact, search out pictures of chick embryos in the library). These learnings were possible because Mrs. Williams took time to allow her children to come to grips with a difficult ethical dilemma arising from the life of their classroom. Teachers consistently find that real-life dilemmas like this one are much more effective at arousing children's thinking and feelings than are "canned" dilemmas from a book or kit.

Elementary school children are not too young to begin to learn the skills of "rational decision making." This methodology, claim a number of philosophers and educators (see, e.g., Hall & Davis, 1975), is a more reflective, systematic approach to solving moral problems than simply confronting children with a dilemma and asking them to debate it. Consider, for example, the real-life dilemma of 11-year-old Andy. He had just made friends with two boys after a month of painful lonesomeness at a new school. Walking home from school with Andy, these boys stole a package from an apartment mailbox, opened it at Andy's house to find two gold-plated medallions, and laughed when Andy said he thought they should return them. Andy wanted to keep his new friends but thought stealing was wrong. What should he have done?

Rational decision making teaches students to ask these questions: What are the alternatives? What are the likely consequences of each alternative for the various people involved? What are the values involved in each course of action? What is the best solution—the one that maximizes the good consequences and is most consistent with the important moral values?

Andy, for example, might tell his parents about the problem, and they might talk privately with the boys about returning the medallions. That wouldn't get the boys in trouble, might have some positive influence on their future behavior (at least with Andy), and would keep alive Andy's chance of a continuing friendship. Rational decision making maintains that children, regardless of their cognitive-developmental stage, can with practice improve in their ability to consider alternatives and consequences in reaching moral decisions. That claim gains credibility from the work of Spivak and Shure (1974) in teaching even preschool-age children to use a simplified form of this cognitive strategy.

The advantage of difficult moral dilemmas is that they create conflict within and between students. This disequilibrium, developmental theory holds, stimulates students to revise their moral reasoning in the direction of greater complexity and adequacy. However, there is a hidden danger in dilemmas, especially for children. This danger was expressed by an elementary school principal who said: "Presenting children with one dilemma after another is likely to be very confusing and disturbing for them. It makes it seem as if it's always hard to know what's right and what's wrong."

Children, especially, need what moral philosophers call "clear cases": instances where moral values are not in conflict and where the right course of action is plain. For example: I shouldn't steal another kid's milk money; I should do my own work on a test; I shouldn't bully a smaller child on the playground; I should keep a promise to go somewhere with a friend even when a better offer comes along. Moral reflection in the classroom should teach children how to act in clear-cut situations like these. It should teach them basic moral values—honesty, promise keeping, fairness, truthfulness, and kindness—and how to apply them to life situations—before it asks them to deal with conflicts between these values.

Classroom moral discussion should also help children reflect on the fact that the hard part of morality is very often not deciding what is right but doing it. Teachers often complain that their students "know the right answers" in discussions about why they shouldn't lie, copy somebody else's homework, or make fun of someone who's different. Why don't they then act according to what they know is right? Children should be challenged to think about that question, to keep track of their own ethical conduct in an "ethics-in-action journal," and to examine the circumstances in life and the weaknesses in character that account for the gap between moral judgment and moral behavior. If they are to make progress in closing that gap, they need to become wise about what helps them hold to the right course when they are tempted to do otherwise. In short, children need to be moral psychologists who understand wrongdoing as well as moral philosophers who can judge what is right and good.

Participatory Decision Making

Participatory decision making, the fourth character development process, involves children in making decisions about classroom rules, plans, and problems. It is important for several reasons: Children have a deeper understanding of rules when they are involved in constructing them; by participating in classroom decision making, students have a chance to apply their moral reasoning to their moral environment and their own moral behavior; members of a classroom feel more accountable to rules and problem resolutions when they have had a hand in making them.

At the high school level, teachers report that it is common for adolescents to see the school's and society's rules in purely pragmatic terms. You follow rules if you don't want to run the risk of getting in trouble; you break them if it suits your purposes and you can get away with it. There is no sense of a *moral* obligation to follow rules, no conception of rules as serving the legitimate purposes of a group or institution. It seems reasonable to suppose that this attitude comes at least in part from students' having had little or no opportunity to participate in making any of the rules that affect their lives.

When the teacher and class make rules together, students get a lesson in the social purpose of rules—"to help us live and work together." Rule making becomes one of the first acts of cooperation and mutual respect in the development of the classroom community. "Rules due to mutual respect and cooperation," Piaget (1965) maintained, "take root in the child's mind" (p. 362).

The class meeting, I believe, is the most important vehicle for participatory decision making at the elementary school level. The class meeting is a meeting of the whole class that emphasizes *interactive* discussion. A skilled teacher deliberately encourages children to interact with classmates' perspectives by asking for their reactions to the last speaker's idea. A class meeting is typically conducted in a circle to facilitate good eye contact, communication, and group cohesion and is held at regularly scheduled times or in response to special needs. To be a positive moral experience, the meeting itself must be governed by agreed-upon rules for mutually respectful talking and listening.

Solving Problems Through the Class Meeting

Teachers use the class meeting as a problem-solving vehicle in a variety of ways, as indicated by the following comments from two second-grade teachers.

> If we're having a problem, I'll get the kids in a circle and deal with it right then. Sometimes I'll have a circle meeting at the

end of the afternoon and say, "Today was a lousy day. What can we do to make tomorrow better?" It helps.

We have something called The Class Business Box. Kids can put in anything they would like brought up at our Wednesday class meeting. One week, for example, somebody wrote that they wanted to talk about "squirting" on the playground. Some kids were filling their mouths with water at the water fountain and then squirting a stream at other people. The kids who had been targets talked about how they didn't like it, we made a no-squirting rule, and that ended the problem.

One advantage of the Class Business Box: It allows a child who might hesitate to bring up a problem in a class meeting to do so anonymously through the box.

The class meeting has been known to solve stubborn moral problems that resist other approaches. A teacher of a first-grade class in an inner-city school held her first class meeting on stealing. She explained:

> Things had been disappearing left and right, and something had to be done. I had tried talking to the class; the ones who weren't stealing were with me, but I wasn't getting through to the guilty parties. I had tried searching children, which recovered a few items, but that wasn't solving the problem. I didn't want to play policeman; I wanted them to internalize the value that they shouldn't steal.

She began the class meeting by reviewing all the things that had turned up missing in recent weeks. Then she asked two important questions; first, "I want you to think of a time when something of yours was taken—how did you feel?" Children spoke freely about that; they said they felt angry and sad—and very happy if they were fortunate enough to get the missing possession back. Then the teacher asked a second question: "How do you feel when *you* take something that isn't yours?" There was silence. Finally one boy spoke up to say, "I don't feel so good when I take something." Other children made similar admissions.

Through this meeting, the teacher accomplished at least two things: sensitizing children to how others felt when they had something taken, and sensitizing them to the fact that they didn't feel very good about themselves when they took something.

After this meeting, to further encourage honesty, she decided to have a Lost and Found Box instead of asking children to bring "found" objects to her desk (something that is threatening for a child who has in fact stolen something). The class decorated the Lost and Found Box and placed it in the back of the room. Soon all sorts of lost things began turning up in the box, and the frequency of missing items sharply declined. The teacher commented:

> What was once an hourly (or more) occurrence [missing property] has become a once-a-day (or less) happening. It's become accepted behavior in our room to be honest—something I did not expect. If children find something that doesn't belong to them, they put it in the box, and they go and find their own things there. If someone does slip and keep something that isn't theirs, it's the kids who pitch in and find it, not me. I hear things such as, "Don't worry, Jimmy, we'll help you find your pencil!" I also hear comments such as, "I didn't keep the eraser this time, I put it in the box," and, "Teacher, I found Lisa's mitten and gave it to her. She thanked me."
>
> I've been using other class meetings to reinforce this honest and thoughtful behavior. The class is very proud of its progress, and so am I.

Sometimes children's moral attitudes and behavior are difficult to change, rooted as they are in their developmental immaturity or in competing values systems outside the school. But time and again, teachers are surprised at their ability to influence group norms positively through the class meeting and at the power of these group norms to influence individual students' behavior.

Expanding Students' Participation in Decision Making

Many teachers use the class meeting only when there is a problem that needs to be dealt with, but its potential is much greater than that. Students can gradually be brought into broader decision-making roles that increase their responsibility for the classroom and stimulate their intellectual and character development.

Some teachers, for example, use the class meeting to involve children in planning a special class project, such as a field trip (Where would they like to go? What do they want to learn? What preparations and arrangements are necessary?) or a class play (Which play would they like to perform? How should roles and jobs be assigned? What audiences would they like to perform it for?).

A fifth-grade teacher goes a step further and makes her students consultants on the curriculum. When she feels her language arts lessons are getting stale, for instance, she'll ask students for their thoughts about something different they'd like to do in spelling or writing. She says she always gets good ideas.

Two teachers who team-teach a combined third- and fourth-grade class allow their students to participate in a variety of decisions that affect their learning. A math group, for example, can decide if they are ready to move on to division or if they need more time on multiplication. The class can decide if they would rather demonstrate their understanding of a just-completed unit on ancient culture by writing stories or by drawing a sequence of pictures.

These teachers comment: "We do not relinquish control of the decision-making responsibility; we structure options clearly. Our children gain a greater sense of worth when they become active decision makers. They show more zest for their studies and are more invested in their products as something *they* value rather than something they do for us."

In the hands of a skillful teacher, then, the class meeting has much potential. It can:

1. Deepen students' sense of shared ownership of the classroom
2. Improve students' moral reasoning, including their ability to take the perspective of others
3. Develop their listening skills and ability to express themselves in a group
4. Develop their self-worth by providing a forum in which their thoughts are valued
5. Help create a moral community that serves as a "support structure"—calling forth students' best moral selves and holding in place the qualities of good character that students are developing
6. Teach the skills and attitudes needed to participate effectively in democratic decision making

This last benefit has special significance in a democratic society. "Democracy," John Dewey (1968) wrote, "is much broader than a method of conducting government. *It is a way of life.* Its foundation is faith in human intelligence . . . faith that each individual has something to contribute, whose value can be assessed only as it enters into the pooled intelligence constituted by the contributions of all" (pp.

59–60). This interactive participation of all individuals, Dewey asserted, is "the keynote of democracy as a way of life" (p. 58).

The class meeting is democracy scaled to the child's world. It enables children to experience the power of their pooled intelligence and learn democracy by living democracy. It enables them to participate in a form of the democratic process that is altogether appropriate to the classroom.

The four classroom processes—community building, cooperative learning, moral reflection, and participatory decision making—reinforce each other; each is needed for the full success of the others. Discussion of moral issues, especially debate, is very difficult when the sense of community is weak, when students don't know or like their classmates. Debating moral issues is shallow without opportunities for real-life decision making. Class discussion is "all talk" if children never work together on substantive tasks. Cooperative learning fails to realize its full potential if children never plan and evaluate their joint endeavors. And, without the group spirit that is born of cooperative activity, participatory decision-making turns into a forum in which students argue for their "rights" with little thought of their obligations or the common good.

Character development, of course, does not stop at the classroom door. It should be stressed that the four processes described in this chapter can also be carried out in the schoolwide environment in ways that support and extend their occurrence in the classroom. A whole-school sense of community can be developed through cross-class adoption (where, for example, a sixth-grade class pairs up with a third-grade class for a weekly activity in which each older student works with his or her younger "buddy"), cross-age tutoring (individual students volunteer to give up a recess or two a week to help a younger child in reading, spelling, or math), and special whole-school events that foster school spirit and pride. Cooperative work can take the form of cross-class field trips, a camping overnight, or a community-service project. School assemblies can be used to foster moral reflection—as, for example, when a school brings in a police officer, judge, and a storeowner for a program on shoplifting. Student councils (with delegates who provide input from each classroom's class meetings) and special-task committees (to combat vandalism, improve bus behavior, reduce fights on the playground) offer students opportunities to participate in meaningful decision making and take on a larger measure of responsibility for the quality of their school environment. (For elaboration of these and other examples, see Lickona, 1990.)

Conclusion

In his thoughtful essay, "Classical Ideas About Moral Education," the philosopher Jon Moline (1982) reminds us of a point Aristotle made long ago: People do not naturally or spontaneously grow up to be morally excellent or practically wise. They become so, if at all, only as the result of lifelong personal and community effort.

The school must clearly be a major part of that effort. Schools certainly can't do it all; they must seek the help of families, churches, youth organizations, and all other groups that touch the lives of the young and shape their values. But schools can do far more, I think, than most of them realize. They have, as this chapter suggests, strategies that are accessible to most teachers.

The first step is for schools to set the goal of fostering students' character development in its cognitive, affective, and behavioral dimensions; the second step is to provide administrative leadership, staff planning time, in-service development, materials, and moral support for teachers—all of which are needed to teach character education effectively. In an era of an already crowded curriculum, systematic character education is a tall order, but given the moral crisis facing our nation and youth, we can surely do no less.

References

Archambault, R. (1964). *John Dewey on education.* New York: Random House.

Dewey, J. (1968). *Problems of men.* New York: Greenwood Press.

Frey, G. (1983). The Middle Ages: The social studies core of the fifth grade. *Moral Education Forum, 8,* 30–34.

Hall, R., & Davis, J. (1975). *Moral education in theory and practice.* Buffalo, NY: Prometheus Books.

Johnson, D. W., & Johnson, R. T. (1984). *Circles of learning: Cooperation in the classroom.* Alexandria, VA: Association for Supervision and Curriculum Development.

Lickona, T. (1990). *Teaching respect and responsibility: The fourth and fifth Rs.* New York: Bantam Books.

Moline, J. (1982). Classical ideas about moral education. In E. Wynne (Ed.), *Character policy: An emerging issue* (pp. 197–203). Washington, DC: University Press of America.

Piaget, J. (1965). *The moral judgment of the child.* New York: Free Press.

Picard, B. L. (1965). *One is one.* New York: Holt, Rinehart, & Winston.

Slavin, R., Sharon, S., Kagan, S., Hertz-Lazarowitz, R., Webb, C., & Schmuck, R. (Eds.) (1985). *Learning to cooperate, cooperating to learn.* New York: Plenum Press.

Spivak, G., & Shure, N. (1974). *Social adjustment of young children: A Cognitive approach to solving real-life problems.* San Francisco: Jossey-Bass.

CHAPTER FIVE

Democracy
in the Elementary School:
Learning by Doing

ETHEL SADOWSKY

AT the Heath School, a kindergarten through eighth-grade school in Brookline, Massachusetts, we take seriously our mandate to educate young people for the essential job of functioning as informed and active citizens in a democracy. We want the children to understand their rights and their responsibilities, to become aware of their obligations to the community, to learn to listen to one another and to the adults in their lives, to ask pertinent questions, discuss, think independently, and reach informed conclusions. The curriculum and teaching approaches at Heath complement the citizenship piece. Children from kindergarten on are encouraged to think originally, to write from their experience and imagination, to figure out math problems by counting, weighing, and measuring, and to learn about science through observation and recording of data. The democratic ethos goes hand in hand with an approach to learning that values the learner as an individual and respects his or her way of learning and thinking.

There are four distinctive approaches to teaching democracy and citizenship to the children of the Heath School. Each of these approaches has pedagogical and philosophical links with the works of Dewey and Kohlberg (see Chapters 1 and 3). One approach takes place within the individual classroom, where teacher and children together discuss and develop the rules and understandings that will govern the class community for the year that they are together. The second effort occurs when an older class of children helps a younger group to learn a new skill cooperatively and caringly. A third method of teaching citizenship takes place in individual classrooms where the teacher presents a project or piece of curriculum aimed at broadening the children's understanding of their role as members of a community. And the fourth way of helping our children learn about the role of citizens in a democracy is in the Heath Community Meeting, a weekly gathering of all fourth and fifth graders. The primary purpose of the meeting is for the children to have a forum where they can raise and discuss issues in the school that are troublesome and work together to find solutions to the problems. A secondary aim is to present models of citizen participation that are exemplary and that the children might want to emulate. In combination, these approaches constitute democratic education at Heath School.

Approach 1
Developing Rules

At the beginning of the school year all of the teachers at Heath take time to work with their students on the rules that will govern the class for the year. These classroom rules supplement and personalize the schoolwide rules that are published each year in the *Heath School Handbook*. Rules are kept to a minimum; they state the expectations of decorum and consideration necessary to maintaining an orderly and cooperative community. It is understood that these rules are subject to change if a group of students feel that they are not working as expected. Although individual classes develop their own set of guidelines, they all focus on similar themes: how to ensure safety (both physical and psychological), promote responsibility, and enhance community life. The way classroom rules are developed in Mrs. Gaskill's fourth-grade classroom is typical of the process other teachers initiate. The format is a whole-group discussion. Mrs. Gaskill sets the stage by explaining that everyone has ideas and needs to share them so that the class can get the best ideas working for everybody. If one person is speaking, no one else can. To get to speak, a person must raise his or her hand and wait to be called on. No one can say another person's ideas aren't good, but the whole class will work together to agree on what the best ideas are.

Discussing Ideas for Order

The discussion begins by focusing on how the group wants the class to run and what agreements they can reach that will make the class a place where everyone—including the teacher—wants to be. For example, Mrs. Gaskill starts by saying that she thinks fourth graders are old enough to know when they need to go to the bathroom or when they need a drink of water. She proposes that the class have a sign-out area on the blackboard where one girl and one boy at a time may leave the room for a drink or a trip to the bathroom. All the students think that this is a neat idea since they haven't had that freedom before. Then she asks what would be reasonable as far as how often a student really needs to leave the room. Most students suggest that about once in the morning and/or once in the afternoon is adequate. The class doesn't make a rule about how many times a day any student can leave the room, but they all basically agree that twice a day is reasonable.

Next Mrs. Gaskill asks if the children think that the teacher should treat all the students the same way all the time. They agree that this would be fair until she asks them questions like: "If someone doesn't do the homework because his or her grandmother arrived from out of town last night and the family all went out to dinner and got home late, is that the same as someone not doing homework because he or she just forgot to take the book home?" This kind of questioning confuses them and they have to sort out for themselves that there are legitimate differences in situations that must be addressed differently. Usually interesting discussion arises on this point, because a lot of fourth graders can think of innumerable exceptions to any situation. Eventually they are willing to agree that the teacher has to deal individually with at least some situations.

Mrs. Gaskill tries to say as little as possible and act as a moderator until it seems that they are ready to accept the idea of difference. She then explains that there will be times when one student will be doing something different and there is no need for anyone else to comment about it. She explains that in order to be fair, they have to act responsibly by being clear and honest in their discussions. The class talks about the impossibility that a teacher can always be completely fair, because ferreting out all the facts in every situation would require so much time that teaching what fourth graders are expected to learn would come to a complete halt. But she promises to do her best at being fair to everyone. Two important goals are achieved in this part of the discussion. The children begin to understand that nothing is perfect, but people can try very hard to figure out things that will serve everyone well. And the children feel positive about the new class and school year because they know they will have access to a teacher who will take their concerns seriously. Fourth graders think it is very grown up to be taken seriously by an adult, especially one in authority. So Mrs. Gaskill listens very seriously to the children's concerns at this meeting, modeling the behavior she will expect everyone to use throughout the year, even though some of the children are silly and push to get the discussion off track or to disrupt the process to see how much it will take to get the teacher to blow her top!

Finally, the group talks about how they would like to treat each other. They all seem to know that they should be kind and not mean. They give examples of what it takes to be kind in school: helping someone with school work, listening if a person has a problem, understanding that everyone has a rough day once in a while, and that sometimes people just need to be left alone for a bit. The children agree that it is never helpful to tease or be mean and that such behavior will be unacceptable in 4G. Then Mrs. Gaskill asks for volunteers to make some rules that aren't wordy but convey all the important ideas. This is a difficult task for most children, but there are always some who can distill the ideas into a code for a class. These are the rules that governed 4G in 1988–89:

> Raise your hand before speaking.
> Appreciate others.
> Be considerate.
> Help others when they need it.

Outcomes

There are several important outcomes of a meeting of this type at the beginning of the year. First, the children begin to think about their classroom environment as one thing they can control to a certain degree. They are essential participants in setting the tone and the rules they will live with all year. Second, the children think about how their behavior is experienced by others, and how they can have good, responsive relationships in the class. Third, they begin the process of recognizing differences as being reasonable, and they learn that they can be comfortable with differences. Fourth, the fourth graders learn that their teacher values discussion as a way for them both to settle problems and to make things happen in their world. And finally, the initial discussion gives Mrs. Gaskill a good reading of each student's thinking level and ability to express himself or herself verbally, important data to have at the start of a new year.

Rule Setting in Other Grades

A similar process takes place in the primary classrooms. In the second grade the teacher, Mrs. Dalsheim, and the children meet on the rug to brainstorm ideas on how 2D can become a caring family with 22 members. The teacher writes down the ideas, and she produces a list of rules stated in positive terms. The children also come up with consequences for breaking a rule, and the teacher modifies them. For example, one ardent second grader suggested that if a child hits another child, he or she should miss recess for the rest of the year. The teacher, with the concurrence of the children, changed the consequence to missing one day of recess. Classroom 2D has one overriding rule: Treat other people the way you want them to treat you. Everyone was able to agree on that one.

In the seventh and eighth grades, the process of making rules to govern the classroom becomes more sophisticated. Mr. Aglietti, social studies teacher, integrates the study of the Bill of Rights with the production of a bill of rights for students. The student document pertains to responsibility regarding classroom behavior, turning in homework, negotiating with the teacher regarding independent projects, decisions on individual vs. group assignments, and rights of privacy. A majority of the eighth graders believe that laws (rules) are necessary, recognizing that without rules, the class—and the school— would be chaotic. They are proud of their bill of rights. Even so, the students are looking for greater empowerment. Some of their issues include the right to wear hats in class, to listen to headsets whenever they wish, except during classes, and to talk back to teachers without consequence. A few feel that their rights to free speech are abridged because they cannot swear in school. Despite these typical early adolescent issues, the students agree that when they violate rules, there should be a consequence. Punishment is essential to ensure justice.

For some of the students, the right of privacy is crucial. Feeling that they have little privacy at home, they want the school to be an environment where they feel independent. They would like the same rights as adults. But they also see that school is a place that is not theirs but rather a shared community, and they accept their responsibility as members of that community. For example, seventh and eighth graders are assigned the task of washing tables and sweeping the lunchroom floor each day after lunch. Although they complain about the unfairness of this job (after all, there are custodians at the school who are paid to do this work), they do it each day. Visitors to the school always remark on this procedure, for the students fulfill the responsibility automatically. On occasion, they send representatives to speak to the younger children about cleaning up their trash more effectively, an indication that they eventually internalize the responsibility and its community aspect.

Mr. Aglietti believes that as the children move from seventh to eighth grade, many of them gain a broader perspective on how the school relates to the outside world. For example, he begins to hear comments like, "If I talk back to a teacher, he will think of that come grade time." They relate this kind of boundary on their freedom to that of a worker who makes trouble in the workplace and risks getting fired. Some see grade/effort/behavior reports as analogous to a paycheck. They start to understand that there are consequences for actions in school and in the world beyond school.

Integrating Bilingual Students: Solving Problems Democratically

In addition to developing rules to which all members of a class agree to adhere, teachers and students often work together to solve problems that threaten the well-being of the whole class or members of the class. An interesting example of creative problem solving took place in Mrs. Lipke's fifth-grade class. The issue was the isolation of a group of fifth graders whose first language is Hebrew. Heath School houses a Hebrew Bilingual Program, comprising about 30 children whose parents have come to the Boston area for a year or two of study or work. Toward the middle of the school year one child in the program complained to the teacher that the bilingual students were systematically excluded from excess activities and from most of the social events that took place out of school. The teacher arranged a meeting for all of the Hebrew bilingual fifth graders, the bilingual teacher, the school's guidance counselor, and both fifth-grade teachers.

The Israeli children spoke of how difficult it was to function in a new land with a new language. They said that they felt discriminated against because they didn't understand the customs or the rules of the games played at recess. As a result, they weren't picked to participate in team games on the playground, although several considered themselves to be excellent athletes. The forum gave these children an opportunity to air their grievances and hurt feelings and to figure out what to do next. They decided they wanted to talk with the rest of the fifth graders, let them know that they wanted to play with them as well as learn with them, and also tell them that when they were excluded from many informal activities, they felt lonely and sad.

When the American children heard what their Israeli classmates had to say, they said they had not realized that they were discriminating against them. They thought that the Israelis had preferred to stay apart, and they had not wished to intrude on their privacy. The discussion was revealing for everyone involved. It led to further talks on how people from different backgrounds can learn to understand one another and even become friends. This kind of classroom exercise is very important in preparing children to live in a complex, multicultural world.

Approach 2
Cross-Age Teaching

A kindergarten to eighth-grade school provides numerous opportunities for the children to practice being good citizens. A class 1 or 2 years older can help younger schoolmates in a variety of ways. In so doing, the older students acquire the satisfaction that comes from teaching. These kinds of activities permeate the school. For example, each spring the third graders keep weekly "Frog Logs," chronicling the development of tadpoles. The kindergartners make three visits to the third grade and fill out simplified logs, with the assistance of the third graders. The logs help children in both grades keep a record of development from egg to tadpole to frog. Similarly, another venture for the kindergartners and third graders centers on sharing of writing. Small groups alternate reading their writing aloud. Other students comment on what they like in the writing. The kindergarten students build self-esteem, and the third graders model good writing and the techniques of commenting positively on a peer's writing.

Another group of third graders spends the end of the school day on Fridays teaching first graders how to play various games, ranging from checkers to Parcheesi. The job of the older children is to bring a game they know how to play well to the first-grade classroom. Each child then explains the game to one, two, or three first graders. They learn to be as clear as possible in their explanation, to encourage the first graders to ask questions and to play the game in a way that permits the first graders to learn the moves and the rules. This kind of activity forces the third graders to be precise in their explanations—a skill that is very useful in a variety of tasks they will encounter throughout their schooling—and it also requires that they adopt a patient, teacherlike attitude with their younger friends. The first graders benefit by learning to play the board games and by experiencing in a positive way some of the grown-up things a third grader knows.

The 1988 Presidential Election: Learning the Issues Together

The presidential election of 1988 was a particularly exciting time at the Heath School, because one of the candidates for president lived in Brookline. Children of all ages talked about the race. The kindergarten held a mock election, which Mr. Dukakis won by a landslide. The seventh and eighth graders kept close track of the candidates' positions on several key issues, and they developed a bulletin board in the classroom to denote where each man stood on abortion, capital punishment, gun control, taxes, aid to education, health care, the homeless, AIDS, and more. The students wrote summaries of the candidates' statements on each of these issues and affixed them to the chart on the bulletin board. Those of us in the school felt that our junior high group spoke more articulately about the critical issues of the campaign than the candidates did.

The week before the election, members of the eighth-grade class prepared and presented a presidential debate to the Heath Community Meeting, a weekly gathering of fourth and fifth graders. Mr. Aglietti moderated the debate, and the students presented the most important issues to their audience, from the perspective of the candidate they were representing. Aware that they were talking to children 3 and 4 years younger than they, the eighth graders carefully explained each topic before presenting the candidate's position. There was also time for the fourth and fifth graders to question the candidates, and the children took advantage of the opportunity. Questions ranged from, "Mr. Dukakis, do you like living in Brookline?" to "Mr. Bush, don't you think there would be fewer murders in this country if there was better gun control?" The candidates gave informed answers. When the schoolwide mock election took place on November 8, Heath went solidly for the Democrat. No doubt the thrill of having a hometown candidate inflated Mr. Dukakis's vote. But the children had listened respectfully to carefully prepared arguments from Republican and Democratic surrogates, and they voted for the candidate they preferred.

Other Opportunities for Cross-Age Learning

Later that month, seventh graders helped first graders prepare for their annual Thanksgiving feast by teaching them how to make simple clay dishes, like the ones the Pilgrims used. Not only did the seventh graders demonstrate some successful ways to form bowls and cups that would hold food and liquid, they encouraged the first graders to decorate their pottery with seasonal designs, and then they fired the dishes. This process required three work sessions, during which the first and seventh graders got to know and like each other. When feast time arrived, the first graders sent invitations to their seventh-grade friends, who participated enthusiastically in the Thanksgiving festivities.

Fifth graders and second graders cooperated to work on a nature scavenger hunt that took place in the park near the school. Small mixed-age groups worked together in several sessions to develop clues of plant and animal life that other groups had to identify in the park. The planning stage took a long time, because the fifth graders, more sophisticated in their understanding of life science than their young friends, learned that they had to help the second graders understand some of the identifying features of a white pine, an oak leaf, or a ginko leaf before they could develop the kind of clues that would be useful. So the fifth graders became teachers to a group of eager young learners, and the scavenger hunt was a genuine success. The bonds that began to form in these sessions have lasted throughout the year.

In the spring of 1989, after the intramural basketball season for the seventh and eighth graders was over, children in grades 3 through 6 requested a Heath School tournament. Mr. Harris, the physical education teacher, agreed, as long as the children understood that everyone who wanted to participate would be able to do it, and everyone would have ample opportunity to play. There were several play-off games, all with large and enthusiastic support sections, until finally only two teams remained. The championship game was a much-anticipated event, attended by children from third grade up—as well as by lots of parents with camcorders. What made the event really special was that the coaches and referees were eighth graders. And these 14-year-olds concentrated on making sure that the players were having fun, that they were good sports, and that they played hard but fair ball. This was a remarkably successful event, one that had the whole school excited. The thing that people talked about was the quality of the play and the lack of tension among the players. Good sportsmanship and fun were the watchwords, and these goals prevailed throughout the tournament.

These kinds of activities—and similar ones that occur continually throughout the year—give children practice in citizenship. One of the obligations of citizenship is participation in the life of the community, helping out when possible and receiving help when needed. Becoming active in the ebb and flow of life at Heath School is not always easy. It can become frustrating to teach a group of first graders how to play checkers; it can try an older youngster's patience to help three tap-dancing fourth graders polish their act for the annual variety show; it takes skill to soothe the egos of members of a losing team that has played its heart out. But ensuring that children have the opportunity to practice the skills of teaching, coaching, mediating, and reaching out extends their understanding of community and participation and prepares them to become the kind of active citizens the country needs.

Approach 3
Understanding Others Through Curriculum Content

Lots of activities take place within each classroom that are designed to expand children's understanding of citizenship. In addition to the Israeli population, the Heath School enrolls children from about 15 different nations. It is very important for the students to gain an understanding of each other's culture, customs, and holidays, and to respect them. Teachers find many opportunities to inform children about the multicultural nature of the school and the nation. In the early grades the teachers invite parents to come to school and speak about their land. In conjunction with the second grade's study of American deserts, Mrs. Dalsheim invited an Israeli parent to show slides of Israel, including some of the Negev. The children were able to point out the similarities in the terrain, and then the class discussed how people lived on Arizona and Israeli deserts. They were amazed to discover the similar adaptations. In the upper grades, the Israeli students were able to inform their classmates about the causes of tension and crisis in the Middle East. Although their perspective was strictly pro-Israel, the discussions brought to the attention of American children the serious problems that exist in that part of the world and the ramifications of these problems on the United States. The children began to follow the statements of various Israeli and Arab leaders, and they learned that tiny countries thousands of miles away from Boston could have a direct impact on their lives.

In the primary grades, children interact with peers from Japan, Peru, Argentina, the Soviet Union, the Netherlands, Switzerland,

China, and Greece. They quickly become aware of language differences, and they help their non-English-speaking classmates begin to acquire facility with English. They also learn that these friends may eat different foods, celebrate different holidays, and know how to do different things. When birthdays occur, they may be celebrated with baklava, rice cakes, a torte, or sweet buns instead of chocolate cupcakes. The children learn to try new foods and to be polite if they don't like what they are tasting.

Exploring Other Kinds of Diversity

Heath children also learn about other kinds of diversity. In the fourth-grade classrooms, there is an Understanding Handicaps Program designed to make children aware of the issues surrounding handicaps. The program deals with four disability areas: visual impairments, hearing impairments, physical handicaps, and mental retardation. Parent volunteers organize and present the class sessions, using simulations, films, videos, games, and books to help demystify the disability under discussion. In addition, the children also meet with a guest speaker who has the handicap being discussed. This program has been going on for several years, and its effect is to promote understanding and lessen fear of people who are disabled. Many faculty members at Heath believe that children would gain true understanding of people with handicaps if they attended school together, and we are working on ways to make this happen. Until that day arrives, the Understanding Handicaps Program is an important way of enlarging children's awareness of human differences.

In Mrs. Hegstad's sixth grade, the children learn about world hunger in a dramatic way: They participate in the Oxfam Fast for a World Harvest, which occurs each year the Thursday before Thanksgiving. Prior to the fast, the teacher prepares the children for the event. She lets them know that participation is voluntary, with parental permission a must, but that all children will do the readings about world hunger and the use of fasting as a political tool and a spiritual act. The class learns about historical figures who have used—and use—fasting to gain attention for their causes, and they discuss why this is an effective tool. They also talk about what they can accomplish by fasting:

Create a symbolic link with hungry people
Raise money for hungry people by having sponsors

Raise our consciousness and that of others about aid to the
hungry

As the day of the fast nears, the anticipation and excitement in
the classroom grow. The children learn that they can have drinks
whenever they wish throughout the day, and bringing thermoses and
cups into the classroom is regarded as a treat. By fast day, everyone
in the sixth grade had received permission. They arrived at school
with ample supplies of liquid nourishment and wore badges reading,
"I'm fasting for Oxfam today. Be nice to me and contribute $ for the
hungry. Thanks." The children experience some pangs of hunger as
the day wears on, and they emerge from the fasting experience with a
heightened awareness of what it means to be hungry and what kinds
of action a rich and bounteous nation might take to alleviate a terri-
ble world problem.

Approach 4
Community Meeting

I believe that our fourth approach, the Heath Community Meeting, is
a unique method of teaching and practicing democracy at the elementary level. Before I became principal at the Heath School in
September 1986, I had been a housemaster at Brookline High School
for several years. (The house system was established at the high
school in the early 1930s. The large school was divided into four
houses—administrative units—each headed by a "master," a term
borrowed from Harvard. The goal was to reduce the size of the
school for the students, make it less anonymous and more personal,
and help the students connect easily with administrators and coun-
selors. Through the years changes have been made in the system, but
the houses remain important entities within the school.) While at the
high school, I participated in the school's town meeting form of
governance. Town meeting is the governing body of most New England towns, as it is of the Town of Brookline—a large municipality of
56,000 people. Brookline's town meeting is representative; town meeting members are elected to represent each precinct and meet annu-
ally in the spring to debate and pass the budget for the town and to
formulate and pass the laws that will govern it. Brookline High School
also adopted a representative form of town meeting, with students
elected by house to represent each class, and with adult representatives from the various departments and houses.

The Town Meeting: A Model for Democracy

From my vantage point as a town meeting member, I considered the strengths of the system to be the empowerment of students; the establishment of a forum in which students and adults in the school could work together collaboratively or adversatively, without repercussions for the students; the development of students' awareness of social responsibility, as they came to understand the needs of the school and how those needs might conflict with the goals of individuals; and the creation of a model classroom in democracy, where town meeting members had the rare opportunity to learn about democracy by practicing it and applying its tenets to real problems.

I also found some weaknesses in the way town meeting developed at the high school. Despite the racial, cultural, and ethnic diversity at the school, almost all the town meeting members were drawn from the same segment of the population—college-bound students with strong academic aspirations. The composition of the body was not representative of the population of the school. This serious flaw had equally serious ramifications. The student body at large knew little and cared less about the decisions town meeting had made, even though these decisions affected the quality of life in the school. Moreover, town meeting did an inadequate job of communicating its agenda and conclusions to the school, thereby increasing the apathy of the majority of students regarding school governance. As town meeting became more entrenched in the school, the procedures of the meeting often seemed to take on a life of their own, separate and distinct from the issues the group was discussing. Some students became enamored of the strategies Robert's Rules allowed, and they monopolized meetings by calling the question, doubting the quorum, and demanding recounts. These complicated delaying tactics frustrated many members who genuinely wanted to address issues of meaning.

With the high school experience under my belt, I thought long and hard about how to adapt democratic structures to fit an elementary school. I also wanted to provide the children with the training and experience that would cause all of them to think of themselves as competent participants in the democratic process. During my first year as principal, I learned about the range of practices in place in the school that foster good citizenship and cooperation. Still, I felt the need to extend the concept of democratic participation and problem solving to the school as a whole. My goals were to:

- Build a feeling for Heath as a community, starting with the youngest children
- Begin to give children a regular opportunity to express themselves in a group beyond the classroom
- Teach listening skills systematically, in a forum larger than the classroom
- Give the children the chance to bring forward their own issues and interests and present them to an audience of their peers
- Build self-esteem by providing a place where children would feel comfortable standing and delivering a poem, a reflection on something they had learned, or a song

Building a Community

These five concepts became the basis of the Heath Family Meeting, a weekly gathering of all children in grades 1, 2, and 3. After 3 years, this gathering has become a firmly established tradition at the school. Under the careful guidance of their teachers, the children regularly speak at the meeting, and they learn to listen to one another.

Once the Family Meeting was in place, it was important to establish a group forum for children as they continued into the middle grades. Thus the Heath Community Meeting was established for grades 4 and 5. (There are weekly class meetings for grades 7 and 8 that are currently being examined for focus and purpose. Grade 6 has no formally established meeting time, but they gather together periodically throughout the year to discuss and plan for a variety of sixth-grade activities.) The weekly Community Meeting, started in 1987, focuses specifically on the rights and responsibilities of members of the school community. At the very first Heath Community Meeting, I spoke to the children about what I thought the group could accomplish. I told them that everyone in a community needs to know how the group is operated—what is OK to do, and what is not OK. Because the Bicentennial of the United States Constitution was being celebrated just as we were establishing the Community Meeting, we had a wonderful way to link our meeting with the purposes of the Constitutional Convention. We talked about why our foreparents developed the Constitution, and we discussed the need for and purpose of charters and rules and regulations in general.

I had Brookline High School's town meeting firmly in mind as I thought about the format for the Heath Community Meeting. Whereas the former group is a representative one, closely replicating the organization of town meetings in large towns like Brookline, I opted for the pure form of town meeting, where every citizen has the right to participate and vote. I conceived of grades 4 and 5 as a small town, with each citizen a member of a body that identifies problems affecting the community and seeks ways to solve these problems. I believed that there would be two major outcomes from the Heath Community Meeting. First, I wanted to empower children, to help them understand that if something is not working well, fourth and fifth graders have both the intelligence to recognize the flaw and the ability to fix it. Second, I believed that the school would run more smoothly if more members of the community accepted a part of the responsibility for making the organization a better place.

Raising Issues to Solve Problems

Recognizing the need to apply theoretical assumptions to practical problems, we worked out a means for children to raise issues occurring in the school that they found troublesome. I attached a large manila envelope to my office door, and I encouraged Community Meeting members to commit their issue to writing and place it in the envelope. The first week the envelope began to fill with problems: saving seats in the lunchroom, cutting into lunch lines, unfair use of playground space, dirty bathrooms, and lack of soap in the bathrooms.

At the next Community Meeting, I presented the list of topics the children had submitted. The issue they decided to work on was lack of soap in the bathrooms. It was a good choice because it seemed to contain enough interest and conflict to hold the children's interest, its intrinsic importance was evident, and it was solvable. We began by discussing the criteria (we called them guideposts) that would shape our discussions and proposals. They were:

- Is it fair? Does it treat everybody in the same way? If it solves your problem but makes matters worse for someone else, then it is not fair.
- Is it consistent? Can you apply the solution to a variety of situations and have it work?
- Is it safe?
- Is it necessary? Here we talked about the problem of making too many rules and regulations. The children quickly acknowledged that it would be hard to remember a whole lot of rules and they might find themselves breaking rules they were unaware of. Thus,

with adult guidance, they submerged their natural bent to make a rule for everything in favor of having a few well-publicized rules or actions in effect.

An Example: Soap in the Bathroom. The following week we began to discuss the issue of lack of soap in the bathrooms. We randomly divided the large group (about 82 students) into eight small discussion groups, each headed by an adult—teacher, student teacher, or me. I had prepared a sheet to help the adults lead the discussion, with this description of the problem:

> Students complain that there is no soap in the bathrooms. The custodians resist stocking them with soap, because it disappears immediately. They also are unwilling to install soap dispensers because they are quickly broken. Still, the principal agrees that the children should have soap to wash their hands. How can we, The Heath Community Meeting, help to make sure that if we install soap dispensers, they will be used for washing, and not broken? What problems are likely to arise? What can we do about them? What are you willing to do?

At the small group discussions, the children were intrigued with finding solutions to how to protect the soap dispensers. The process required that the adult group leaders record all of the suggested remedies, without discussion as to their viability. Ten minutes were allotted to generating ideas. After that, groups would examine the proposals in light of the four criteria we had developed. They would then bring an agreed-upon solution to the whole group for a vote. In this part of the process, the children's imagination took flight, yielding solutions such as,

> Employ a guard to watch the dispensers
> Install television monitors
> Hire fingerprinters
> Have the custodians check the dispensers every 5 minutes
> Put alarms on the dispensers
> Get a watchdog to patrol the bathrooms

These fanciful solutions (or similar ones) emerged in each group. On hearing them I had a moment of considerable self-doubt. Could these 9- and 10-year-olds possibly believe that placing alarms on soap dispensers was a realistic solution to a minor, if troublesome, community problem? Had I badly miscalculated their ability to assess a situation and then develop a reasonable remedy? Would they merely play with the issues that they had raised, as a diversion from the classroom, and be unable or unwilling to see them as real concerns requiring their attention?

Debating the Issue. Fortunately, someone emerged in each group to point out the impracticality or pitfalls of such actions. In the group I led, for example, one student was able to argue persuasively against the fingerprinting idea. She attacked it on both practical and libertarian grounds, saying it would be very expensive to do all that fingerprinting, and someone might be falsely accused of breaking a dispenser who had left fingerprints while using it appropriately.

Each of the teacher/leaders reported that a similar process had occurred in the group she led. When the time came to assess the proposals and decide upon the one the group would present to the whole forum, someone was able to point out the flaws in proposed solutions that required electronic installations or the hiring of guards, human or canine. The small size of the discussion groups and the interaction of fourth and fifth graders helped to elicit thoughtful criticism and to yield workable solutions.

The Solution: Soap Dispensers. The consensus was this: The soap dispensers would be installed. Heath Community Meeting members, in pairs, would visit each classroom, explain the problem about the lack of soap, and describe how the Heath Community Meeting had worked out a solution. The children would request cooperation from all the students to use the soap dispensers for the intended purpose and not destroy them. "The soap dispensers are for everybody's use, and if they get broken, no one will have them," they decided to say.

There were ample volunteers to speak to the primary classes, and several children agreed to talk to grade 6. Finding speakers for grades 7 and 8 was more difficult, but ultimately two fifth-grade girls agreed to do it. I rehearsed their presentations with them, and, except for an episode of the giggles in an eighth-grade classroom, the explanations and requests for cooperation went well.

Working through the problem of no soap in the bathrooms enabled us to establish a method for attacking other problems. There was a process to follow: defining, brainstorming, reaching consensus, and implementing the solution. In addition to the four guideposts we had previously identified, we added one more—Is it workable? Our experience with the soap dispenser problem showed us that although some solutions might generate unbridled enthusiasm—think of the fun it would be to have gentle watchdogs stationed in each boys' and girls' room—they simply would not work. The process used to deal with the problem of no soap in the bathrooms worked well. The members of the Heath Community Meeting acquired relevant information about a problem they had brought forth as a serious concern; they designed a remedy that satisfied them; and they used their skills to see that the remedy was implemented.

Other Issues

Since that first foray into democratic problem solving, the Heath Community Meeting has found many other issues deserving of their attention. For example, they complained that there was no safe place to lock their bikes when they rode them to school. We spent several meetings seeking a solution to that problem. We invited the director of the Parks Department of the Town of Brookline to come to a meeting, hear the need from the children, and help us decide on the type of bicycle rack that would meet the needs of the school. Community Meeting members surveyed the school to learn how many children might ride their bikes on a given day. They decided that they needed a rack that could accommodate up to 30 bikes. Mr. Willis, head of the Parks Department, told the children that his department would be willing to pay up to $250 for a bicycle rack for Heath. He worked with a small committee to select the perfect rack, and then a setback occurred. The department had used up its entire budget for the year and could not keep its commitment. Although the children were disappointed, they felt that they could raise enough money to purchase a rack. As they were making plans for bake sales and a school fair, a nearby college came to our rescue. Having heard of the need for a safe place for bikes (the daughter of an administrator at the college was a member of the Heath Community Meeting), the college offered us an appropriate alternative to the rack the children had selected. Mr. Willis offered to pick up the rack, strip it, repaint it, and install it in front of the school. Thus the children learned how public and private groups cooperate in problem solving.

Community Meeting members also worked together to devise appropriate safety rules for the use of a new playground structure that was installed in 1988; they allocated funds for the purchase of play equipment (soccer and basketballs, jumpropes, frisbees, etc.) to be used at recess, after conducting a survey of children's needs and preferences; they discussed and argued about the wisdom of taking turns each day to clean the cafeteria (a suggestion bravely put forward by two fourth graders), and while turning down the notion of giving up part of their recess—even three or four times a year—they agreed to take greater responsibility for cleaning up their own debris at lunchtime; and they conducted an evaluation of the Heath School Arts Festival that became a part of my evaluative report to the Parent Teachers' Organization. They do not seem to run out of issues that require attention, although they periodically become bored with the problem-solving format.

The Community Meeting: Varying the Format

We respond to the need for variety at Community Meetings in several ways. One of them is to bring in guest speakers who do something or know something the children care about or ought to know about. We have had reporters from the *Boston Globe*, members of the community orchestra, college students in various fields, members of the police and fire departments, parents in a variety of careers who represent the cultural diversity of the school, and teachers at different grade levels speak to the group. At the time of Martin Luther King, Jr.'s birthday, one parent spoke to the children about participating in civil rights marches in the 1960s. She described the kind of training in passive resistance that all the participants received, and she told the children why they followed the model of passive resistance. The children seem to enjoy these sessions, and they have an endless stream of questions for the guest speakers. They learn how people in many different careers view their responsibility as members of a community and as citizens.

Another goal of the Heath Community Meeting is to build in children the understanding that each of us is a member of a lot of different communities. The fourth and fifth graders belong to the Community Meeting, but they are also members of their class, the school, their family, perhaps a religious organization, their neighborhood, the town, the state, the country, and so forth. So at times we also share our skills and energy with members of different communities. A week before Valentine's Day, the meeting became a great workshop for the production of valentines, made for veterans in a nearby hospital. The children produced hundreds of cards with friendly messages. On Valentine's Day, a parent and several children went to the hospital and delivered the cards to the veterans. Once a month, faculty members at the school join with other schools in Brookline to prepare a hot meal for homeless people in the Boston area. The children support this effort, both by raising money to help pay for the meals and by periodically baking homemade brownies as a special treat for the diners. Before they became involved in the dinner project, we had a discussion about who the homeless were and how they got that way. One child said, "The homeless could be any one of us," and he went on to explain how people "like you or like me" could suddenly find themselves without a place to live or other necessities of life. Other children offered their understanding of the problem in a meeting that was especially moving.

The Koosh Ball Incident

On occasion, an issue for discussion at the Heath Community Meeting will be proposed by an adult. Such was the case with the Koosh ball incident. After recess on the Friday before the Columbus Day weekend, Mrs. Gaskill greeted me with these words, "Conan roofed Henri's Koosh ball." I immediately translated the fourth-grade idiom into "Conan has thrown Henri's soft rubber ball, covered with soft elastic spikes, onto the low roof of the building adjacent to the playground." There is no access to the roof except by climbing onto it—an activity that is not permitted. The custodians will not retrieve objects that land on the roof. I was pleased that it was a Friday with a long weekend ahead. I hoped, not too optimistically, that the problem would disappear before the children returned to school after the holiday.

By Tuesday the Koosh ball issue had taken on new ramifications. On Columbus Day Jim, a fourth grader who lives very close to the school, climbed a tree onto the roof, retrieved the blue and red Koosh ball, and brought it to school, claiming it as his own. Henri quickly made a counterclaim, insisting the ball was his whether Jim had rescued it or not. Mrs. Gaskill attempted to resolve the issue, but each boy adamantly stuck to the belief that the Koosh ball was his. After nonproductive discussion, Mrs. Gaskill sent the boys to see me. It was clear that both Jim and Henri firmly believed that the ball was his. Henri had received the ball as a gift from his dad who had paid for it and presented it to Henri. Jim agreed that it had been Henri's, but after it was abandoned on the roof, he had taken the risk of retrieving it. Without his initiative to recover the ball, it would have remained there, and it would have been lost to Henri forever. Therefore, it belonged to Jim.

I referred to the rule against students' climbing on the roof, but I indicated that because this event had occurred on a school holiday, I would not impose sanctions. I also said that I considered it a friendly community gesture on Jim's part to rescue the ball for his friend. Jim rejected this reasoning, stating emphatically that he would not have taken the risk of climbing up to the roof had he not expected to own the ball. Neither boy was willing to concede that the other had any justifiable claim to the ball. Harking back to a biblical precedent, I suggested that I cut the ball in half and give one half to each boy. Neither found this an acceptable solution.

The boys did agree, however, to have the issue presented to the Heath Community Meeting the next day. They further agreed to abide by the decision of the meeting. In the meantime, I held the ball in my custody. By meeting time just about everybody knew about the Koosh ball incident, and most of them had made up their minds who should have it. A few agreed with Jim that possession was the decisive factor. He had gone after the ball, and he deserved to keep it. Most of the children strongly disagreed with this point of view. They developed alternative scenarios to support their perspective. If it had been a wallet with Henri's name on it, could Jim possibly claim it as his? If the ball had been caught in a tree and released a few days later by wind and rain, wouldn't it still be Henri's? If Jim's father had bought a Koosh ball for him, wouldn't he expect to keep it under these circumstances? (Jim said he would not, but the children disagreed.) One child, Cindy, said that in this case everyone knew the ball was Henri's; but, she added, even if that were not known, and Jim had found a Koosh ball on the roof—or anywhere—without knowing who the owner was, it would be his responsibility to try to find the rightful owner before claiming the ball as his own. This is how she would want to be treated if she lost something important, and she believed that others would want to be treated this way, too.

The discussion of the Koosh ball episode lasted about 15 minutes, and the consensus of the Heath Community Meeting was that the ball should be returned to Henri. Jim agreed with this decision, both boys shook hands, and the event was concluded. What was of special interest to me was that no one raised the role Conan had played in this episode. On reflection, I concluded that adding Conan's participation to the equation made the problem too complex for the children to deal with, and so they simplified it in a way that made it manageable.

Late in the year Cindy brought a similar level of moral reasoning to another dilemma. Brookline's recreation department asked to use several rooms in the Heath School as a base for a summer day camp. Although I did not bring this issue to the meeting, one of the children had heard about the request and raised it for discussion. The general feeling was that the children preferred to have the school closed in the summer, so that "nothing would happen to it." They were particularly concerned that an installation of handmade tiles, representing the work of each child and teacher in the school, not be damaged.

I explained that the classroom areas, and the hallway where the tiles were on display, would not be accessible to the campers (most of whom were not Heath students). The students were still reluctant to share the school. At this point Cindy said, "If we aren't going to use the school in the summer, and if other people want it, and if most of the school is going to be locked and secure, then I think we should let them have it. We don't need it and they do." There was agreement that this reasoning made sense. Having a youngster in the group who is able to articulate a level of thinking higher than that of the group is very beneficial to the group process.

Conclusion

Over the past 2 years, the Heath Community Meeting has been established as an integral part of the school program. It complements the work the teachers and children do in class on a daily basis. It provides a forum in which children are asked to cooperate with one another in finding solutions to problems; where they are reminded in substantive ways that they are members of a community with the obligation to help that community improve and grow; where they are given the opportunity to hear and respond to one another's thinking—and perhaps to elevate their own thinking; and where they periodically have the satisfaction of seeing tangible change they have been able to design and implement. My hope is that fostering this kind of activism in fourth and fifth graders will cause them to think of themselves as doers, able to identify areas that need improvement and armed with the skills to make improvement happen. Surely these are qualities that all citizens should possess.

These four approaches to teaching democracy at the Heath School mesh with one another and are enhanced by a curricular approach that emphasizes inquiry, cooperation, and respect for divergent thinking. We want our children to learn to ask important questions, identify issues and arenas that require attention, and know they have the skills and the power to make things better. Providing opportunities for children to implement their solutions to problems in class, on the playing field, and at meeting time is a critical step in our goal to prepare the youngsters to become active, questioning young adults, prepared to take on the vital role of citizens in a democracy.

CHAPTER SIX

Development and Practice of Democracy in a K–8 School

ROBERT J. WEINTRAUB

I had been the principal of the City Magnet School in Lowell, Massachusetts, for 7 years when I replaced the principal at the Runkle School in Brookline, who had taken a 1-year leave of absence. As founding principal of the City Magnet, I had helped create a "microsociety school," where teachers guided students in grades K–8 in the development and operation of their own small society within the school building. The school is based on John Dewey's (1938/1963) assumption that "there is an intimate and necessary relation between the processes of actual experience and education" (p. 20) and on George Richmond's *The Micro-Society School* (1974).

The curriculum at the City Magnet is unique. It is a curriculum that links the world inside the schoolhouse, where students are active participants in developing their own society, with the world outside, where the macrosociety's institutions serve as models for the microsociety. Children learn about math and economics as they develop and work in their own banks and businesses, conducting transactions in their own school currency; about writing and economics as they publish and market their own newspapers, books, and magazines; and about government, democracy, and economics as they conduct their own comprehensive system of government.

The microsociety today is very different from the one that greeted the children when the school first opened in September 1981. In each curriculum strand, teachers established an initial "process-oriented" structure. The curriculum then grew from student experience within that structure. In the government strand, teachers organized and supervised a constitutional convention. A three-page constitution was created by students and teachers at that convention. That original constitution has become a 14-page document that defines roles and responsibilities for students, teachers, and parents in executive, legislative, and judicial branches of the school's government. The original four-page code of laws that was created by the school's first legislature is now a 20-page document that constitutes the school's standards for student behavior. The process of developing the school's comprehensive government reflected—and continues to reflect—the voices of students, teachers, and parents. In the process, the children—and the teachers and parents—learn a lot about democracy and government and, having worked together, also experience a strong sense of community.

I came to my new position at the Runkle School with a commitment to process-oriented, experiential, and democratic education. I was also eager to define that commitment with a new group of children and teachers.

Getting Started: The Teachers Define Some Basic Rules

Before the 1987–88 school year ended, Runkle's principal arranged for me to meet with all of the teachers. I did so, in small groups, and listened to their assessment of the school's strengths and needs. Several themes emerged from these discussions. The Runkle School faculty was superb—talented, caring, and hard-working. They were very proud of their outstanding academic program. This was a great school. The teachers felt strongly, however, that standards for student behavior needed to be clarified and enforced. And they also wanted to develop an increased sense of responsibility within the student body. Establishing student democracy at Runkle seemed to address both of these concerns and also to mesh with the process-oriented education that already characterized the school.

Before the 1988–89 school year began, eight teachers and I, the Task Force on Standards for Student Behavior, met to discuss clear guidelines for conduct. At the City Magnet School, the teachers and I had established Executive Orders—nonnegotiable standards for student behavior. At Runkle, we drew up the Ten Commandments. The practice of democracy in schools sometimes doesn't sound very democratic. Democracy in schools, however, must always be guided by what's best for children and by the elements that define great teaching. Clear—and fair—standards for student behavior are always a starting point when adults work with children. So during the first 2 days of the new school year when I visited every classroom and announced the Ten Commandments, I felt I was not being undemocratic; I was helping to establish a climate within which great education—and great school democracy—could flourish. I said to each class, "The teachers and I believe that the Ten Commandments are fair and reasonable guidelines for student behavior. Most of you will have no trouble following these rules, and you will have a safe and productive school year. If, however, you *do* have difficulty following these rules," I added, "I can promise you that this will *not* be a pleasant school year for you."

I then read the rules to the children, as outlined in Figure 6.1, and discussed the consequences that we established should the rules be violated.

The Ten Commandments provided a system from which moral, character, and citizenship education could grow and flourish. They defined a school climate characterized by decorum and civility.

Student democracy, nourished and cultivated by the teachers, is the visible and dynamic organism that can grow from the system. Student democracy provides a *voice* for the student body to express its opinions. Often the student perspective can be translated into policies that make a real difference in the quality of the lives that students lead at school. They become enfranchised citizens of their own school-based society while simultaneously learning a lot about how the world outside of school works, including the vocabulary of that world. In the process, excitement is generated, adults and children work together in the development of a school community, and the faces of the children are alive.

Structuring Democracy: Involving the Faculty and Students

During the fall of the 1988–89 school year, the Student Government Task Force—seven teachers and I—met every other week to develop a structure for student government at Runkle School. The discussions were animated and intense. The teachers wanted to make sure that the student government would fit well into the culture of this school. On January 10, the task force presented to the faculty the final draft of a position paper that described such a democratic structure. The faculty approved the recommendations of the task force. In part, the position paper said,

Figure 6.1 City Magnet School Rules

THE TEN COMMANDMENTS	CONSEQUENCES
1. All children in the Runkle School community must feel safe here. Therefore, no child shall threaten or cause physical or psychological harm to another child in the school community.	—Referral to the principal or vice-principal —Communication with parent
2. Adults in the Runkle School community must be treated with respect. Therefore, children shall be respectful, in language and behavior, of all adults in the school community.	—Two written apologies: one to the victim and a copy to the principal —Communication with parent
3. Individual and school property must be respected. Therefore, children shall not steal or cause damage to individual or school property.	—Replace item —Repair item —Two written apologies: one to the victim and a copy to the principal —Communication with parent
4. Students shall always walk within the school building.	—Repeat behavior in the correct manner
5. Children shall not carry or use any item that may be considered a weapon.	—Confiscation of the item and communication with parent
6. Skateboards shall not be allowed in the school building or on school grounds.	—*First Offense:* Confiscate and return at the end of the day —*Second Offense:* Confiscate and notify parent —*Third Offense:* Notify parent and confiscate for the remainder of the year
7. Food will be allowed only in the dining hall unless specifically sanctioned by a teacher.	—Food will be confiscated outside of dining hall, including the recess area —Communication with parent
8. During the school day, children will be allowed to use phones in the building *only in case of emergency*	—Communication with parent
9. Neither "Walk-men" nor any portable stereo system will be allowed in the school unless sanctioned by a teacher.	—Same as for Commandment 6
10. Children shall not be in possession of gum in school or on school grounds.	—Fines —School cleaning

Civic education can help us to see that not all problems have solutions, to live with tentative answers, to accept compromise, to embrace responsibilities as well as rights—to understand that democracy is a way of living, not a settled destination (Gagnon, 1988, p. 44). We would say that democracy is a system of self-government that obligates citizens to participate but does not guarantee that one's point of view will triumph. Democracy is a system that provides a voice for the diverse perspectives of those governed. And, through these voices, democracy offers at least an opportunity for problems to be identified, solutions proposed, ideas generated, and programs created that give wings to the ideas.

The task force proposed a *Town Meeting* model at the primary level—grades K–3—and a *representative* model at the intermediate and senior levels—grades 4–8. Once a month, representatives from both structures would meet to share their experiences.

The primary children would participate in class (community) meetings, scheduled by the classroom teacher.

In the representative model, it was proposed that each class in grades 4–8 elect one representative and one alternate. The election campaign would consist of the following phases: a *Democracy Assembly* for grades 4–6 and another for grades 7 and 8, at which time the *possibilities* and *limitations* of the proposed democratic structure would be explained; a nomination process in the individual classes; the preparation by each candidate of a position paper on the nature of representation, including the candidate's view of his or her role as a representative; oral delivery of the position paper in individual classrooms; and an election. Voting and tabulation of votes would be accomplished in the computer lab, using a program that was designed by two seventh graders working with the computer teacher.

On January 24 and 25, the two Democracy Assemblies were held. Before the assemblies, every student received a paper entitled "A Guide to Runkle Student Government." In part, this guide said,

You are citizens of the Runkle School. Today, we are announcing that the Runkle School will have a House of Representatives. There will be one representative and an alternate representative from each homeroom class in grades 4–8. In order to be a candidate from your class, you must be nominated—by yourself or by a classmate. All nomination papers must be received by homeroom teachers by 2 p.m. on Friday, Jan. 27, 1989.

All candidates will then have two weeks to prepare a position paper. The topic for the paper is, *The Kind of Representative That I Will Be.* There are really three kinds of representatives. The first kind is elected by his/her fellow citizens and says, "I was elected. Therefore, my fellow citizens obviously trust me to make decisions. I will make these decisions to the best of my ability." She/he is called a *trustee*.

The second kind of representative says, "I was elected by my fellow citizens. Therefore, I must always check back with them to find out what they are thinking and my decisions will reflect their opinions." She/he is called a *delegate*.

The third kind of representative says, "Sometimes I'll do what I think is best and sometimes I'll do what the community wants me to do." She/he is called a *politico*.

Every candidate was required to have a faculty coach. The coach would help students in the preparation of the paper. The Student Government Task Force wanted to link the electoral process to the school's academic program. The requirement that each candidate have a coach provided that academic linkage and also ensured that every candidate—not only the candidates with interested parents—would have appropriate guidance.

At the Democracy Assemblies, the initial structure that the faculty had proposed for student government at the Runkle School was discussed. The limitations of student government were explored. Students, for example, could not pass laws that contradicted existing local, state, and federal statutes. The possibilities of student government were also discussed. Students certainly could petition local, state, or federal officials if they were interested in establishing a new law or questioned an existing one. In fact, several years before, fourth-grade students at this school successfully lobbied the state legislature to establish the corn muffin as the official muffin of the Commonwealth of Massachusetts. The dynamic nature of student government was emphasized. One student asked if we could write a constitution. The answer to that question was repeated many times during the Democracy Assemblies—"*You* will determine the direction of *your* student government."

The week of February 13 was Democracy Week at the Runkle School. On Monday, 53 students presented position papers to their classmates. A fourth grader said, "I may be small, but in my heart I'm tall. I'm running for student government because my friends trust me to make a correct decision." Another fourth grader said, "I will *definitely* not be afraid to speak up, though I'm only in fourth grade and there will be eighth graders. I *will* stand up for my class' rights if I make a suggestion and a seventh or eighth grader says, 'Shut up, you wimpy fourth grader.'"

A sixth grader said, "I would like to tell all of the voters that this election is not for you to vote for a friend, but for you to vote for someone who you think is intelligent and would be a good representative." (In fact, the election results surprised those who believed that this would indeed become a popularity contest. All of the more "popular" candidates were defeated by candidates who were perceived as less "popular" but more serious and thoughtful in their position papers.)

A seventh grader said, "If I am elected your representative, I will be your delegate. I believe that the purpose of a representative is to represent. Because, as Abraham Lincoln once said, 'No man is good enough to govern another man without that other's consent.' About popularity," he continued, "I would hope that I don't have to be popular to win this election. I mean, popular in the sense that you want to dance with me, or like the clothes I wear, or my hairstyle, or the earring that I don't wear, or even like me personally. The important thing is that you vote for who you think is the better candidate. So, my motto in this election is, 'Maybe We Could.' Maybe we could change something, or do something, instead of just standing by."

The election was held on Tuesday. There was tremendous anticipation as the votes were tabulated. I was besieged by students in the hallways asking, "When will we know who won?" In the afternoon, winners were announced over the public address system. High-pitched screams echoed through the building at the announcement of each winner.

Inauguration Day was Wednesday. All of the children in fourth through eighth grades and their teachers filled the school's multipurpose room. The winning candidates and alternates, dressed more formally than usual, sat at the front of the room. One by one, they stood and presented their "winning" position papers to a very attentive and enthusiastic audience. With the end of the presentations, all of the newly elected representatives and alternates were asked to stand, and I said, "I hereby proclaim that these Runkle citizens constitute the first Runkle House of Representatives."

Implementing the Democratic Structure

On Thursday at 7:30 a.m., 30 minutes before school began, the House of Representatives convened for its first meeting. I explained that this was *their* government and they needed to select their own leadership and make decisions about how to conduct the meetings. I asked them if the name "House of Representatives" was OK. They liked it. One representative then suggested that they elect a Speaker of the House.

The first few meetings resulted in a number of decisions. Seventh grader Peter Campo was elected Speaker of the House. I was given veto power. "It's important for Dr. Weintraub to have absolute veto power," said a seventh grader during this discussion. "Perhaps we would override his veto and bad things would happen," he continued. Another student said, "We should trust Dr. Weintraub to know what's right and wrong." (I was quite surprised by the students' willingness to grant me absolute veto power. It is important to listen to the voices of the children, however, and in this case I sensed that their inexperience with democracy made them somewhat insecure. At the beginning, at least, my veto would provide a comforting moral safety net.)

Alternates were invited to the meetings "so that they'll know what's going on in case they have to take over." The meetings were scheduled every week beginning at 7:15 a.m. instead of 7:30—"We need more time to discuss things; there's a lot to do," said the representatives—and would follow Robert's Rules, with decisions made by majority vote. A bill was defined as a motion that was passed by the House. I would then consult with the faculty on the bill—I compared the faculty to a "senate"—and, if I signed the bill, it would become a school law. I also created official Runkle House of Representatives stationery with the names of each representative, each alternate, and the faculty advisors listed in the left margin. It was very official looking and the children loved seeing their names in print. Each child was given several copies of the stationery to take home.

The First Debate: Lunch and Recess

The first major discussion focused on a policy that I had changed early in the school year. Before this year, children could eat lunch—or not eat lunch—and leave the cafeteria independently to walk or run out to the playground. In an effort to contain the children, with the hope that they would eat lunch at a more leisurely pace, I had decided they must remain in the cafeteria for at least 15 minutes before going out for recess. Beginning in September, this new policy was the target of regular criticism by students at all grade levels.

Not surprisingly, the first substantive issue raised by the new student government had to do with this policy. Speaker Campo called the meeting to order and said, "A lot of students are proposing that we be allowed to finish our lunch and just go out to recess." "Yeah," "Definitely," "Absolutely," greeted this suggestion. The seventh- and eighth-grade representatives were particularly vocal. Their lunch and recess period is 30 minutes long. All of the other grades have 45 minutes for lunch and recess.

Sixth grader Alex Zonis asked the seventh- and eighth-grade representatives, "How much time do you get for recess?" Seventh grader Sandy Rossman responded, "Fifteen minutes." Looking directly at Alex, he quickly added, "You'll get that next year."

I suggested that a motion be presented. Seventh grader Daniel James said, "I move that when a Runkle student is finished with lunch, he or she may leave the cafeteria freely and go out to recess." The motion was seconded. Peter, a quick study on Robert's Rules, said, "Is there any discussion?" James said, "You know, a lot of the confusion in the lunchroom is caused by people gathering around the door waiting to go outside." He was right. Despite the efforts of the cafeteria supervisors to keep the children at their tables, there was an inexorable movement toward the doors as the clock approached the end of the 15-minute waiting period. As the clock struck the quarter-hour, there was a stampede. So, for me, there was some attraction in this new/old proposal.

The volunteer faculty advisors—the vice-principal, the guidance counselor, and I—offered the adult organizational perspective. We had several concerns about the bill. Vice-principal Robin Pickett asked, "What about the cleanup responsibilities? What happens if, as a result of the earlier recess, students bug out on their cleanup responsibilities?" Fourth grader Andrew Sharfman responded, "There should be consequences."

I added, "The teachers are also concerned about seventh and eighth graders who do not go out at all. They report that there are always seventh and eighth graders hanging around the halls, making noise, sometimes running around the building during recess time." "We'll speak to all of the kids in homeroom tomorrow morning and tell them that they have to go out," responded Speaker Campo.

Brenda Stein, the school's guidance counselor, said, "If adopted, this new rule will have an impact on the adults in the building. There will have to be adult supervision of an earlier recess."

Brenda, Robin, and I were asking the legislators to embrace responsibilities as well as rights.

In response to Brenda, seventh grader Rossman suggested that "one or two of the cafeteria supervisors can go outside with the kids." I said, "Sandy, I appreciate your suggestion. It illustrates an important difference between the legislative and executive branches of government. The legislative branch passes bills. It is the responsibility of the executive branch to approve—or disapprove of—the bill. If the bill is approved, it becomes a law and the executive branch then translates the law into reality. If this bill becomes a law, we'll make sure that there is adult supervision for the earlier recess."

Sensing that I was supportive of the bill, at least as far as seventh and eighth graders were concerned, the fourth, fifth, and sixth graders wanted to make sure that the bill included them. I said, "It is a little more complicated with the fourth, fifth, and sixth graders. If you go outside as soon as you finish your lunch—let's say it takes you 5 minutes to eat—you could go outside at 12:20. The first, second, and third graders will still be on the playground at that time, and there really isn't enough room out there for all of you. And," I continued, "you're so much bigger than the first, second, and third graders; I'm a little afraid that they might get hurt."

"But the little kids mainly hang around the climbing structures and we play on the basketball courts," responded a fifth grader. "That's not really true," I said. "There are always second and third graders playing football and baseball on the basketball courts."

Peter Campo said, "It's getting late; can't we reach a compromise?" "How about letting the fourth, fifth, and sixth graders out at 12:25 instead of 12:30?" asked a sixth grader. "That would give the little kids 25 minutes by themselves," he added. "That might work," I said.

Peter became very animated. He summarized the discussion, echoing my interest in student responsibilities that go along with student rights. "Dr. Weintraub seems agreeable to changing the policy on going outside after lunch, but we can't be hanging around the building and we have to be careful of the little kids," he explained. The bill was passed unanimously. During the day, I asked many teachers their feelings about the bill. They were supportive. The next morning, on Runkle House of Representatives stationery, I issued the following memo to the Runkle faculty and staff. It was signed by me and Speaker of the House Peter Campo.

On Monday morning, March 6, the Runkle House of Representatives proposed and approved a bill that modifies and clarifies the rules regarding recess time. The bill allows the seventh and eighth graders to proceed outside for recess upon completion of their lunch. It also allows the fourth, fifth and sixth graders to proceed outside for recess at 12:25 p.m.

The bill also obligates the children to go directly outside when they leave the cafeteria. The House agreed that there shall be no loitering inside of the schoolhouse during recess time. Further, the fourth, fifth and sixth graders agreed to be sensitive to the needs of first, second and third graders, with whom there is now a five minute overlap—12:25–12:30—of recess time.

I have approved House Bill #1 for a one week trial period, beginning today.

The students were delighted. They viewed this event as a major victory. They had changed a school policy. It was the fulfillment of Daniel James's campaign theme, "Maybe we could." In school democracy, it is very important to provide students with the sense that they really can accomplish something, that they really can make a difference, that their voice really counts. There were smaller victories, previously noted, when the House began its work. This decision, however, was the first time that students achieved a significant policy change. It provided the student legislators with tremendous credibility among their peers, and it bestowed a sense of legitimacy upon the student government.

During the next week, the vice-principal and I carefully monitored the halls and recess area. Almost no one was in the building and there were no problems between younger and older children at recess.

Peter opened the next meeting of the House by asking, "Were there any problems with House Bill #1?" One eighth grader replied, "Some eighth graders would rather do their homework than go out to recess." Peter responded, "Well, they can't do that." A fifth grader reported that "there was no trampling of first, second, and third graders." I said, "I am satisfied with the performance of all students affected by the new law ..." A fourth grader interrupted, saying "bill." A seventh grader responded, "Dr. Weintraub signed the bill; it's now a law." A government curriculum had been born and students were already incorporating the vocabulary of government.

At the next meeting, a fourth grader presented a motion that stated, "Fourth, fifth, and sixth graders may leave the cafeteria when they finish their lunch and are required to then go outside for recess." It passed unanimously and I signed it the next day.

The Skateboard Issue: A Lesson in Constitutional Government

Toward the end of the April 3 meeting of the Runkle House, Paulo Souza, an eighth grader, said, "Several of my friends in the eighth grade have asked me to bring up the topic of skateboards." Speaker Campo responded, "What about skateboards?" Paulo said, "They think that skateboards are legal and that we should be able to bring them to school." "But at the beginning of the year Dr. Weintraub said that they were illegal," responded Campo, "and that's why there's a commandment against them."

I said, "You know, I *think* that they are illegal, but I'm not positive. Can someone call the police department and ask the police about this issue, and then report back to us next week?" Fourth grader Andrew Sharfman volunteered to do this.

At 7:15 on Monday morning, April 10, the 20 members of the House gathered, as they did each week, around several large tables in the school library. Orange juice and Dunkin' Donut munchkins were served.

Andrew Sharfman raised his hand. Peter called upon him. "I asked a policeman if skateboards are legal," Andrew said. "He said that you're not allowed to use them in the street but you can use them on the sidewalks."

Nora Liss, a fifth grader, said, "I talked to a lawyer and she said that skateboards are legal."

After consulting with Peter, I decided to get my *Brookline Public Schools Policy Manual.* I returned with the manual and searched through the index. There was no policy on skateboards.

Peter said, "Well, it seems that it's legal to use them, but once we got them to school where would we put them?"

Andrew, a skateboard owner, replied, "We could have a place for them."

Ali McVey, a third grader, said, "If two people had the same kind of skateboard, how would we know whose belonged to who?"

I again consulted with Peter. Peter announced, "We're thinking of inviting someone to discuss this issue with us."

Seventh grader Daniel James asked, "Who makes the laws in Brookline?"

I replied, "The selectmen."

Daniel said, "I move that we invite the selectmen to our next meeting in order to discuss the issue of skateboards in town and in the schools."

Peter said, "We have a motion; is there a second?" Several representatives seconded the motion. "Any discussion?" asked Peter. There was none. It was time for a vote. "As we have decided, only the representatives may vote. An alternate can vote only if the representative from that class is not here today. All in favor? All opposed? Abstentions?" "What's an abstention?" a voice called out. "That's when you choose not to vote at all," explained Peter. (Peter has become a government instructor.) "OK, it's unanimous. The motion passes," Peter reported. I asked Peter to see me at the end of the meeting so that we could act on this motion.

At the end of the meeting, before they left the library, the representatives worked to restore the library to what it looked like before we entered—the tables were separated and arranged as before; and the orange juice containers, the used cups, the munchkin box, the napkins, and the crumbs were thrown away. Peter then walked up to me as I gathered my papers. "Peter, could you please prepare a letter, either today or tonight, inviting the selectmen to our next meeting?" I asked. "I'll have it typed on House stationery and we'll mail it," I continued. Peter agreed.

The next morning, Peter handed me the following letter:

Dear Selectman:

We, at the Runkle School House of Representatives, would like to invite you to our next meeting. We would like to discuss the issue of skateboards in town and at school. We think that this issue needs clarification. Thank you for your interest. The next meeting of the Runkle House of Representatives is Monday, April 24, at 7:15 a.m. in the school library.

Sincerely,
Peter M. Campo, Speaker

On Monday, April 24, at a little after 7:15 a.m., John Alden, chairman of the Brookline Board of Selectmen, arrived at the Runkle School library.

I introduced Mr. Alden to the representatives. I thanked him for getting up so early in the morning to be with us, and I turned the meeting over to Peter Campo.

Peter began, "We've been talking about skateboards and it is unclear what the rules are regarding skateboards. Several of our representatives did some research on this issue, and some people think that skateboards are legal, others think they are illegal."

Mr. Alden replied, "I don't know of any law or regulation that would bar you from using skateboards. I've never heard of anyone being arrested in Brookline for use of a skateboard." He added, "What do you think the laws should be?"

Peter was the first to reply. "They should not be allowed in school," he began. "They'd take time away from teaching," he continued. "I have a skateboard and when I use it, lots of people stop me and ask me lots of questions. And kids would talk about whose skateboard is the best," he concluded.

Jacob Samansky, an eighth-grade skateboarder, said, "I think that we should be able to ride skateboards to and from school."

Peter replied, "Where are we going to put them when we get to school?"

Andrew Sharfman, the fourth-grade skateboarder, replied, "We can tie them up to the bike rack."

Sixth grader Alex Zonis asked, "How are you going to tie a skateboard to a bike rack?"

Andrew said that he had done it before. "You tie a bike chain around the skateboard and then attach it to the bike rack. You can do it," he said.

Mr. Alden asked, "What about the safety issue? Are skateboards dangerous?"

Peter responded, "When you start out, you do fall a lot and get bruised."

Alex said, "People who skateboard should wear a helmet."

Seventh grader Andrew Vann said, "The school is held responsible for student safety, you know. Maybe they *are* too dangerous for us at school."

Liz Dolen, a fifth grader who was not a member of the House of Representatives but was attending as an interested student, said, "Why can't we make rules for the use of skateboards? You know, where we can use them, how long we can use them for."

Ramah McVey, a sixth grader, responded, "Who would keep track of the time? Would someone have to come out to recess with a stopwatch?"

Peter added, sarcastically, "So now we're going to come to school with a skateboard, tie an intricate knot around it, tie it to the bike rack, untie it at recess, use it while someone with a stopwatch times us, then tie it up again."

Andrew Scharfman sensed that any use of skateboards was in jeopardy and tried to salvage a compromise. He suggested, as Jacob did before, "You could have no skateboarding at school, but you could just ride your skateboard to school."

I tried to clarify the issues that had been raised. "It seems that we're talking about three issues—skateboarding as recreation during recess at school; skateboards as transportation to and from school; and the problem of what to do with the skateboards once they are at school so that they are protected."

Edward Lassner, a sixth grader, suggested, "Why don't we do what we did when we were deciding about a salad bar—ask our classes?"

There was unanimous agreement that this was a good idea. And, before the meeting concluded, Mr. Alden agreed to check with the chief of police on the definitive regulations governing the use of skateboards. I thanked him and used the opportunity to illustrate the limitations of student government. "Our school laws cannot be created in isolation," I explained. "The school is part of the larger society and we cannot make laws that contradict the laws of the government beyond the schoolhouse—at the town, state, and federal levels."

At the May 1 meeting, representatives reported on the responses of their classmates. Nora Liss offered that no one in her fifth-grade class had a skateboard and therefore skateboards were not really an important issue for them. Ramah McVey reported that although her classmates wanted skateboards, only two had them. Sara Rosen, a fifth grader, said, "Only a few kids have skateboards."

Peter Campo, returning to his theme that skateboards cause trouble in school, said, "I remember when, a few years ago, someone brought a skateboard and everyone said, 'Ooh, where did you get it?' The teacher got very mad," he concluded.

The discussion was turning against allowing skateboards at school because so few students seemed to have them. Sandy Rossman, a seventh-grade representative, then raised his hand and spoke with some passion. "If only 17 students want to ride skateboards, I think that we should allow them to do that," he said. "We are the representatives of *all* of the students, and just because only a few want this, we still represent them; they still count," concluded Sandy.

Sandy's comments offer another illustration of how experiential curriculum provides impromptu experiences that are opportunities for great teaching. I was able to link Sandy's comments to the world outside of school—in this case, to the U.S. Constitution. Sandy, operating in the Runkle School House of Representatives, had articulated a concept that is in the spirit of the equal protection clause of the Fourteenth Amendment to the Constitution. I was able to say to the House membership, "Sandy's argument is a very important one. He is saying that *every person* within our school community is important and that representatives must represent every student. There is an amendment to the U.S. Constitution, the Fourteenth Amendment, that says something very similar to what Sandy is saying here today. The Fourteenth Amendment was passed in 1868, 3 years after the Civil War ended. The equal protection clause of this amendment promises that the laws of this country will protect *every* citizen."

Sandy's argument carried the day. The House voted, 5 to 3, to approve the following motion:

> Skateboards shall be allowed outside the building. They may not be taken inside. They may be kept locked or unlocked on the bike racks. Keeping your skateboard on the bike racks is strictly at your own risk. Skateboards will be used only as a means of transportation, ridden to and from school. Skateboards will only be allowed to be ridden and used by children in grades 4–8.

The vote, as it turns out, was anticlimactic. On May 3, the Runkle House of Representatives received the following letter from George P. Simonetti, chief of police in Brookline.

> The Chairman of the Board of Selectmen, John Alden, has asked me to explain the law relative to skateboards. Under the Town of Brookline, Traffic Rules and Regulations, Article 9, Section 1(b):
>> No person shall ride upon any skateboard or similar device on any public way, sidewalk, or other public place within the Town of Brookline, said place being covered under these rules, except as otherwise authorized by the Transportation Board.
> This regulation was put in several years ago after several serious accidents involving young people. Many of these injuries were head injuries resulting in long-term disability to the young person.
>> The rule was adopted after public hearings and testimony from medical and legal areas within the community and was not started to take away a pleasure that the young people have.

Peter called the May 8 meeting to order and said, "I would like to read this letter that we received from Brookline's chief of police." After reading the letter, he read the motion on skateboards passed at the previous meeting. He then said, "Can I have a motion declaring this bill null and void?" The motion passed, without discussion, 6 to 3. I said, "Do you remember the Democracy Assemblies in January? At those assemblies I said that there are limitations on student democracy. This is an example of one."

The students were very accepting of this "defeat." It was really the first time a motion of theirs did not become binding school policy. Throughout the year, they had managed to meet earlier and more often than teachers had initially planned; they modified and clarified rules regarding recess time; and, during a meeting with Brookline's director of food services, they had reached a compromise and gained a chef's salad as an entree choice at lunchtime every Thursday. The skateboard discussion provided important insights into constitutional democracy and the limitations of student government. It was also a lively and not very forgettable lesson in local government.

The Writing Center: Two Perspectives Collide

Two teachers, a first-grade teacher and a fifth-grade teacher, were coordinators of the school's Writing Center. There had been some recent vandalism in the center, a room on the first floor of the school building. On May 14, the House received a letter from these teachers. Speaker Campo read it to the representatives. In part, it said, "Could you please bring up the problem of the damaged typewriters and materials in the Writing Center? How can we solve this problem and still keep the Writing Center student-centered, without having to monitor it?"

Sixth grader Ed Lassner spoke first. "Perhaps people are coming into the Writing Center from the halls. Maybe we should lock up the typewriters."

Sixth grader Ramah McVey said, "I have an idea. If there are keys to the Writing Center, then we would know who's in there at certain times and we can find out who's responsible for the damage."

"How would we know when the damage occurred? Who would check on the condition of the center?" asked seventh grader Dan James.

"How about a schedule that tells who is in there at certain times?" suggested another representative.

"Maybe we could buy a video camera like they have in banks?" suggested Dan James, with some sarcasm.

"Or, we could get plastic cards to let us in," he added. The representatives laughed.

Peter said, "Kids are going down there and messing it up. Maybe only teachers and parent volunteers should be allowed in."

I responded, "The teachers have asked us for ideas that will solve the problem and keep the Writing Center student-centered."

A fifth grader then said, "You know, if we're honest about it, we'd say that we do not do a lot of writing in the Writing Center. Maybe we write for a few minutes, maybe we conference for a few minutes, but then we talk to our friends," she added.

The discussion changed. It was confession time. Representative after representative confirmed the sense that the students were not fulfilling their responsibilities in the Writing Center. "When there's no teacher around, there's no work done," said one. "Why do we have to go to the Writing Center to write? Why can't we write in the class-room where there is a teacher to supervise us?" added another. "It's not just us," said seventh grader Sandy Rossman. "You can ask any student in the school," he added, "and they'll say that they mainly fool around in the Writing Center." Only one representative spoke in favor of using the Writing Center as an unsupervised space. Fourth grader Andrew Sharfman said, "I like the Writing Center. It is a quiet place for us to think and write."

I said, "It seems that there is a very strong feeling here that most of you are not using the Writing Center as the teachers would like." I added, "Can't we try to come up with some ideas to make it work better?"

There was silence. I suggested the creation of an "Accountability Form" that would be returned to the teacher after a student used the Writing Center. The form would have space for the student to de-scribe the work that he or she accomplished during the time spent in the center. And there would be a space for students to state the condition of the center when they arrived and when they departed.

"Who's going to write down that the center was in good condition when they arrived and vandalized when they left?" asked a cynical seventh grader. A fifth grader added, "Kids will show teachers work, but not necessarily work that was done in the Writing Center."

I expressed disappointment in the body's failure to create solu-tions; in the group's inability to trust itself with the independence that teachers wanted to provide.

"Dr. Weintraub," said Peter Campo, solemnly, "at our age we just cannot resist the temptation that is offered by a Writing Center that is not supervised."

A motion was proposed. "I move that the Writing Center shall be shut down for all unsupervised student purposes until the end of the school year or until the student government comes up with a better idea." The motion passed, 9 to 1. Anticipating an uncomfortable situation with the teachers, I reinforced our lawmaking process, explaining to the representatives, "You have just passed a bill. I will now consult with the teachers and decide whether or not to sign it."

Some of the representatives did not listen carefully to that explanation. When I approached the teachers later in the morning, they were very angry. Several representatives had returned to the home-rooms reporting that the House had shut down the Writing Center. The teachers felt that the student government had crossed into the domain of academic policy. "How can students close down a class-room?" asked one of the teachers. "And representatives in grades 4 through 8 had closed the Writing Center for students in grades K through 3," added the other teacher. "It's unacceptable," one said. "I have been a strong supporter of student government, but I'm not sure that I can support it any longer," she added.

I explained that the House had passed a bill that morning. I had not signed it and it was not law. "Well, that's not what they understand," replied one of the teachers.

There were two more House meetings on the subject. I attempted to move the members closer to the teachers' position, toward adopting accountability mechanisms. The representatives, however, maintained their stance that an unsupervised Writing Center could not work for students. I did not sign the bill, and the Writing Center remained open. For the first time, I had exercised the veto that had been granted to me. Impromptu experience again provided me with a great teaching moment. I said to the House members: "This situation reminds me of similar conflicts in bicameral legislatures at the state and federal levels. The House maintains one position and the Senate holds another. A conference committee, comprised of representatives from both houses, is convened to work out a compromise. In our case, the teachers have a point of view and the students have a different opinion. The teachers are like the Senate, the students like the House. The teachers will be meeting this coming summer, as they have in past summers, to evaluate and plan for the continued development of the Writing Center. Although you will not be there, your voices will be there. Your voices are really the House contribution to a conference committee."

After this meeting, I met with the two teachers. I said, "It is true that the students were unable to solve the problem the way we might have wanted them to. But in our planning we need to pay attention to their perspective."

The conflict between teacher and student perspectives was not comfortable. Neither is the contentiousness that often characterizes democracy beyond the schoolhouse. Democracy at the schoolhouse is not really very different from democracy beyond it. It is not always comfortable, nor efficient. However, it is alive; it has everything to do with the lives that are led within the school building; and I believe that it is effective.

During the summer, the two teachers did meet and the voice of the Runkle House of Representatives was heard. In the fall, parents were asked to become more involved in the daily supervision of the Writing Center. And, where five or six students were last year allowed to work in the center at one time, now only two or three at a time would be permitted. The teachers would not abandon their goal of instilling more independent student learning. In moving toward this goal, however, they would be more attentive to the developmental ability of children to become independent learners.

Conclusion

The magic of student democracy is that it encompasses two essential ingredients found in great schools—effective teaching and dynamic participatory structures. During the 1988–89 school year, Runkle students learned about government, democracy, and citizenship as they assumed citizenship and practiced democracy within their school. Students were also given a structured forum within which their voices could be heard and their perspective incorporated into the ongoing development of their school.

I return to Paul Gagnon's (1988) statement that democracy teaches us that not all problems have solutions, that we sometimes have to live with tentative answers, that we must accept compromise, that we need to embrace responsibilities as well as rights, and that we should understand that democracy is a way of living, not a settled destination. With faces that were almost always vibrant and engaged, and demonstrating the power of Dewey's relationship between experience and education, the representatives achieved many of these understandings during the first term of the Runkle House.

References

Dewey, J. (1963). *Experience and education.* New York: Macmillan. (Original work published 1938).

Gagnon, P. (1988). Why study history? *The Atlantic, 262*(5), 43–66.

Richmond, G. H. (1974). *The micro-society school: A real world in miniature.* New York: Harper & Row.

PART III

The Character Education
or Direct Approach
to Moral Education

The four chapters in this section also share a unifying theme. For these authors, children are best served by curricular environments carefully planned in advance by concerned adults. Thus these programs use an external orientation to motivating children. The themes emphasized in school are known beforehand, and the reinforcements are carefully thought out and implemented. The school programs' emphases are on establishing early good habits in a controlled setting so that when their young students mature, those habits will be ingrained and will generalize.

William Bennett begins this section by defining terms. The focus, according to Bennett and supplemented by the authors of the other three chapters, is on influencing proper behavior in youth. Character traits such as honesty, courage, persistence, and responsibility are repeatedly mentioned by these authors, representing behaviors that are *right*, behaviors toward which students should strive.

Both Bennett and Edward Wynne stress that there are eternal themes to be taught to young children and that precious time is wasted if the profession attempts to "reinvent the wheel" (Bennett's term) by having children discover those themes. Rather, these traits of character, "the dispositions to do certain kinds of actions in certain situations" (Wynne's words), must be communicated directly by example, by a shared sense of purpose between adults and children in schools, by a clear code of behavioral expectations, and by reinforcing public ceremonies (e.g., school awards assemblies).

The chapters by JoAnne Martin-Reynolds and Bill Reynolds and by Richard Sparks demonstrate how the character perspective takes on concrete form. Martin-Reynolds and Reynolds describe school practices in three rural districts. Their research shows that community support for their schools and the subsequent values imparted by them is high compared with a national sample. In those rural schools, publicly stated community values were reinforced by curricular programs emphasizing good role models in literature (including the Bible), self-control, and respect, and by incentives for attendance, academic excellence, and citizenship.

The final chapter in this section, by Sparks, documents in detail how character education is implemented in one school. Regardless of the ethnic or socioeconomic background of the students, the program documented in Chapter 10 is a model for effective education that pervades an entire school and each of its teachers and students. The school's curricular and co-curricular programs and the incentives for student participation through the Block FW Award and the Patriotic Classroom Award (the school's nickname is the Patriots) is detailed along with its positive results.

Collectively, these four chapters provide both the philosophic and practical basis for the direct instruction of values to children. This approach to education for character development justifies the role of adults as authoritative mentors who must take the responsibility of guiding their young charges along the path to adult moral literacy.

CHAPTER SEVEN

Moral Literacy and the Formation of Character

WILLIAM J. BENNETT

THE term "values" may suggest that judgments of right and wrong, noble and base, just and unjust, are mere personal preferences, that things are worthwhile only if and insofar as individuals happen to "value" them. As a friend once said, when he hears the word "values" he reaches for his Sears catalog.

Rather than reach for a catalog, we need to reach for a new term. Because these issues are not matters of mere personal taste, let me propose that we reconsider the enterprise now known as "the teaching of values." Let me suggest that we relabel that enterprise as the effort to help form the character of the young and to aid them in achieving moral literacy—that, I think, is what we should be about.

Forming character must begin in the home, starting in the earliest childhood years, but after that, schools must help—because as President Eliot of Harvard once reminded us, "in the campaign for character no auxiliaries are to be refused." And the school can be a mighty auxiliary. There is fairly general agreement as to what elements constitute good character in an individual. You won't find many people who are going to argue: "No, honesty is not a part of good character," or "No, courage isn't really admirable." We all agree

This chapter is based on an address delivered to the Manhattan Institute, New York City, October 30, 1986. Published in *Our Children and Our Country* (pp. 77–85) by William J. Bennett, 1988, New York: Simon and Schuster. Reprinted by permission.

on the value of these things. Now, we may disagree on cases involving these traits, or when there are conflicts among competing claims, but we still maintain our allegiance to good character as a virtue, as something worth preferring.

But despite the beliefs of the majority of Americans, no sooner does anyone begin to point out how important it is to "teach values" in the schools than others immediately begin to raise the specter of awful complexity. As soon as someone starts talking about forming character at school, others claim that it just can't be done, that we won't find a consensus on what to teach or how to teach it. I have heard this complaint on and off, mostly on, in the fifteen years I've been writing on this issue.

A *New York Times* columnist recently wrote that if the people urging schools to teach values—including, he wrote, Governor Mario Cuomo and myself—were asked to define those values, they would probably find it hard to agree. And a *Washington Post* columnist, also writing about the Secretary of Education and the governor of New York, gave us this analysis: "In the United States, the most heterogeneous nation in the world, one man's values can be another man's anathema. . . . Does it really make any sense to add still further to [our schools'] burden, to insist that they provide the answers to questions of values upon which we mature adults cannot agree?"

And sometimes it is one and the same person who calls attention to the importance of teaching values and then immediately thinks better of his suggestion. So Governor Cuomo, talking about his plans to bolster the teaching of values in New York schools, immediately demurred: "You probably won't be able to get a consensus view on values, so it probably won't go anywhere, but we'll try."

Governor Cuomo is right to stress the importance of teaching values—but he shouldn't be so doubtful that it can be done. I agree there are hard cases. I agree there is not a consensus on everything. But nevertheless this task can be done, and should be done. It has been done for most of American history. While a certain amount of caution and prudence is of course healthy—no one wants to impose a moral straitjacket on children—we do not want to present them with a moral vacuum either. There is no reason for excessive timidity, in suggesting a role for our schools in the formation of character. In fact, there is an increasingly broad consensus today as to the importance of this task. My message is that it can be done, and that we should demystify this subject so we can get down to business.

The first mistake is to say that we cannot agree on "values." Well, we cannot agree on everything. But we can agree on the basic traits of character we want our children to have and our schools to develop. And we can agree that there ought to be such a thing as moral literacy.

What do I mean by "moral literacy"? Professor E. D. Hirsch of the University of Virginia has pointed out that being literate entails more than recognizing the forms and sounds of words. It is also a matter of building up a body of knowledge enabling us to make sense of the facts, names, and allusions cited by an author. This background knowledge Hirsch calls cultural literacy. For example, someone who is unsure who Grant and Lee were may have a hard time understanding a paragraph about the Civil War, no matter how well he reads. Likewise, a reader who isn't familiar with the Bill of Rights will not fully understand a sentence containing the words "First Amendment." Understanding a subject, then, involves not just the possession of skills; it also depends on the amount of relevant prior knowledge a reader has, on his cultural literacy.

So it is with "moral literacy." If we want our children to possess the traits of character we most admire, we need to teach them what those traits are. They must learn to identify the forms and content of those traits. They must achieve at least a minimal level of moral literacy that will enable them to make sense of what they will see in life and, we may hope, will help them live it well.

So the question is: How does education form character and help students achieve moral literacy?

It seems that some have forgotten the answer. Some educators have turned to a whole range of mostly dubious "values education" theories, wherein the goal is to guide children in developing "their own values" by discussion, dialogue, and simulation. It is not unusual to hear educators say they should be neutral toward questions of right and wrong. I believe these views are mistaken.

For example, in 1985 *The New York Times* ran an article quoting New York area educators proclaiming that "they deliberately avoid trying to tell students what is ethically right and wrong." The article told of one counseling session involving fifteen high school juniors and seniors.

In the course of that session the students concluded that a fellow student had been foolish to return $1000 she found in a purse at the school. According to the article, when the students asked the counselor's opinion, "He told them he believed the girl had done the right thing, but that, of course, he would not try to force his values on them. 'If I come from the position of what is right and what is wrong,' he explained, 'then I'm not their counselor.'" Now, once upon a time, a counselor offered counsel, and he knew that an adult does not form character in the young by taking a stance of neutrality toward questions of right and wrong or by merely offering "choices" or "options."

We would do well to remember that the Greek word *charakter* means "enduring marks," traits that can be formed in a person by an almost infinite number of influences. But as the theologian Martin Buber pointed out, the teacher is different from other influences in one important way: The educator is distinguished for all other influences "by his *will* to take part in the stamping of character and by his *consciousness* that he represents in the eyes of the growing person a certain *selection* of what is, the selection of what is 'right', of what *should* be." It is in this will, Buber says, in this clear standing for something that the "vocation as an educator finds its fundamental expression."

To put students in the presence of a morally mature adult who speaks honestly and candidly to them is essential to their moral growth. And it seems to me that this is why many teachers entered the profession in the first place—because they thought they could make a positive difference in the lives of students, in the development of their character, to make them better men and women.

We must have teachers and principals who not only state the difference between right and wrong, but who make an effort to live that difference in front of students. In this business of teaching character, there has never been anything as important as the quiet power of moral example. I once visited a class at Waterbury Elementary School in Waterbury, Vermont, and asked the students, "Is this a good school?" They answered, "Yes, this is a good school." I asked them, "Why is this a good school?" Among other things, one eight-year-old said, "The principal, Mr. Riegel, makes good rules and everyone obeys them." So I said, "Give me an example." And another answered, "You can't climb on the pipes in the bathroom. We don't climb on the pipes and the principal doesn't either."

This example is probably too simple to please a lot of people who want to make this topic difficult, but there is something profound in the answer of those children, something educators should pay more attention to. You can't expect children to take messages about rules or morality seriously unless they see adults taking those rules seriously in their day-to-day affairs. Certain things must be said and certain examples must be set—there is no other way. These are the first and most powerful steps in nurturing character and developing moral literacy in the young.

When it comes to instilling character and moral literacy in schoolchildren, there is of course the question of curriculum. What materials and texts should students be asked to read? The research shows that most "values education" exercises and separate courses in "moral reasoning" tend not to affect children's behavior; if anything, they may leave children morally adrift. So what kind of materials should we be using instead?

The simple answer is, we don't have to reinvent the wheel. And we don't have to add new courses. We have a wealth of material to draw on—material that virtually all schools once taught to students for the sake of shaping character. And it is subject matter that we can teach in our regular courses, in our English and history classes.

The vast majority of Americans share a respect for certain fundamental traits of character. Because they are not born with this knowledge, children need to learn what these traits are. They will learn them most profoundly by being in the presence of adults who exemplify them. But we can help their grasp and the appreciation of these traits through the curriculum. That is, we can invite our students to discern the moral of stories, or historical events, of famous lives.

Let me mention just a few examples. There are thousands.

Do we want our children to know what honesty means? Then we might teach them about Joan of Arc, Horatius at the bridge, Harriet Tubman and the Underground Railroad.

Do we want them to know about kindness and compassion, and their opposites? Then they should read *A Christmas Carol* and *The Diary of Anne Frank* and, later on, *King Lear*.

Do we want them to know about loyalty to country? Then we should want them to know of Nathan Hale, about the Battle of Britain, and the siege at Thermopylae. They should know that men such as Lieutenant Elmo Zumwalt have served their country willingly, nobly. And they should understand the contrary examples of men like Benedict Arnold and John Walker.

We want our children to know what faithfulness to family and friends means, and so they should know how Penelope and Telemachus and even an old dog waited twenty years for Odysseus to come home. We want them to know about respect for the law, so they should understand why Socrates told Crito: No, I must submit to the decree of Athens.

We want them to know about persistence in the face of adversity, and so they should know about the Donner party, and the voyages of Columbus, and the character of Washington during the Revolution and Lincoln during the Civil War. And our youngest should be told about the Little Engine That Could.

We want our children to recognize greed, and so they should know King Midas. We want them to recognize vanity, and so they should read "Ozymandias" and learn about Achilles. We want them to know about overreaching ambition, so we should tell them about Lady Macbeth.

We want our children to know that hard work pays off, so we should teach them about the Wright brothers at Kitty Hawk and Booker T. Washington's learning to read. We want them to see the dangers of an unreasoning conformity, so we should tell them about the Emperor's New Clothes and about Galileo. We want them to see that one individual's action can make all the difference, so we should tell them about Rosa Parks, and about Jonas Salk's discovery of a vaccine against polio.

We want our children to respect the rights of others, and so they should read the Declaration of Independence, the Bill of Rights, the Gettysburg Address, and Martin Luther King, Jr.'s "Letter From Birmingham City Jail."

There are other stories we can include, too—stories from the Bible: Ruth's loyalty to Naomi, Joseph's forgiveness of his brothers, Jonathan's friendship with David, the Good Samaritan's kindness toward a stranger, Cain's treatment of his brother Abel, David's cleverness and courage in facing Goliath. These are great stories, and we should be able to use them in teaching character to our children. Why? Because they teach moral values we all share. And they shouldn't be thrown out just because they are in the Bible. As Harvard psychiatrist Robert Coles recently asked, "Are students really better off with the theories of psychologists than with the hard thoughts of Jeremiah and Jesus?" Knowing these hard thoughts is surely part of moral literacy, and it does not violate our Constitution.

These, then, are some of the familiar accounts of virtue and vice with which our children should be familiar. Do our children know these stories, these works? Unfortunately, many do not. They do not because in some places we are no longer teaching them. Why should we go to the trouble of picking up the task again?

First, these stories and others like them are interesting to children. Of course, the pedagogy will need to be varied according to students' level of comprehension, but you can't beat these stories when it comes to engaging the attention of a child. Nothing in recent years, on television or anywhere else, has improved on a good story that begins "Once upon a time . . ."

Second, these stories, unlike courses in "moral reasoning," give children some specific reference points. Our literature and history are a rich quarry of moral literacy. We should mine that quarry. Children must have at their disposal a stock of examples illustrating what we believe to be right and wrong, good and bad—examples illustrating that, in many instances, what is morally right and wrong can indeed be known.

Third, these stories help anchor our children in their culture, its history and traditions. They give children a mooring. This is necessary, because morality, of course, is inextricably bound both to the individual conscience and the memory of society. Our traditions reveal the ideals by which we wish to live our lives. We should teach these accounts of character to our children so that we may welcome them to a common world, and in that common world to the continuing task of preserving the principles, the ideals, and the notions of greatness we hold dear.

I have not mentioned issues like nuclear war, abortion, creationism, or euthanasia. This may come as a disappointment to some people, but the fact is that the formation of character in young people is educationally a different task from, and a prior task to, the discussion of the great, difficult controversies of the day. First things first. We should teach values the same way we teach other things: one step at a time. We should not use the fact that there are indeed many difficult and controversial moral questions as an argument against basic instruction in the subject. We do not argue against teaching physics because laser physics is difficult, against teaching biology or chemistry because gene splicing and cloning are complex and controversial, against teaching American history because there are heated disputes about the Founders' intent. Every field has its complexities and controversies. And every field has its basics.

So too with forming character and achieving moral literacy, or teaching values, if you will. You have to walk before you can run, and you ought to be able to run straight before you are asked to run an obstacle course. So the moral basics should be taught in school, in the early years. The tough issues can, if teachers and parents wish, be taken up later. And, I would add, a person who is morally literate will be immeasurably better equipped than a morally illiterate person to reach a reasoned and ethically defensible position on these tough issues. But the formation of character and the teaching of moral literacy come first, the tough issues later, in senior high school or college.

Further, the task of teaching moral literacy and forming character is not political in the usual meaning of the term. People of good character are not all going to come down on the same side of difficult political and social issues. Good people—people of character and moral literacy—can be conservative, and good people can be liberal; good people can be religious, and good people can be nonreligious. But we must not permit our disputes over thorny political or religious questions to suffocate the obligation we have to offer instruction to our young people in the area in which we have, as a society, reached a consensus: namely, on the importance of good character, and on some of its pervasive particulars.

I have spent much time as Secretary of Education traveling the country, visiting schools and teaching classes. I have taught seventh-graders the Declaration of Independence, and eleventh-graders *Federalist* No. 10 and the story of the Constitutional Convention. To third-graders I've taught the story of Cincinnatus returning to his farm when he could have had an empire. And they got it. To the third-graders too, I've taught how nothing but George Washington's exemplary character stood against a mutinous army of unpaid soldiers bent on besieging the Continental Congress in Philadelphia, and how that shining character itself was enough to make those men turn back.

I have taught these lessons, and others, to American children. I have tried to teach them directly and unapologetically. I have talked to teachers and parents about these matters as well. And when I have very publicly done this in our classrooms, no one has ever stood up and said, "You shouldn't be teaching these lessons. You are indoctrinating our children, corrupting them, you are not respecting parental prerogative. This isn't the right stuff for our children to learn." On the contrary, people have been pleased. It has been my experience, in many trips across this country, that students and parents welcome such discussions; they want more, and most teachers and principals are not opposed to giving them more. There is a very broad, and very deep, consensus out there, and we are failing in our duty if we ignore it. Objections noted, cautions observed, let us get down to, and back to, the business of the moral education of the young.

CHAPTER EIGHT

Character
and Academics
in the Elementary School

EDWARD A. WYNNE

CONSIDERABLE controversy has arisen about how to transmit moral values to young people, particularly those in elementary schools (Nucci, 1989). At the heart of the problem, undoubtedly, is the long-term trend toward social disorder among young people (Wynne & Hess, 1986; Office of Educational Research and Improvement, 1988). We have seen rising rates of youth suicide and homicide, out-of-wedlock births, criminal arrest, and drug use. Such patterns of conduct raise urgent questions about whether our schools should do more to address these problems. Although most of these alarming behavior patterns do not surface at the elementary school level, educators, parents, and communities realize that preventive programs in moral education should begin in the primary grades.

This chapter presents one perspective on this controversy. I have adopted the ancient concept of "character" as a theme. The roots of the word *character* are taken from the Greek word "to mark." It suggests a focus on observable conduct (Peters, 1955). Before the conclusion of this chapter, readers will be offered a variety of practical and tested pro-character suggestions to apply in elementary classrooms and schools. These suggestions have been derived from the practices of public and private elementary schools operating in a variety of environments, from prosperous suburbs to ethnic neighborhoods and inner-city ghettos. However, as a first step, I would like to sketch the overall controversy surrounding moral education.

The "Modern" Moral Education Position

One strain of philosophical analysis can be called the modern position. Proponents of that position are relatively optimistic about the merits of giving students a major say in their own moral education. They believe strongly in students' self-direction and are often critical of overt adult direction or monitoring.

Though I call this position modern, it has deep historical roots. It can be traced back at least to Rousseau, who opened his influential text *Émile* (1761/1972) with a powerful criticism of intrusive adult efforts to shape the minds of growing children.

John Dewey was another notable proponent of such perspectives, stating as early as 1897 that "the child's own instincts and powers furnish the material and give the starting-point for all education," and that "education, therefore, is a process of living and not a preparation for future living." Rather than learning from the experiences of others, education, from Dewey's perspective, was a continuous reconstruction, or reinvention, of experience (Gutek, 1970, p. 195). It is important to recognize, in discussing Dewey, that many of his alleged "pronouncements" are due more to his overenthusiastic interpreters than to his direct statements. His prose is often obscure and ambiguous and invites uncertainty (Hirsch, 1987). Indeed, one writer has commented,

> Dewey's language . . . is a principal factor in the persistent problems of measuring the effects of his work against his intentions, and of distinguishing the latter from the interpretations of his disciples. . . . In a way, Dewey may be said to deserve whatever confusions came to be associated with his name. It may be no compliment to professional educators that they so easily understood Dewey while philosophers shook their heads. (Dworkin, 1959, pp. 13–14)

Many theorists, in the tradition of Rousseau and Dewey, have favored general, emotive terminology—like "educating for democracy"—without articulating precise policies to advance such ends. Of course, American pupils should be educated for democracy. But this proposition provides no clue as to what such education should consist of. Some may take it that education for democracy requires pupils to vote on all key matters of school policy. The notion of one person, one vote is essentially what democracy means to millions of American adults, but surely other interpretations of "educating for democracy" can be defended.

For example, someone may argue, as did John Adams (1971), that citizens in a democracy should be dedicated to "Republican virtue." This implies a willingness to display considerable self-restraint, perhaps to accept greater personal frugality precisely because democracy gives them the power to vote excessive benefits to themselves. However, I do not believe that many education theorists dramatically urge American schools to strive to educate pupils toward frugality (e.g., by encouraging students to walk to school or even to be responsible for school campus cleanliness) as part of education for democracy.

In sum, when theorists' propositions are allegedly "distorted" and misinterpreted, sometimes the theorists should share the blame. Poor communication, or colorful language with popular appeal, can lead to unclear, illogical applications.

It is significant to note that Dewey worked to found the famous Laboratory School at the University of Chicago to help advance his principles. In 1905, the principal of the school, in an article for an education periodical, presented the school's basic rationale as follows (De Pincier, 1967, p. 59): "The School recognizes the utter futility of trying to teach anyone anything when he is not in a happy frame of mind." This was the principal's interpretation of Dewey's propositions! Once again we have a strong emphasis on the consensual definition of values: Do not stress values that may make pupils unhappy: that is, don't delay their gratification.

In our own era, researchers such as Lawrence Kohlberg (1981, 1984) and popularizers such as Raths, Harmin, and Simon (1966) have reemphasized what I call the modern approach. They have undertaken to justify consensual methods of teaching morality. Although information is lacking as to the extent to which such methods are actually applied by teachers, various surveys of texts and readers used in American schools have found that published prose presented to pupils is heavily affected by consensual themes (Vitz, 1986; Hirsch, 1987; Lewis, 1947).

Various research findings have often been cited to justify the modern position (Leming, 1981), although some researchers have been critical (Swindler, 1979). But the research *issues* involved confront enormous technical and philosophical barriers: What are the objectives of such consensual approaches? What should they be? What measures would show that their desired effects have been attained? What possible secondary consequences result from applying such approaches? How do we know such consequences are good or bad?

A simple instance can help demonstrate this complexity.

Kohlberg was a proponent of establishing "just community schools" (1985). In such schools, pupils actively participate in defining the norms of conduct. One newspaper article described the tensions that ensued in such a just community high school project (initiated under Kohlberg's general auspices) before a school outing (Hand, 1989). A controversy arose among the pupils about the propriety of prohibiting "weapons and sex" on the outing. After lengthy discussion, the majority of the pupils and teachers adopted the prohibition. Since the article emphasized that the school had many potential delinquents among its students, we must assume that the proposals were completely serious; if the "vote" went the other way, some pupils would have brought knives or the like to the outing, and others would have come and engaged in sex.

This story, published in *The New York Times,* may be seen as controversial. Thus I called and spoke with an employee of the school, who verified the incident. The story is also congruent with two separate stories personally reported to me, by informed persons, of problems with evident drug use by students in just community schools. The problems arose because the adult staff believed it was inappropriate to prohibit such use without the assent of the students.

Assume we tried to evaluate the just community school described in the *Times* article. It is possible that research might show that the "no-sex rule" was actually observed and that many pupils said they found the discussion helpful. But many other philosophical and research issues related to the incident remain problematic.

- Is it wise to dedicate large amounts of school time to such discussions (e.g., compared with teaching math)?
- Were there other rules that adults might see as warranted (where pupil consensus might not develop) that were not promulgated (e.g., against drug use or vulgar language on the picnic)? What are the effects of avoiding such prohibitions?
- If the program was shown to have any beneficial effects, such as improving general discipline, is it possible such benefits could have been obtained by other, less problematic approaches (e.g., bringing in a more able school principal)?
- Is it wise to "teach" pupils that basic principles and conventions generally accepted by responsible adults should be considered de novo, and possibly rejected, by each successive adolescent cohort? Must each generation try to completely reinvent society?

The weapons-and-sex vote has other important implications for moral education policies in elementary schools. We will discuss them later in this chapter.

The Traditional Perspective: Character Education

The traditional perspective about transmitting morals to children can be derived from classical (Greek and Roman) authors and many subsequent authorities as well as recent anthropological research (Wynne, 1985–86; Durkheim, 1961; Read, 1968). Proponents of this approach expect adults to shape and determine the immediate behavior of the young, to form their character. As children mature, increased emphasis should be given to developing discretion and applying individual judgment. But first, a strong base of good habits and belief in moral values must be established.

For example, Plato, who was a student of Socrates, described Socrates' teaching methods—relying on probing, somewhat open-ended questions—in sympathetic terms. But Socrates' students were young men between the ages of 15 and 20, who had undergone lengthy and rigorous preliminary training (such as memorizing long passages from Homer) (Bowen, 1972). Socrates himself emphasized law-abiding conduct and patriotism to the state of Athens. Even Plato and Aristotle, who disagreed about educational approaches, both recognized that education in more speculative matters should be reserved for adulthood (Bowen, 1972).

Finally, Plato in *The Republic* and Aristotle in the *Nicomachean Ethics* presented careful psychological analyses of the ways in which morals are shaped, emphasizing the central role of adults in managing the education of children. Both emphasize that moral values are not innate but rather traits of character, dispositions to take certain kinds of actions in certain situations, that must be cultivated in the young. As Aristotle said, "We become just by the practice of just actions, self-controlled by exercising self-control, and courageous by performing acts of courage. . . . Hence it is no small matter whether one habit or another is inculcated in us from early childhood; on the contrary it makes a considerable difference, or, rather, all the difference" (Aristotle, 1962, pp. 34–35).

In America during the early 19th century, Horace Mann and other activists vigorously promoted creating the public common school to teach appropriate character to the children of immigrants, who were thought to possess values at variance with mainstream American thought (Cremin, 1957). Mann's proposals formed a central theme in American education until well into the 20th century (Tyack & Hansot, 1982), although his ideas were criticized by some as attempts to suppress the values and beliefs of certain ethnic groups (Glenn, 1988). Underlying Glenn's analysis is the assumption that the children's parents, and not the state, should form the children's values and beliefs. No one was suggesting that the children themselves should "independently" determine their own character.

Research regarding both modern and traditional approaches is inconclusive. However, the traditional approach has been tested by time, with many parallels existing between the moral education techniques proposed during 3,000 years in the Torah, Plato's works, the Roman Catholic *Baltimore Catechism* (1943), and the writings of Horace Mann. Cross-cultural studies in anthropology can supply equivalent insights into how character is formed in non-Western cultures (Eisenstadt, 1956). A number of researchers and contemporary educators have also concluded that traditional approaches are more likely than modern techniques to generate good conduct in pupils (Leming, 1981; Bennett & Delattre, 1978; Pritchard, 1988; Ryan, 1986).

Many questions, however, remain unsettled: What sorts of adults are created by such pro-character approaches? What sorts of adults should we want in our society? Can we, or should we try to, create a new and better adult through applying novel approaches? Would the outcome be better or worse? Is it right to experiment with children in such innovations? Toward the end of this chapter I will consider some of these questions. But first we need some more background data.

A Contrast

Figure 8.1, summarizes and contrasts the important elements of the modern and traditional pro-character approaches. The differences between these methodologies should be readily apparent.

Research Findings

Over the past 20 years, my pupils and I have studied about 200 of the 2,000 elementary and secondary public and private schools in and around Chicago. These schools were selected in a semirandom fashion. (A major factor determining whether a school was studied was

Figure 8.1 Modern and Traditional Approaches: A Contrast

MODERN	TRADITIONAL
1. Pupils participate actively with adults in defining central values and prohibitions.	**1.** Adults and their institutions define central values and prohibitions.
2. Pupils learn a "right" way of reasoning to achieve the proper state of mind leading to moral efficiency.	**2.** Pupils' day-to-day good conduct, displayed through deeds or words, is the test of a school's moral efficiency.
3. Pupils, it is assumed, will regularly choose "good" values.	**3.** Pupils, unless precautions are taken, may choose seriously bad values.
4. Moral discourse is the central mode of transmitting values.	**4.** The school curriculum and environment transmit good values; moral discourse is one of several means of instruction.
5. Dramatically better ways of transmitting morality, it is assumed, can be discovered and/or invented.	**5.** The traditional ways of transmitting morality, it is assumed, are generally sound.
6. Prohibitions are not made clear and prompt punishment for undesirable actions is not emphasized.	**6.** The individual is held partly responsible for the morality of his or her school or class, as a collective entity, and vice-versa. Clear prohibitions are published, and prompt punishments are established for individual or group misconduct.
7. The academic program is sometimes of secondary importance.	**7.** The academic program is always of primary importance.

whether it was convenient for my students to reach; but the students came from all over the Chicago area–suburbs, ethnic enclaves, ghettos. Thus the long-term sample had many random elements.) Because of the length and semirandom nature of the studies, some schools were observed several times over a number of years. This proved a good form of verification and also provided historical data. From 1982 to 1987, I also worked with the For Character School Recognition Program, an elaborate enterprise covering the same 2,000 schools. That program enabled me to study descriptive statistical and narrative data from over 300 schools purporting to focus their programs on both pupil character and academics.

The quality and quantity of descrptive data collected on the schools varied somewhat over time and were affected by factors such as variable levels of student care in completing and recording observations and availability of relevant school-related documents. In general, the data included reports of structured interviews with principals, teachers, students, and parents; copies of relevant school documents; written descriptions (and sometimes photographs) of the school and classroom environment; and, in the For Character program, a 60-item questionnaire returned by the schools and analyzed by computer. (I also interviewed some 25 principals whose schools were identified as sympathetic to traditional perspectives.) This work has been published in a variety of forms (e.g., Wynne, 1980, 1981, 1987).

In the 1988–89 school year, I also conducted a thorough study of one strongly pro-character urban elementary public school (Wynne, 1989). That study included more than 100 site visits. During the 1989–90 school year, I studied a pro-character suburban high school. All of these studies have focused on two questions: How hard did the school work at transmitting good character to pupils? How did the school go about teaching morality?

Regrettably, the studies provided little information about the formal *subject matter* presented to pupils and its potential moral content. Furthermore, analysis of comparative test scores was considerably confounded by our inability to separate out and compare students of like socioeconomic status and to distinguish schools that rigorously adhered to one conceptual approach. One exploratory study, however, did report favorable statistical relationships between pro-character focus and academic emphasis in some schools (Wynne & Iverson, 1989).

Thus it is artificial to portray the theories (and practice) of teaching morality in a rigorous bipolar fashion. Of the 500 schools summarized here, most take an approach that falls somewhere between traditional and modern. Furthermore, the methodology applied was only semiquantitative and much of the data does not lend itself to simple classification. Therefore, I have made descriptive, qualitative analysis of schools at each end of the moral education spectrum to illustrate the sharp contrast.

• About 10% to 15% of the schools could be described as strongly traditional; perhaps 5% or fewer were strongly modern.

- Strongly pro-modern high schools tended (1) to dissolve in 2 to 3 years or (2) to shift quickly in mildly pro-tradition directions. Some pro-modern elementary schools showed stability.
- Many schools with indeteminate characteristics showed substantial modern tendencies.
- Pro-tradition schools appeared in all types of environments—suburbs, ethnic enclaves, ghettos—but they were more often associated with (1) stable community environments and/or (2) strong principals. There was a mild tendency for them to be private and/or church related.
- Pro-tradition schools often maintained their thrust over a number of years, especially if they were run by the same principal.
- Many schools in more disordered communities adhered to modern approaches, and tended to maintain such approaches for many years.
- There was no evident relationship between a school's level of financing and its moral philosophy or practices.

The Practices of For Character Schools

The practices of For Character schools vary according to many factors—pupils' age range, whether the school is public or private, and the community it serves. Still many common themes exist in such schools.

- Adults model good moral conduct. They work diligently; are obedient to school rules and policies; display goodwill and consideration toward colleagues, pupils, and parents; are basically optimistic about their work; and take pride in the school and their community.
- Pupils are encouraged and even required to engage in many forms of service. They are teachers' aides, tutors, and crossing guards; deliver presentations at assemblies; and participate in service activities and clubs, student councils, athletic teams, and fund-raising for the school. On appropriate occasions, faculty explain to pupils the broader rationales for such activities. Faculty also develop diverse and often elaborate ways to recognize students publicly for good conduct.
- Discipline and monitoring are stressed. Typical forms of misconduct are clearly prohibited by well-publicized rules vigorously and fairly enforced. Prompt penalties are applied to violators. Prohibitions are essentially similar to those that might apply to adults who work in banks, offices, fast food restaurants or the like.

- A relatively uniform sense of purpose exists. Adults and children alike give the same concrete answers when asked about matters of school policy.
- Academics are taken seriously. Significant amounts of homework are regularly assigned, collected, graded, and returned. Diverse efforts are made to improve the quality and quantity of instruction provided by teachers. Pupils are grouped to facilitate instruction. Pupils who do not know the required materials are not passed on. Frequent, rigorous exams are administered. Honor rolls, report cards, and recognition assemblies are used to emphasize the value of academic excellence.
- There are often occasions for good-spirited fun, in the form of Halloween parades, homecomings, dress-up days, dances, teacher appreciation days, balloon releases, different kinds of assemblies, and parties and dances.
- Ceremonies are an important means of stressing school values. Assemblies, daily classroom flag salutes, awards assemblies, and occasions for "appreciation" are standard events. Symbols are identified to facilitate such processes. School pride is an important theme.
- School documents—teacher handbooks, newsletters, notes to parents, discipline codes—are clearly written and provide persuasive justifications for the schools' policies.
- Parents, visitors, and observers are welcomed. These schools solicit parent cooperation, support, and advice. When the faculty believe parents are acting ill-advisedly, they are willing to risk awkward confrontations to try to change patterns harmful to children.

In elementary schools, many of the preceding activities are classroom-based. In departmentalized schools, they are more often schoolwide. In either case, the activities receive strong support from the central administration. The principals stress good communication and appropriate delegation. But there is an understanding that one person is in charge.

I conducted a revealing interview with a group of eighth-grade pupils in the elementary school I studied in depth (1989). That school served a low-income community, with 60% of its pupils from families entitled to federal lunch subsidies. The pupils I interviewed had spent time in other elementary schools before transferring to their present school. When asked to compare their current school with the one they attended before, they identified certain consistent differences. They said their present school

Was cleaner

Made them work harder at academics (the teachers "made you learn")

Had teachers who were stricter on discipline

Offered more "activities" in the form of assemblies, parties, fun at recess, dress-up days, clubs, student council, and opportunities for students to help others and the school

Was preferable over their previous school

Some readers may recognize certain parallels between the characteristics I have identified and some of the findings of the "effective schools" research (Brookover & Lezotte, 1979). Such parallels are not merely coincidental. True, the effective schools research focuses largely on practices related to better academic learning. But For Character schools, as noted, are strongly committed to such learning. It is not really surprising that educators who work hard to improve students' academic learning are also willing to work hard to transmit good moral values to their pupils. Indeed, some research has even found strong positive relationships between good character values (e.g., dedication to honesty, diligence) and greater academic success (Hanson & Ginsburg, 1988).

Implications for Elementary Schools

The preceding data show it is quite possible to run a relatively traditional, For Character, public school in contemporary America. But it is not necessarily easy, especially if the school's approach to teaching values must be totally redirected.

The broad principles for undertaking such a shift are easy to sketch. The incumbent (or incoming) principal must have clear goals for his or her school. There must be a group of powerful allies, for example, influential parents, teachers, or upper level administrators. The principal must model the values he or she wants to transmit: diligence, determination, politeness, solicitude, tact, and foresight.

A multipronged program should be planned for shifting the school gradually toward a traditional approach. Matters such as rigorous classroom instruction, pupil discipline, and enrichment of the school's extracurricular program (in individual classrooms and throughout the school) comprise one element of the plan. In addition, adult-to-adult and adult-to-pupil communication must be intensified, so that successes can be reinforced and problems can be dealt with quickly and effectively. Staff meetings need to stress rigorous standards of commitment. An effort must be made to enhance the ceremonial life of the school and to encourage faculty and students to support each other.

The principal and key staff will achieve these objectives through a variety of measures. First, they will prepare and circulate appropriate handbooks and other documents. The principal will, of course, be responsible for hiring and evaluating teachers. Careful records will be kept on the process of school improvement. The principal and key staff members will need to explain often to parents, staff, and pupils the basic rationales for the changes undertaken. Where necessary, the principal must confront and subdue dissident pupils, teachers, and parents opposed to the basic aims of the program.

The process of change can be exhausting for many of the persons concerned, but it need not be bleak. Although For Character schools may be difficult to create, they are much less work to sustain. Once the necessary structure has been established, many homeostatic forces begin to operate. For example, excellent communication makes it easy to identify and repair trouble spots. Furthermore, people like to work in a school where human relations are warm and supportive and students demonstrate discipline and careful attention to academics. Conversely, in many schools where teachers do not work so hard to instill character in their students, their professional pride is diminished because lax discipline and poor learning often prevail.

Finally, many people have chosen a career in education in part for moral concerns. For Character schools, where strong positions are taken on behalf of helpfulness and in favor of learning and discipline, gratify such motives.

Implications for Classrooms

Individual teachers in For Character schools are regularly instructed as to how they can manage their classes to improve their students' character. The age and academic potential of the pupils determine what policies are appropriate. In all cases, however, the For Character policies are comprehensive in their approach to academic learning, discipline, encouraging helpful behavior, and developing class spirit, cohesion, and pride.

The focus of academic learning is "academic press." This means making pupils work hard at learning through well-organized, efficient instruction; significant assignments and homework; regular and frequent grading; emphasis on grades; appropriate variations in instruction; sophisticated use of test-score data for purposes of evaluation or instruction; and good communication with parents about academic expectations and pupils' successes and difficulties.

Discipline is most effectively implemented through developing clear, appropriate classroom rules and norms, communicated in writing to students and their parents. A clear, yet simple, system of punishment for infractions is part of this communication. Parents must be supportive. Faculty can encourage helpful behaviors among students by providing opportunities for them to be of help to the class or school, by monitoring their conduct, and by designing formal systems of recognition for good conduct (such as notes to parents, certificates, buttons, pins, etc.).

Developing class spirit first requires the teacher to regard the class as an entity. Appeals must be made to the pride of the group. Sometimes the teacher should allocate privileges and punishments—parties, restrictions at recess—on the basis of group conduct or misconduct. Questions about conduct can be discussed with the class in toto. Class projects can be identified and planned collectively. A flag salute ceremony is a useful way to heighten group identity. Where feasible, well-designed cooperative learning projects can enhance academic support among pupils.

Conclusion

Certain issues bear close scrutiny. Few public school principals or teachers would let pupils vote on weapons or sex; likewise, few would refuse to suppress drug use in school because they could not attain pupil assent. Thus, in one sense, the incidents described earlier are aberrations. However, such incidents are the predictable outcome of reflexively prating about "education for democracy." They are also entirely consistent with the pronouncement of the University of Chicago's Laboratory School's early principal that the aim of education is to keep the pupils happy. After all, sex, clothes, drugs, and the demands of academic work are important issues directly affecting the young. It is no secret, furthermore, that young people are often unhappy about adult policies governing such matters. Thus, if we want to teach them democracy and keep them happy, should we not let them vote on these issues? Furthermore, in elementary schools, one can recognize plausible adaptations of such principles: downplaying discipline, failing to make appropriate academic and character-related demands on pupils, and generally applying so-called permissive perspectives.

We must also recognize a reality. The "just community" activities are fully supported by nationally established scholars, tenured at some of the most prestigious universities in the world. The proposals have been screened by an elaborate process of intellectual gatekeeping. They have been funded by reputable foundations. By all reasonable criteria, such proposals represent part of mainstream academic thinking. The major reason we do not have far more such activities in schools is that very few practicing educators will tolerate them. Nor will many parents.

The "reinvent the world" approach advocated by many scholars has understandable psychological roots. All reflective adults wish on occasion that some important things in the world could be changed dramatically. And so we may be tempted, from time to time, to offer this unlimited option to the young. Maybe they can do better.

I recall a famous remark by Thomas Jefferson (Padover, 1956, p. 56) to the effect that every 20 years a society should be affected by a new revolution—freedom is sustained by the blood of martyrs. And, again, Jefferson wrote about the inability of the past to constrain the future. However, despite such colorful language, 25 years after the start of the American Revolution he began the first of his two terms as President. His dramatic rhetoric about revolution and radically overthrowing the hand of the past did not guide his real-life, postrevolutionary activities. Indeed, in actually dealing with young people, Jefferson displayed a quite traditional perspective: Adults should set the key policies and rules, and the young should respectfully obey and learn (Honeywell, 1964).

Similarly, in our own era, many intellectuals should be more willing to get on with the complex and realistic problems of educating the young. They should steer clear of letting their personal semi-utopian impulses guide their proposals and their rhetoric. After all, it is objectively possible for deliberate changes to make the world worse.

Persons concerned about education for democracy and other semiconsensual themes have an obligation to state their objectives and premises in more explicit fashions. In practice, they must answer the question: What does "education for democracy" actually mean when one is dealing with other people's children? If they do not believe pupils should vote on weapons and sex, they have to say so in clear, strong language. Otherwise it is fair that they receive the scorn and incredulity most citizens direct toward educational programs premised on strongly consensual policies.

Now, to some more concrete observations. If one generalizes from my wide Chicago sample, the information outlined portrays a mixed picture. Penetration of the formal curriculum by modern perspectives has been widespread. But very few schools and classrooms are strongly dedicated to such perspectives in their day-to-day policies. There are many schools and classrooms whose policies have been moderately affected by such perspectives. A substantial proportion (about 10% to 15%) of schools are dedicated to traditional, For Character, perspectives, with many more applying a number of these.

For educators sympathetic to traditional perspectives, the scene is moderately heartening. Such perspectives have shown remarkable vitality. They have persisted despite disdain among academics and the devotion of much of the formal curriculum—history, literature, social studies, reading—to modern perspectives. Furthermore, it is evident that there is increased public, and even some intellectual, sympathy for the application of traditional approaches.

It may not be wildly optimistic to propose that, if traditional approaches have shown such vitality under such severe stress, they may flourish even more in a climate of moderate intellectual sympathy. At least that is my hope.

References

Adams, C. (1971). *The life of John Adams: Vol. II.* St. Clair Shores, MI: Scholarly Press.

Aristotle. (1962). *Nicomachean ethics.* New York: Bobbs-Merrill.

Baltimore Cathechism. (1942). *Father Connell's the new Baltimore catechism, no. 3, being the text of the official revised edition, no. 2.* New York: Benziger Bros.

Bennett, W. J., & Delattre, E. (1978). Moral education in the schools. *The Public Interest, 50,* 81–98.

Bowen, J. (1972). *A history of western education: Vol. 1. The ancient world.* New York: St. Martin's Press.

Brookover, W., & Lezotte, L. (1979). *Changes in school characteristics coincident with changes in student achievement.* East Lansing, MI: College of Education, Michigan State University.

Cremin, L. (Ed.) (1957). *The republic and the school.* New York: Teachers College Press.

De Pincier, I. B. (1967). *The history of the laboratory schools.* Chicago: Quadrangle Press.

Durkheim, E. (1961). *Moral education.* New York: Free Press.

Dworkin, M. S. (1959). *Dewey on education.* New York: Teachers College Press.

Eisenstadt, S. N. (1956). *From generation to generation.* New York: Free Press.

Glenn, C. (1988). *The myth of the common school.* Amherst, MA: University of Massachusetts Press.

Gutek, G. (1970). *An historical introduction to American education.* New York: Thomas Y. Crowell.

Hand, D. (1989, April 9). Morality lessons? Hear, hear. *New York Times Special Report on Education,* p. 53.

Hanson, S. L., & Ginsburg, A. L. (1988). Gaining ground: Values and high school success. *American Educational Research Journal, 25*(3), 344–365.

Hirsch, E. D. Jr. (1987). *Cultural literacy.* Boston, MA: Houghton Mifflin.

Honeywell, R. J. (1965). *The educational work of Thomas Jefferson.* New York: Russell & Russell.

Kohlberg, L. (1981). *The philosophy of moral development: Moral stages and the idea of justice.* New York: Harper and Row.

Kohlberg, L. (1984). *The psychology of moral development: The nature and validity of moral stages.* New York: Harper and Row.

Kohlberg, L. (1985). The just community approach to moral education in theory and practice. In M. Berkowitz & F. Oser (Eds.), *Moral education: Theory and application* (pp. 27–87). Hillsdale, NJ: Erlbaum.

Leming, J. (1981). The limits of rational moral education. *Theory and Research in Social Education, 9,* 7–33.

Lewis, C. S. (1947). *The abolition of man.* New York: Macmillan.

Nucci, L. (Ed.) (1989). *Moral development and character education: A dialogue.* Berkeley: McCutchan.

Office of Educational Research and Improvement (1988). *Youth indicators: 1988.* Washington, DC: U.S. Department of Education.

Padover, S. K. (1956). *A Jefferson profile as revealed in his letters.* New York: John Day.

Peters, R. S. (1955). *Ethics and education.* London: Allen & Unwin.

Pritchard, I. (1988). Character education: Research and related prospects. *American Journal of Education, 96,* 469–495.

Raths, L. E., Harmin, M., & Simon, S. B. (1966). *Values and teaching.* Columbus, OH: Charles E. Merrill.

Read, M. (1968). *Children of their fathers.* New York: Holt, Rinehart & Winston.

Rousseau, J. (1972). *Emile, or on education.* B. Foxley, Trans. New York: Everyman. (Original work published 1761)

Ryan, K. (1986). The new moral education. *Phi Delta Kappan, 68,* 228–233.

Swindler, A. (1979). *Organization without authority.* Cambridge, MA: Harvard University Press.

Tyack, D., & Hansot, E. (1982). *Guardians of virtue.* New York: Basic Books.

Vitz, P. (1986). *Censorship: Evidence of bias in our textbooks.* Ann Arbor, MI: Servant.

Wynne, E. A. (1980). *Looking at schools.* Lexington, MA: Heath/Lexington.

Wynne, E. A. (1981). Looking at good schools. *Phi Delta Kappan, 62,* 377–381.

Wynne, E. A. (1985–86). The great tradition in education. *Educational Leadership, 43,* 4–14.

Wynne, E. A. (1987). *Chicago area award winning schools.* Chicago: University of Illinois at Chicago.

Wynne, E. A. (1989). *A year in the life of a school.* Unpublished manuscript, College of Education, University of Illinois, Chicago.

Wynne, E. A., & Hess, M. (1986). Long term trends in youth conduct. *Educational evaluation and policy analysis, 8,* 294–308.

Wynne, E. A., & Iverson, B. (1989). *Academics in For Character schools.* Unpublished manuscript, College of Education, University of Illinois, Chicago.

CHAPTER NINE

Character Development in Small Rural Schools: Grades K–8

JOANNE MARTIN-REYNOLDS

BILL J. REYNOLDS

RURAL school districts and their communities across the country have certain advantages in providing environments that encourage shared values. Their long history of community schools, of pride and involvement in the work of the schools, and their traditions of hard work, resourcefulness, and productivity seem to provide many opportunities for communicating community expectations for student attitudes, values, moral and ethical behavior, and academic performance.

Rural schools comprise approximately 67% of all schools in the United States, and one third of all students live in rural America. Rural and small-town communities serve as the residence and employment site for as many as 80 million Americans (Dunne & Carlsen, 1981). The term *rural* brings to mind sparsely populated areas, distant from an urban center, and a bucolic setting not unlike the ones landscape painters often render. In recent times, however, the agricultural economy in many states has been affected adversely by lower land values, poor, drought-stricken yields in many standard crops, lower prices for some types of meat, diminished animal herds because of drought, and bankrupt lending institutions.

The three districts in this study were selected not because they were examples of exemplary programs in moral education and character development but because they were representative of small rural districts throughout the nation, suffering from similar troubles and coping in similar ways. Each of their communities was classified as rural by the U.S. Census definition: having a population of less than 1,200 residents or people living in open country. Their policies and practices, especially in the elementary schools, are the focus of this chapter.

One of the districts is situated in the middle of a rich agricultural region with many residents who draw their income from agriculture. However, many small plants, businesses, and shops also exist within the district. Teachers in the district largely live outside it and commute to school. A second district is located in a small rural community, with students and their families representing a blend of rural and suburban lifestyles. Agriculture is the major industry. However, more than 60 small businesses and industries are located within the boundaries of the school district. The majority of teachers live in the district. In the third district, according to the 1980 census of population and housing, 1% of the population are self-employed and nearly 80% are private-wage or salaried workers. Many residents commute to large nearby cities to work, such as Toledo. The majority of the teachers in the district do not live in the district but live elsewhere and commute to school.

The districts differ in available school facilities. One has all students in one building, K–12; another has two buildings, one in each of two small neighboring towns. One of the buildings houses grades K–4 and the high school, and the other is the middle school for grades 5–8. This arrangement has dual advantages: The high school students serve as volunteer tutors for the elementary students who need extra help in reading or math, and there tend to be fewer harassing or teasing problems among the older and younger pupils with this age spread. The third district has an elementary building for grades K–6 and a second building for grades 7–12, both located in the same community. Most students come from white middle- and lower- middle-income families with a small Hispanic population in each district. In some districts, migrant workers' children account for a small portion of the student population in early fall.

Any social-class differences are largely based on income-class lines rather than racial lines. Twenty percent of the community members reported income levels below $20,000, 50% between $20,000 and $40,000, and 19% above $40,000.

Schools and Values

Do teachers teach values? Yes, say many recent researchers, only the methods differ (Benninga, 1988; Lickona, 1988; Ryan, 1986). Directly or indirectly, verbally or nonverbally, we all communicate our ethical standards to those around us. And schools are key environments in which a society's values and acceptable standards of behavior toward each of its members are communicated daily.

The age-old question is, of course, What values should be taught? How are they chosen? Who decides? What role does the community play? Should the means be indoctrination or reasoning or a combination of both (Benninga, 1988)? How aware are our teachers, most of them recently trained to be consciously value-neutral (Ryan, 1986), of their own role in teaching values?

What school programs and policies can be identified as teaching values, either formally or informally? What are the shared school and community expectations for adults and children in school? What are community attitudes toward school, teachers, administrators? The manner in which schools address these questions and others provides evidence of what are valued, accepted, and expected by the community as objectives for its schools.

Questions such as these were at the center of in-depth research conducted in three rural school districts in northwest Ohio from 1986 to the present. The research was designed to investigate whether opportunities and environments existed in small rural schools to foster student character development. The researchers took a historical perspective in order to find a working definition of character.

For centuries, most societies have relied on schooling to provide moral and intellectual growth for children. From Plato to Dewey, philosophers have viewed education as a way for children to become morally and intellectually sound. For the classic philosophers such as Plato and Socrates, a virtuous person was just, temperate, courageous, and wise, a fit citizen in whom these virtues were evident in behaviors and actions toward self and others. Men like Madison, Hamilton, and Jefferson, influenced by these classical writings, incorporated such principles in the Constitution of this nation. They also based their recommendations for the role and purpose of schools and education in America on these virtues. Hence, until recently, schools in the United States were held accountable not only for student academic achievement but for the direct transmittal of these societal values. But, in recent times, the values to be taught are not clear. In addition, there is no clear consensus on which values are to be taught.

In some homogeneous communities and their schools, however, shared values and expectations are easier to identify and agree upon than in other more diverse populations. The point is made in a slightly different way by Dunne (1983), who claims that small rural communities see the school "as the primary vehicle by which local values are transmitted to future local citizens" (p. 139). In other words, the more pluralistic and heterogeneous the population, the more difficult it is to achieve consensus regarding community values.

The following description illustrates one example. Scarlet and gray ribbons flap in the breeze from stop signs, streetlights, and bushes. It's homecoming. But for this district of 844 students, the ribbons symbolize more than sports. Students, community members, parents, teachers, and school administrators are all participants, caught up in the spirit of the school and community, sharing the enthusiasm with friends and family. This close bond among all students, especially when kindergartners through 12th graders are housed in the same building, becomes a setting for personal involvement for students, teachers, and parents. This small rural district uses one building for all classrooms, administrative and school-board offices, and all sports, music, and drama activities. "In a small school like ours," notes the superintendent, "you get to know the parents and the kids. Because of that closeness, you can anticipate student needs and work to meet them, involving both parents and students" (Kisiel, 1988, p. 17).

This closeness and personal attention focused on parents and students are supported and promoted by formal and informal policies, from school-board members to classroom teachers, many of whom have been living and working in the district for one or two generations. How have these districts communicated their priorities to the schools? Through the Board of Education is an obvious answer, but other more subtle means are also important. The methods and enthusiasm of the administrators and teachers are key components in what is taught. Teachers put programs and ideas into practice. Their support and the personal attention they pay to parents and students are critical. But, as noted above, the key question is, What school programs and policies can be identified as teaching values, either formally or informally? To begin to answer this question, it is important to examine a number of variables, including teacher and parent attitudes, community expectations, and school policies and programs. Because the character traits embodied in the cardinal virtues have been deemed prerequisite to effective citizenship, they were selected as standards by which to identify behaviors and values appropriate for student character development in this case study of three small, rural districts.

Teacher Attitudes Toward Schools and Students

Teachers ($N = 160$) and community members and parents ($N = 1,245$) were asked to grade the schools in a fashion similar to that used in Gallup's national sample of teachers (1984) and community members (1985). The perceptions of the community members and teachers in the rural schools were more positive than national averages. Figure 9.1 illustrates the percentages of A and B grades given to schools, teachers, and administrators by the teachers and community members. Mean composite scores of teachers and community members in the three districts were used for the ratings.

As noted in Figure 9.1, the rural elementary teachers were generally less positive than the rural high school teachers in grading their schools but significantly more positive than the Gallup sample. Ele-

Figure 9.1 Percentage of Rural School Teachers and Community Members Rating the Schools A and B

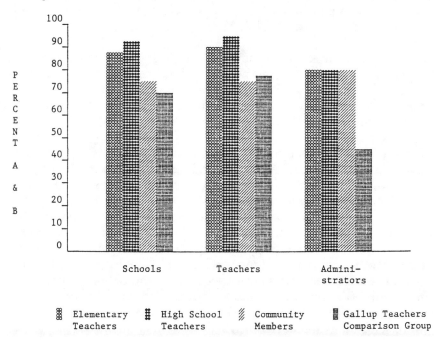

Figure 9.2   Mean of Courage, Justice, Temperance, Wisdom

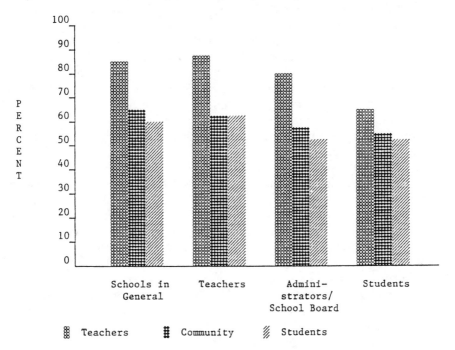

mentary teachers rated themselves highest (91% A or B) and administrators lowest (79% A or B). However, they were consistently higher than Gallup Poll teacher participants on all factors.

Teachers, community members, and students were next asked to rate the level of emphasis given to the cardinal virtues (i.e., courage, justice, temperance, and wisdom). These data are provided in Figure 9.2. Figure 9.2 illustrates the mean percentage of agreement across the four categories (courage, justice, temperance, and wisdom) for each of the response groups. On the average, teachers agreed more so than did students or the community members that schools in their community (85%), the teachers (88%), the administrators and school board members (79%), and the students (64%) operated in a manner reflecting the virtues of courage, justice, temperance, and wisdom (Pertner & Olson, 1987). The mean percentage of agreement for community members was very similar to that of the students. These data indicate that the teachers, overall, feel very positive about their schools and the people who inhabit them in terms of the cardinal virtues and how they rate them. This positive attitude about their work signals an enthusiastic staff, overall, a group satisfied with their jobs and the people with whom they work.

To further corroborate these data, teachers were asked their perceptions of how often certain problems occurred in their schools. Teachers responding A (most of the time) and B (fairly often) reveal that all feel their greatest problems *in school* to be incomplete assignments and too lenient punishments for misbehavior (see Table 9.1), but that, with the exception of leniency, the national comparison sample rated each in-school problem area considerably higher than did the rural teachers.

The rural teachers rated out-of-school problems such as lack of respect for the law, one-parent families, and a decline in teaching manners higher than did the national sample. Rural teachers saw skipping classes as definitely not occurring often in the schools, with 0% choosing most of the time or fairly often, either at the elementary or secondary level. Compare this figure with the 35% figure from the Gallup survey of teachers and you have a realistic picture of the data concerning teachers' perceptions of students' cutting classes nationwide (in some large districts nearly 40% a day) as compared with the local rural school data. Stealing, use of drugs and alcohol, and carrying firearms at school were not perceived as problems occurring often either locally or nationwide.

Parent/Community Data

Parents and communuity members were surveyed not only regarding grading the schools and attitudes toward the cardinal virtues but also regarding character traits and behaviors important for children and youth. In Table 9.2, evidence of opinion of traits illustrating the cardinal virtues such as self-discipline (84%), commitment (61%), persistence (51%), prudence (40%), moderation (42%), and honesty (83%) were ranked as very important.

Separate findings indicate that 83% of the community members polled were in favor of teaching moral education in their schools. This is similar to national rankings. For nurturing responsibility at home, 94% of the parents reported having chores for children to do at home. The majority of these tasks tended to be cleaning chores, such as making own bed, picking up own room, doing household cleaning, caring for pets, washing dishes, and mowing lawns. Eighty-nine percent reported maintaining bedtime and curfew hours for their children.

Table 9.1 Percentage of School Problems Rated A and B

	ELEMENTARY TEACHERS	HIGH SCHOOL TEACHERS	COMBINED RURAL TEACHERS	GALLUP TEACHERS COMPARISON GROUP
Assignments	47	50	49	76
Behavior	22	19	21	47
Truancy	16	24	20	47
Talk Back	12	13	13	43
Leniency	43	46	45	50
Legal Pressures	46	50	48	65
Student Mandatory Attendance	37	55	46	66
Lack Respect for Law	79	81	80	74
No Home Discipline	93	92	93	94
Decline in Teaching Manners	59	67	63	48
Decline in Teaching Morals	56	68	62	0
One-Parent Family	84	76	80	42
Cheating on Tests	14	18	16	40
Sloppy Dress	18	14	16	37
Skip Classes	0	0	0	35
Stealing	7	3	5	32
Use Drugs in School	7	5	5	17
Sell Drugs in School	0	3	1	13
Drink Alcohol in School	3	1	2	10
Weapons in School	0	1	3	8

The data indicate parents' efforts to foster values such as responsibility, cooperation, and teamwork within the family structure through family chores and expectations. Parents and community members rated fostering values such as self-esteem, self-discipline, self-respect, honesty, and respect for others as very important. The high ratings on self items appeared to outdistance ratings of virtues such as temperance, moderation, and prudence by a wide margin. One might speculate that this reflects our society's emphasis on individualism, an emphasis that writers like Oldenquist (1987), Ryan (1987), and Wynne (1982) characterize as a national preoccupation with self to the detriment of building a sense of community.

School District Policy Statements

General school district policies and those specifically for elementary children in the three districts speak both broadly and specifically to student character development and district expectations for moral education. The following board policy statements, contained in the *Philosophy of Education,* are examples.

Table 9.2   Selected Character Traits Important for Parents to Foster in Their Children as Ranked by Community Members in Three Rural School Districts ($N = 1263$)

CHARACTER TRAIT	VERY IMPORTANT (%)	IMPORTANT (%)	NOT IMPORTANT (%)	NO OPINION (%)
Positive self-image	85.2	13.3	0.3	1.2
Self-discipline	83.8	14.8	0.7	0.7
Responsibility for self	81.0	18.0	0.5	0.5
Responsibility for others	57.6	36.1	3.9	2.4
Responsibility for tasks	71.3	26.4	1.4	0.9
Sound study habits	67.3	30.8	0.8	1.1
Respect for self	83.4	15.0	0.4	0.9
Respect for others	82.0	16.8	0.4	0.8
Respect for school rules	73.0	25.3	0.4	1.3
Pride in accomplishment	70.1	28.4	0.7	0.8
Pride in schoolwork	66.7	31.9	0.6	0.8
Commitment	60.8	35.3	1.5	2.4
Persistence	51.4	43.1	1.8	3.7
Value of work	59.7	37.2	1.1	2.0
Self-reliance	62.0	34.9	1.1	2.0
Fairness	65.5	32.4	1.0	1.1
Moderation	42.3	47.1	3.7	6.9
Prudence	39.6	46.2	4.2	10.0
Sense of justice	55.8	40.9	0.8	2.5
Careful judgment	56.8	40.5	1.2	1.5
Respect for truth	83.2	15.7	0.5	0.6
Honesty in dealing with others	82.8	15.9	0.5	0.8
Courage in coping with life's tasks	64.4	34.1	0.7	0.8
Enthusiasm	50.7	46.0	1.6	1.7
Achievement	53.2	43.7	1.7	1.4
Self-confidence	76.8	21.9	0.7	0.6
Attainment of goals	50.9	45.1	1.8	2.2

"An education . . . will help each student . . . develop mentally, morally, physically and socially . . . through disciplined thought, enlightened vision and mature appreciation of our cultural heritage" (*Hopewell-Loudon Student-Parent Handbook*, 1985–86, p. 2). Another district's policy identifies self-discipline as "a result of learning to follow rules and regulations in the total environment, recognizing the rights of others" (*McComb Local Schools Curriculum Guide*, 1986–87, p. 2).

Good conduct expectations in each district's elementary teachers' handbooks speak specifically to acceptable student behavior in school. "We must also be responsible for the perpetuation of the highest standards and ideals of good (student) conduct in and out of the classroom" (*McComb Middle School Parent-Student Handbook*, 1989, p. 2). "Parents want teachers to place special emphasis on instruction in matters of honesty, cooperation, respect for rights of others, purity of speech, and other desirable qualities of conduct" (Edmonson, in *McComb Teachers' Handbook*, 1985–86, p. 27).

Good conduct rules and regulations adhere to the Ohio Code for legal processes and procedures in all three districts. Discipline policies are clearly spelled out for students, teachers, and parents and follow due process requirements for all grade levels. At the same time, however, each district has incorporated some unique policies that reflect its community's priorities and values. In one district, the flag is specifically mentioned in the parent-student handbook as a symbol of our obligations and respect for our nation. Another district policy states that:

> Teachers should attempt to build in students a deep appreciation and pride for our building and equipment to the extent that students become conscious of their responsibility in helping to keep both building and equipment neat and attractive. (*McComb Teachers' Handbook*, 1985–86, p. 28)

The vandalism policy for this district states that "pupils will pay in full for all damages plus be subjected to whatever punishment the administrator and/or board of education deem necessary or wise" (*McComb Middle School Parent-Student Handbook*, 1989, p. 5).

Homework and good study habits for elementary students are also included routinely in the elementary handbooks and newsletters sent home to parents. The bond between parents, teachers, and administrators at the elementary level in support of student habits and study schedules is strongly supported through frequent written and oral communication. One district recommends that parents use the following rules regarding homework to ensure that students will develop good study habits.

> Set aside a certain time each night for homework or reading. The area should be quiet, well lighted and free from distractions. We recommend a bedtime of no later than 8:30 p.m. on school nights for students K–3 and 9:30 p.m. for students in grades 4–6. Television viewing time should be limited to one and one-half hours per evening. (*McComb Elementary School Handbook*, 1988–89, p. 14)

Incentives

Incentives for attendance, academic achievement, and good conduct toward others are used to encourage students to do their best both academically and in their relationships with others. Specific practices in each district are summarized below.

Attendance

Attendance in school is rewarded and encouraged. As noted by one elementary teachers' handbook, "Regular school attendance develops positive attitudes toward school, encourages promptness and promotes the habit of dependability." Further, "Every parent has the responsibility to make certain his/her child attends school regularly and without tardiness" (*McComb Elementary School Handbook*, 1988–89, p. 3).

Rewards for perfect attendance and a 4.0 grade point average include half-days off and field-day experiences. Students in one district who achieve perfect attendance for the first three quarters of each school year are given a half-day off without being counted absent. The half-day off must be taken anytime during the first week of the subsequent quarter. A note indicating parental permission must be turned in to the principal prior to the free half-day off. The policy is meant to develop good practices of attendance and responsibility. It is not meant to encourage students to attend school while ill or injured. The principals report that attendance averages about 98% to 99% daily.

Academics

Academic achievement is emphasized and rewarded through a variety of means. One district has the following reward policy for all students:

Students who earn straight A's any quarter will be rewarded for their effort. The following schedule will be used: First quarter: students will be rewarded with a free lunch at school. Second quarter: students will receive a pass to all school events for the third nine weeks. Third quarter: students will be treated to breakfast served in the school cafeteria. Fourth quarter: students (any who have received all A's any quarter) will be treated to a day at Cedar Point [an amusement park]. (*Hopewell-Loudon Student-Parent Handbook*, 1985–86, p. 31)

The motto of the middle school principal is "A happy kid is a teachable kid." The principal's academic honor roll pins go to all seventh- and eighth-grade students who achieve all A's and B's during a 9-week grading period. A waterproof tote bag goes to each student who makes the honor roll three times during the school year. To further personalize attention to students, teachers and the principal at the middle school have initiated a conference with each of the students on a regular schedule to establish a one-to-one period of time for each student. Students can initiate conferences and talk to the teacher about any topic. During the first year, 23% of the conferences were student initiated; during the second year, 50%.

Additional rewards for attendance and academic performance are tummy pleasers as well as pride pleasers. Each grading period, students receive free steak dinners at Ponderosa for perfect attendance. Any day of the year, students can receive a certificate for a Burger King sandwich, fries, and a Coke for any good thing they may have done. Students can be caught being good for just being a nice guy to being on a winning team or helping another person.

Citizenship

Good conduct and rewards for citizenship are often integrated with awards for academic achievement and attendance. At the middle school, the Principal's Pride bulletin board recognizes students with photos for good papers, improvement in homework, attendance, and so on. The Wall of Fame recognizes students for outstanding achievement in academics, leadership, citizenship, athletics, music, and art. All schools have end-of-year awards for citizenship, academic achievement, and attendance.

Classroom teachers use a multitude of rewards for their students to reinforce everything from good behavior to good academic work. Some use stickers, some make signs and posters, and some have parties and take star students out to dinner. But as one teacher noted, "I want my students to achieve and to be good in class because it makes them feel proud of themselves, not necessarily because they might get a reward for it. I don't want them just to be good for the special recognition."

Teachers as Role Models

The school policy manuals have relatively few recommendations for the behaviors of teachers. One district's handbook states that teachers have a duty to "conform to social standards acceptable to this community in order to increase (their) usefullness (sic) to the school and to (their) standing in the community" (*Gibsonburg Teachers' Handbook*, 1985–86, p. 2). No mention of any requirements beyond those of the state of Ohio for teachers were found, that is, "good moral character and compliance with the code of ethics established by the profession."

Another district's handbook lists a "bridled tongue and diplomatic contact with parents" (*McComb Teachers' Handbook*, 1985–86, p. 26) as the greatest single help a principal can have. It maintains that the teacher is the most important factor in building educational goodwill in the community. In the third district, teachers are asked to build a caring image of themselves, the school, and the students through their interactions with the students.

Students as Role Models

Student role modeling and cross-age tutoring are used in all three districts but especially in those that have high school and elementary students in the same building. Students are used as role models for younger students through programs such as Teen Talk, a self-esteem-building program for elementary students with high school youth as the group leaders. This is a part of the elementary guidance program in one district and has been incorporated into the drug education curriculum as well.

Selected Classroom Practices

Examples of selected classroom practices used in the districts to reinforce community values and policy statements are illustrated below. In some cases, the method is unique to the district. In other instances, the approach is used in all three districts.

Values Through Fables

Sixty-five first graders listen intently as the superintendent takes up the tale of Blue Bunny at the point where he left it at his last visit. The storyteller carefully weaves his sequel of the tale of the adventures of Blue Bunny, a charming but rascally rabbit, curiously reminiscent of his more famous cousin, Peter. Carefully building to a suspense-filled ending, the storyteller uses bright illustrations on a flip chart to dramatize Blue Bunny's attempts at confronting problems (usually created by not listening to his mother's advice) and then trying to solve dilemmas as best he can.

> Blue Bunny walked along happily on his way to school. He was looking forward to seeing his friends and playing with them at recess. Blue Bunny's favorite time was recess. He whistled happily as he walked along. He paused to shift his book bag. He had brought his library book home to read and his mother had packed his lunch for him so his tote bag was heavier than usual today. His mother had wanted him to walk to school with his older sister Sally, but he had been too busy eating breakfast and watching television to hurry this morning. So, he was not ready to go when Sally started down the path for school.
> "A few more steps and I'll be able to see the playground," thought Blue Bunny. "This bag is heavier than I thought." Suddenly, Jimmy Cottontail, one of the older bunnies, walked past. "Hi, Blue Bunny. What's in your bag?" he asked. Blue Bunny hesitated. He didn't know Jimmy very well and he felt a little bothered by the way Jimmy was looking at him. "My lunch and a library book," he answered. "Well, I'm kind of hungry," Jimmy said. "Give me your lunch. I can eat it on the way to school." Blue Bunny was shocked. "My lunch?" he stammered. "But my mother fixed it for me. It's mine. What will I have to eat?"
> "I don't care about you," said Jimmy. "I'm hungry now. Give it to me! And, if you tell the teacher, I'll get you." Blue Bunny was really frightened now. He felt his heart pounding in his chest. His eyes were stinging. He felt like crying. What'll I do? he thought desperately to himself. (Dyer, 1989)

Sensing the children's growing empathy, Mr. Dyer pauses. "How many agree that Blue Bunny is probably pretty frightened by now?"

When most of the class raise their hands, he asks, "What should Blue Bunny do?"

The children's hands begin to wave eagerly. Their discussion is lively and touches on several possible solutions and behaviors for Blue Bunny. The children finally decide that Jimmy Cottontail may be hungry and needs help, but Blue Bunny can't just give him his lunch without defending his rights. Mr. Dyer (1989) sums up the children's comments.

> You know something, boys and girls? This was really a good discussion. Sometimes, life is complicated and we have to face problems in dealing with others. And sometimes, that means that we have to take a stand. In some cases, it could mean that we'll get hurt in the process. If we try to avoid the hurt, if we run away from our problems, they usually have a way of coming back again. It takes courage for all of us to face hard choices. But, sometimes facing a problem helps us find solutions. We must all respect the rights of others to what is theirs. These are things we do and value as adults as well as children. This is part of our responsibility as citizens no matter whether we are adults or children.

The issue of courage in fighting for one's own property and rights against a bully is a common one for elementary children. As most parents and teachers know, children can be cruel to one another in many ways, not just physically. Moreover, courage is not always bravery in the face of danger. Facing difficult odds or dealing with difficult tasks, sorrow, or loss requires persistence and a willingness to persevere, a special kind of courage. In the story above, however, more than just courage is being discussed. Justice, fairness, and truth are major concepts that children at this age are learning to understand and value. Elements of each are examined in the discussion and are related to responsibilities of citizenship in a democracy.

In an amusing and interesting way, Mr. Dyer's personal approach to teaching values like truth, honesty, courage, integrity, and responsibility mirror the values that the community wishes to pass on to its children through a formal and integral part of the language arts curriculum of the school. His Blue Bunny stories are well known in this community of 1,500 residents. Of the 840 children from kindergarten through 12th grade in this district, all but the juniors and seniors have heard the *Tales of Blue Bunny*; this is Mr. Dyer's ninth year as superintendent. Each story has a message to convey about acceptable and unacceptable behavior in dealing with everyday life, emphasizing traits necessary to citizenship in a democracy and embodied in the cardinal virtues.

Values Through Discussion

In another setting, Mrs. Smith asked her sixth-grade class to consider a moral dilemma in a story about Heinz (Hersh, 1979) and his wife who is ill (Anderson, 1987). Each student wrote out a solution and gave reasons for the solution prior to class discussion. When Mrs. Smith asked for hands of how many thought Heinz was justified in stealing the drug to help his wife, 21 students said he was right to steal the drug, although their reasoning varied.

> "The druggist is greedy."
> "The price is too high."
> "Heinz loved his wife and had to steal the drug to save her."
> "Heinz should go back to the druggist and bargain with him to
>   lower the price."

This approach to teaching values is incorporated in Kohlberg's (1981) levels of moral reasoning and judgment. It is also closely associated with values clarification as found in certain guidance materials and kits. Guidance programs like *Developing Understanding of Self and Others* (Dinkmeyer, 1970) and *Transactional Analysis for Tots* (Freed, 1974) develop basic values such as understanding and accepting self, consideration of others, recognition of responsibility, acceptance of differences, and respect for feelings. Stories are used to help students make choices involving value judgments, moral reasoning, and standards of behavior. Teachers' lesson plans incorporate these kit materials as well as other activities such as Good Deed bulletin boards and "Just Say No" films and videos. Since the state of Ohio requires elementary guidance programs and counseling, all of the districts have some type of program like these.

Values Through Critical Thinking

One district's elementary school has adopted the CoRT Thinking Program by deBono (1973) as a means to aid students' ability to generate alternatives to problems and to help students analyze problems without fear of being wrong. The students are given instruction during the regular school day. The principal noted that "the feeling of self-worth that students receive from contributing to a group effort has helped our students understand that it is desirable to be a person who has the courage to be himself . . . and, indirectly, aided open-mindedness." The staff defined a person of good character as one who

> displays the ability to stick to a set of principles; a person who can risk unpopularity, a person who has the courage to be himself/herself, who is open-minded, and who does not deceive himself/herself. . . . Formal instruction of thinking skills can be used to provide the opportunities for students to meet these character building requirements. (Pertner & Olson, p. 88)

This district used a measure of children's self-perception (Children's Affect Needs Assessment, 1987) as a post-test measure of the effect of the CoRT thinking program with district fourth graders. The mean score for the class was 13 on a 15-point scale, indicating strength in the five affective areas being measured (respecting others, self-awareness, self-control, values/decision making and group cooperation). The district also undertook a study to examine the relationship between their fourth- and sixth-grade level students involved in formal thinking instruction and control group students with no training in thinking skills in 10 other school districts in Ohio, Texas, and Massachusetts. It was hypothesized that students with formal instruction in thinking could generate more ideas and reflect less egocentrism than those without such instruction in response to selected questions. A significant difference was found at the .03 level for the rural students' ability to generate alternative solutions reflecting less egocentrism than that of the comparison groups.

Values Through Literature

Another example of a program of instruction using stories to teach moral education in another rural district's elementary school has been a part of the regular curriculum for nearly 50 years. Sponsored by a countywide nondenominational coalition, these 20-minute lessons are incorporated into the weekly curriculum as a regular part of the time allotted for language arts instruction. Volunteer consultants spend their time in the schools teaching these lessons focusing on moral and ethical standards. Classes in the K–4 building are integrated into the time allocated to language arts/reading and children's literature. Old Testament stories and songs are a part of this curriculum. Emphasis is placed on students learning to tell the truth, to be fair to others, and to be brave in times of danger. To illustrate wisdom, the instructor uses the story of Solomon, who chose the gift of wisdom to govern his people better. However, in accumulating great wealth and power, he lost sight of good judgment. The story of Daniel dramatizes courage. Moses breaking the tablets illustrates losing control and destroying something valuable in the process, thus the virtue of temperance.

The central thrust of the classes is nondenominational, using the Old Testament as classic literature. Parents may request that their children be excused from the sessions, but in 50 years, only one parent has done so. In the middle school, emphasis is placed on relating contemporary lifestyles and problems to similar dilemmas confronted by people depicted in the Bible. The Middle Eastern crises of today are compared wtih political and social unrest in biblical times. The instructor also spends a few weeks each year working with the social studies classes to discuss the religions of the world.

The scenes above took place in rural school districts not unlike thousands of other similar small rural districts throughout the nation. These instances illustrate the kinds of classroom interactions that teachers and students have daily. They are the kinds of interactions that covertly or overtly convey values and moral choices teachers and students make every day. In some cases the values are taught directly, in others they are the result of shared discussion. Although all districts use, to some degree, a values clarification approach, all three also have unique programs that teach values more directly. In almost all instances, the district approaches reflect shared community and school values, formally or informally transmitted to students and adults through daily contact.

Discussion of Related Findings

Is it possible to determine outcomes of these policies and procedures on student conduct and behavior? Although there is no direct cause and effect evidence, there are comparative student data available based on the districts' high school population ($N = 700$) and the national high school sample of students in urban, suburban, and rural schools ($N = 58,000$) in *High School and Beyond* (1980). Answering questions patterned after the national study, rural school students reported cutting class less often (14%) than the national sample (34%). Sixty-three percent were never late for school as compared with 40% nationally. Ninety percent reported spending from 1 to more than 10 hours a week on homework compared with 73% of the national respondents. A greater percentage of rural students (59%) reported being enrolled in college prep courses than did the national sample (35%).

The rural students in both elementary and secondary settings exhibit high rates of daily attendance, ranging from 95% to 98% for all three districts as estimated by superintendents using average daily attendance figures. Graduation rates of students are high (95%) in all three districts. This means a 5% dropout rate as compared with 20% nationally and, in some urban settings, 40%. Sixty-five percent of the rural students reported receiving grades in school of mostly A's and B's, whereas 48% of the national sample reported such grades. Patterns of participation in school extracurricular activities were similar to those reflected in the national data with these exceptions: 57% of the rural students participated in athletics compared with 43% nationally; 33% participated in band compared with 15% nationally. Although it cannot be inferred that these data give direct evidence of results of school and community policies and practices on student behavior, other studies indicate that schools recognizing student accomplishments tend to have higher pupil achievement levels (Rutter, Maughan, Mortimore, & Smith, 1979; Wynne, 1980) and that consensus by teachers and administrators on curriculum and discipline are correlated with high achievement (Rutter, 1979) and school spirit (Wynne, 1980).

Conclusions

Generally speaking, these rural districts' staff, parents, and community members have common perceptions of expectations for their schools and for acceptable student behaviors in school. They also are in agreement regarding ways to achieve those expectations. Local teacher and community attitudes toward school are more positive than those reflected in national samples. In addition, more than 60% of all parents, students, and community members felt that the schools and the teachers operated in a manner reflecting courage, justice, temperance, and wisdom.

Teachers and community members have different perceptions of problems in the schools but are supportive of measures to reduce them. The rural teachers see lack of discipline in the home as a major contributor to problems in school (93%). Local teachers worry about one-parent families and students' lack of respect for law and order more than did those teachers surveyed by the Gallup Poll. Despite differences in degree, however, these contemporary social problems are being felt by all segments of society as contributing factors to problems in school. Additionally, as in other communities, income-class differences exist, but as Sizer (1984) notes, it is the commonalities of shared experiences that help to shape the values of youngsters in any community, and school experiences play a major role.

High standards for student attendance, achievement, and good conduct are integrated into the school day in both formal and informal ways. Incentives and reward systems are used extensively to encourage and sustain good conduct as well as academic achievement and attendance. Programs for building self-esteem, honesty, and cooperation work collaboratively with a more direct approach such as story telling to illustrate moral values and decision making. Teachers consciously work carefully to teach values such as truth, honesty, justice, and tolerance. Teachers are aware of being role models, of exemplifying moral conduct, and of teaching moral reasoning without imposing personal values.

Have we answered the question of whether or not teachers teach values in these three rural districts? The answer is yes, in both formal and informal ways and by direct and indirect methods. The question concerning what values is harder to pinpoint, but for the most part, they are values stressing truth, honesty, justice, courage, good judgment, tolerance of others, fair play, respect for parents and teachers, and respect for rules and good conduct both in and out of school; in short, the characteristics of good citizenship as embodied in the cardinal virtues.

All across the country, in schools in rural, suburban, and urban settings, common routines, common daily experiences, and common problems shape students' values and views of the world in which students live. A consistency of value expectations among parents, teachers, and administrators charged with the education of children leads to general agreement on the purpose of education, ultimately working to the benefit of those children. When community, family, and school values are mutually shared, students are given clear signals about expectations for ethics and moral views. Even though we all may fall short of these expectations at one time or another, the standards are still there to strive for and achieve.

References

Anderson, R. (1987). The teaching of social studies and character development. In J. Martin-Reynolds & M. S. Hurley (Eds.), *Character develop-*

ment in the schools (pp. 73–78). Bowling Green State University: *American Secondary Education.*

Benninga, J. (1988). An emerging synthesis in moral education. *Phi Delta Kappan, 69,* 415–418.

Children's affect needs assessment. (1987). Canton, OH: Grow With Guidance.

deBono, E. (1973). *CoRT thinking curriculum.* Elmsford, NY: Pergamon Press.

Dinkmeyer, D. (1970). *Developing understanding of self and others.* Circle Pines, MN: American Guidance Service.

Dunne, F. (1983). Good government vs. self-government: Educational control in rural America. *Phi Delta Kappan, 65,* 254.

Dunne, F., & Carlsen, W. (1981). Small rural schools in the United States: A statistical profile. Washington, DC: The National Rural Center.

Dyer, R. (1989). *Tales of blue bunny.* Oral stories as told by R. Dyer, McComb Local Schools.

Edmonson, J. B. (1985–86). Cultivating goodwill in the community. In *McComb Teachers' Handbook,* 1985–86 (p. 27). McComb, OH: McComb Local Schools.

Freed, A. (1974). *Transactional analysis for tots.* Sacramento: Jalmar Press.

Gallup, A. (1984). The Gallup Poll of teachers' attitudes toward the public schools. *Phi Delta Kappan, 66,* 97–107.

Gallup, A. (1985). The 17th annual Gallup Poll of the public's attitudes toward the public schools. *Phi Delta Kappan, 67,* 35–47.

Gibsonburg teachers' handbook. (1985–86). Gibsonburg, OH: Gibsonburg Exempted Village Schools.

Hersh, R. (1979). *Promoting moral growth from Piaget to Kohlberg.* New York: Longman.

High school and beyond. (1980). University of Chicago: National Opinion Research Center.

Hopewell-Loudon student-parent handbook. (1985–86). Bascom, OH: Hopewell-Loudon Local Schools.

Kisiel, R. (1988, October 22). Rural schools build character, study finds. *The Toledo Blade,* p. 17.

Kohlberg, L. (1981). *Essays on moral development: Vol. 1. The philosophy of moral development.* San Francisco: Harper and Row.

Lickona, T. (1988). Four strategies for fostering character development in children. *Phi Delta Kappan, 69,* 419–423.

McComb elementary school handbook. (1988–89). McComb, OH: McComb Local Schools.

McComb local schools curriculum guide. (1986–87). McComb, OH: McComb Local Schools.

McComb middle school parent-student handbook. (1989). McComb, OH: McComb Local Schools.

McComb teachers' handbook. (1985–86). McComb, OH: McComb Local Schools.

Oldenquist, A. (1987). The inward making of a person: Character, culture, and the role of schools. In J. Martin-Reynolds & M. S. Hurley (Eds.), *Character development in the schools* (pp. 15–21). Bowling Green State University: *American Secondary Education.*

Pertner, J. & Olson, T. (1987). Thinking skills and character development. In J. Martin-Reynolds & M. S. Hurley (Eds.), *Character development in the schools* (pp. 88–91). Bowling Green State University: *American Secondary Education.*

Rutter, M., Maughan, B., Mortimore, J., & Smith, A. (1979). *Fifteen thousand hours: Secondary schools and their effects on children.* Cambridge, MA: Harvard University Press.

Ryan, K. (1986). The new moral education. *Phi Delta Kappan, 68,* 228–233.

Ryan, K. (1987). The emergence of character development. In J. Martin-Reynolds & M. S. Hurley (Eds.) *Character development in the schools* (pp. 9–14). Bowling Green State University: *American Secondary Education.*

Sizer, T. (1984). *Horace's compromise.* Boston: Houghton Mifflin.

Wynne, E. (1980). *Looking at schools: Good, bad, indifferent.* Lexington, MA: D. C. Heath.

Wynne, E. (1982). Facts about the character of young Americans. In E. Wynne (Ed.), *Character policy* (pp. 3–9). Washington, DC: University Press of America.

CHAPTER TEN

Character Development at Fort Washington Elementary School

RICHARD K. SPARKS, JR.

"To serve their rightful role in society, schools need to focus jointly on the educational goals of character development and academic learning" (Wynne & Walberg, 1985–86). That precept is axiomatic, especially in light of the current emphasis on excellence in education and the quality indicators for effective schools. Although implementing effective school curricula for character development has been problematic, the call for schools to act is clear.

To implement goals and strategies for character development successfully, schools must establish firm philosophical and functional positions regarding three fundamental questions. First, what does "character" mean? Second, how should the energy and resources of the school be organized and allocated to provide for the character development of its pupils? Finally, by what criteria should the school's effectiveness with respect to character development be assessed? As is the case in most curriculum development efforts, the first and last of these questions must be addressed at the outset. That is, what exactly does the school wish to accomplish and how will the results be measured and evaluated? The remaining question, the "how" question, must follow.

The faculty of the Fort Washington Elementary School in the Clovis Unified School District (Clovis, California) has attempted to address these questions in a practical, systematic way. The result is a thoughtfully conceived, well-articulated approach to character development which has yielded some tangible results over the past 5 years.

At the time the approach described in this chapter was first implemented in 1984, Fort Washington was a medium-size school (450 kindergarten through sixth-grade students) located in a suburban community northeast of Fresno, California. Based on a 94% return of the annual parent survey of school effectiveness conducted in 1984, over 60% of the chief household breadwinners indicated having a college or university degree, and nearly 80% classified themselves as having professional, executive, or managerial occupations. Compared with the other 17 elementary schools in the district, Fort Washington was the least endowed with respect to racial, ethnic, and cultural diversity. Underrepresented minorities comprised approximately 12% of the student population.

Rapid growth in population was projected in this essentially middle-class, homogeneous community over the next few years. The projections proved accurate, for by 1989 Fort Washington emerged as the largest school in the district with 900 students. While the school increased in size, however, the ethnic composition of the community and student body remained essentially the same.

The impetus for the staff's attention to developing a coordinated, articulated approach to character development came from two sources. First, although Fort Washington was known for the successful academic performance of its students, the faculty perceived a strong need to expand the program by promoting more student participation in a broader range of experiences such as athletics, student service, music, and art. Those activities existed at the time; however, participation was not regarded by students or parents as a priority. There was a need, therefore, to establish student participation in a wide range of activities as an essential part of a well-rounded school experience leading to success in adult life.

Second, in anticipation of rapid population growth, there was a strong need to maintain the cohesiveness of the community and the effectiveness of the school program. Practical methods to articulate and communicate the school's philosophy, goals, and expectations for student performance and conduct to a large number of newcomers who had not participated in the evolution of the school were essential. *Newcomers* in this context applies to staff members as well as students and their parents.

As the ideas that grew from these needs continued to evolve into the articulated approach described in this chapter, its impact on the community and the school climate, and its success in promoting desired student qualities and behaviors, were most encouraging. Furthermore, lest the reader discount the generalizability of this approach to other types of school populations, a comment addressing that point at the outset may be useful. By 1988, the essential elements of the Fort Washington program had been replicated in at least five other elementary schools and one of the intermediate schools in the district. The impact on the school and the positive results with respect to student behavior at each of these schools closely parallel the Fort Washington experience.

Three Principles Underlying Character Development at Fort Washington

The Fort Washington approach to character development is guided by three basic principles that are grounded in the district's philosophy of education. The icon for Clovis Unified School District's (CUSD) philosophy and goals is the "Sparthenian," which represents its emphasis on three domains of human development: body, mind, and spirit. The term "Sparthenian" was formed by combining two ancient Greek cultures to represent the best attributes of each: the Athenian culture, which was known for its intellectual, cultural, and artistic pursuits, and the Spartan culture, which emphasized physical and competitive goals.

The spiritual domain of the Clovis Sparthenian embodies the character of the individual. Thus, by including it as one of the three essential goal areas, CUSD has affirmed that developing strong character is an educational commitment equal to developing a sound mind and body. Consequently, a districtwide committee composed of teachers and administrators was established to articulate the CUSD philosophy and goals for character development. Input and review by teachers, district officials, community members, and students made up an important part of the process. As a result, the principles underlying the Fort Washington programs reflect the principles and goals that emerged from this committee's work.

Definition

The first principle concerns the operational definition of *character*. In a broad sense, character is a function of

1. One's sense of right and wrong
2. One's standards of what is good and just

3. One's judgment of what constitutes good and bad human behavior

Although there are many ways to describe character, in essence they involve two dimensions. One is focused on the individual's beliefs, moral reasoning, and system of values; the other is focused on the individual's actions and conduct. The distinction between these points of departure in describing character is evident when contrasting the concept of character development that traditionally has been the thrust of American education and the concept of moral education that gained prominence during the 1960s and 1970s.

It must be recognized that character development and moral education are neither synonymous nor discrete, for one's values and level of moral reasoning are central to the concept of character. Our basic assumption is that there is a reciprocal relationship between thought and deed. That is, individuals act in accordance with their perceptions, values, and beliefs, and, in turn, the actions and behaviors an individual chooses in resolving dilemmas and making decisions are manifestations of those perceptions, values, and beliefs. Based on this assumption, an educational environment in which virtuous conduct is consistently nurtured, valued, and reinforced is presumed also to have an impact on the formation of one's values and moral reasoning. As individuals interact in a school environment where desirable behaviors are clearly communicated, systematically nurtured, and consistently reinforced, the values underlying those behaviors will become internalized and, ultimately, characteristic of the individual.

Because we lean toward the traditional concept of character development, an essential goal at Fort Washington is to develop individuals who, through their actions and conduct, exhibit certain qualities perceived to be positive traits of character. Specifically, the goal is to provide a school environment that fosters the development of individuals who are honest, responsible, respectful, dedicated, perseverant, self-respecting, and concerned for others. These "character qualities," which were developed by a district committee composed of teachers, are viewed by the faculty and community as requisites for leading a successful, fulfilling life and for responsible, contributing membership in society. For the most part, these qualities do not require elaborate explanation. The descriptors in Figure 10.1 have been included under each of the qualities to clarify the faculty's interpretation and to facilitate the communication of school goals.

Figure 10.1   Fort Washington Elementary School Desired
Character Qualities

HONEST	PERSEVERANT
Trustworthy	Industrious
Truthful	Self-disciplines
Ethical	Diligent
	Resourceful
RESPONSIBLE	
Dependable	SELF-RESPECTING
Accountable	Self-accepting
Conservation-minded	Confident
	Resilient
RESPECTFUL	Health-minded
Courteous	
Obedient to legitimate authority	CONCERNED FOR OTHERS
Patriotic	Friendly
	Helpful
DEDICATED	Considerate
Courageous	Fair
Involved	Cooperative
Faithful	Civic-minded

Although no hierarchy exists among these qualities, two seem to be especially worthy of further comment: perseverance and concern for others. With respect to perseverance, a desired outcome of the Fort Washington program is students who:

1. Are eager to seek and accept challenges
2. Understand that there are many criteria for judging success and that those criteria may differ depending on the goal
3. Understand that both success and failure are necessary realities of life
4. Have learned to appreciate each success and to treat each failure as a learning opportunity
5. Choose to "stay in the game" and not quit in the face of failure

Concern for others is also viewed as an essential character trait at Fort Washington. This quality has to do with compassion, social consciousness, prosocial conduct, and duty—that is, getting along in a complex society. Cooperation, interdependence, and teamwork are emphasized in Fort Washington classrooms to reinforce the idea that both the individual and society benefit when people work together in collaborative and supportive ways toward achieving common goals. Activities and experiences that promote understanding and appreciation of cultural, ethnic, and racial diversity are emphasized in the school environment. We live in a world community, and students must learn to become participants in the human experience—thinking beyond self and finding fulfillment in service to others.

In creating a school environment conducive to the development of character, perseverance and concern for others are the cornerstones. They encompass and support the other qualities: responsibility, respect, dedication, and self-respect.

Philosophical Approach

The second principle underlying the Fort Washington program has to do with the school's basic approach to character development. The philosophical basis of the program begins with a recognition that the desired "character qualities" cannot be "taught" in isolation (i.e., a lesson here, a discussion there). They are developed over time as the student interacts within the total environment of the school.

The school should be the training ground for entry into the adult world as a rational, competent, reflective individual. The experiences provided to students in school become the building blocks of their success in life and extend the home experience. The school is, in one sense, a laboratory for students, a place where young people should assume a variety of roles and engage in diverse activities in order to explore and develop the many facets of their unique personalities and talents. A comprehensive array of curricular and co-curricular activities must be offered to provide students the opportunities to test themselves and their abilities, to experience success and failure in many contexts, and to encounter and address issues relating to morals and values in situations meaningful to them. The lessons students learn from these experiences must be valid and useful in the world of adult society.

In addition to exploring interests and developing talents, diverse opportunities to participate help students grow in other ways. Learning how to be a participant is an important part of preparation for adult life. Participation means assuming obligations, responsibilities, and commitments to one's self and to others. It means learning and practicing skills of leadership and followership, cooperation with others in the pursuit of goals, and prosocial conduct. The school environment must provide experiences for students that draw them out and enable them to contribute to others and to their society. Self-esteem is rooted in an individual's sense of being needed, useful, and competent.

There is yet another facet of the school environment considered by the Fort Washington faculty to be crucial in facilitating the character development of students—communication. The goals, standards, rules, and expectations of the school and classroom must be clearly defined, understood, and communicated to all participants, including all students, staff members, parents, and indeed the community at large. The mission of the school and the goals of the individuals within the school must be aligned.

The values of our school are embodied in written standards, goals, policies, procedures, traditions, and forms of student recognition. Consistency, therefore, is crucial to ensure that (1) the school's policies, goals, and procedures do in fact emanate from and reflect a core of central values and (2) the adults associated with the school share a common interpretation of the goals, standards, and policies and of their relationship to the central values of the school.

It is incumbent upon all school personnel, secretaries, custodians, and aides as well as teachers, to provide an environment that includes a broad range of experiences for students—an environment that communicates clearly and consistently, formally and informally, what are the desired qualities. In the school setting, students must have the opportunity and encouragement to explore their interests and talents and to test themselves and their abilities. They must have the opportunity to experience success and failure in a variety of relevant contexts.

Assessment and Outcomes

The third basic principle underlying character development at Fort Washington addresses the problem of assessment and desired outcomes. Well-intentioned efforts to provide programs for character development have been handicapped by the elusive nature of assessment and evaluation of results. In all areas of the curriculum, character development included, a school faculty must be able to examine the cause-and-effect relationship between the instructional program or strategy and its impact on the student.

The goal of character development at Fort Washington is to nurture and support certain student behaviors, those that reflect the desired character qualities. Behavior is overt, observable, and can be assessed. Therefore, observing individual and group behaviors provides a means to determine the effects of the strategy to promote the desired character qualities.

These principles are aligned with Ryan's effort to link the concepts of moral education and character development with what he calls the "five E's of the new moral education: Example, Explanation, Exhortation, Environment, and Experience" (Ryan, 1986). Conceptually, these elements are the key threads that form the fabric of Fort Washington's character development program.

Three Major Program Components

In a functional sense, three major components of the Fort Washington program illustrate how the above-mentioned principles have been incorporated into our educational program. The Co-curricular Program, the Exemplary Patriot Award Program, and the Patriotic Classroom Award, in combination, are essential vehicles for communicating expectations and for identifying, encouraging, and monitoring the development of desired behaviors.

Co-curricular Program

A comprehensive co-curricular program is provided for students at Fort Washington School in grades 4 through 6. This program includes interscholastic athletics (tackle football, volleyball, cross country, wrestling, basketball, track, paddle tennis, and baseball), choral and instrumental music, oral interpretation and drama, spelling team competition, art festivals, student government, and journalism. These activities are not considered "extras." Rather, they are an integral part of the total educational program. Participation in the co-curricular program is a *highly valued behavior* at Fort Washington. In fact, it is a school goal that 100% of the fourth- through sixth-grade students participate in at least some co-curricular activity—a goal that has been achieved!

The co-curricular program provides opportunities for teachers to work with students not only in skill development but also in shaping attitudes about themselves and others. It provides a relevant context for dealing with issues concerning values, ethics, and social judgment. Teachers and coaches, both in and outside the classroom, make conscious efforts to set and model high standards with respect to appropriate social interaction, right and wrong, and concern for others.

A significant aspect of the co-curricular program is the Fort Washington Code of Participation. This code, which sets the conditions for student involvement, emphasizes personal commitment and responsibility. It is a means of telling students that when one chooses to be involved, one also assumes obligations. In essence, the code stipulates that participants maintain a satisfactory level of scholarship, demonstrate satisfactory behavior and citizenship, and contribute in a positive way to the group effort. Each of these behaviors is defined behaviorally for the students. For example, students must maintain a C average in their classroom work and must not receive unsatisfactory marks in citizenship to participate in the co-curricular programs. Furthermore, co-curricular teachers, coaches, and advisors are explicit in their expectations and requirements for all aspects of participation such as attendance, conduct, adherence to practice or rehearsal schedules, and care of equipment and materials. A "no quit" provision requires students to participate through the duration of an activity. Students agree and are held to the Code of Participation when they elect to join a school activity. This code, as simple as it may appear, is a significant factor in setting the norm for student conduct in the school. Students have come to know that they are part of a group and have a responsibility to that group and to themselves. The attainment of group goals is dependent upon each member's performing to the best of his or her ability.

Exemplary Patriot Award (Block "FW")

Most schools have student awards that provide incentives for students and a means of acknowledging their accomplishments. More importantly, the goals, expectations, and values of the school can be communicated through the criteria for student recognition. Such is the case with the Exemplary Patriot Award.

The Exemplary Patriot Award, initiated in the fall of 1984 and named after the school mascot, is the highest award a student can earn at Fort Washington. Also known as the Block "FW," it is available to fourth-, fifth-, and sixth-grade students and is awarded at the end of each semester. The criteria for earning this award reflect a broad base of participation, achievement, and service. In order to earn the Block "FW," a student must accrue points in five distinct categories: (1) Curricular (scholarship and physical fitness); (2) Co-Curricular; (3) Athletics; (4) School Service and Leadership; and (5) Effort and Citizenship.

This award has been designated for grades 4 through 6 for three basic reasons. First, in the younger grades (K–3), character traits, citizenship responsibilities, and interpersonal relationships are developed more appropriately in the context of the "family." As the classroom is a family, teachers at those grade levels concentrate on those attributes, attitudes, and behaviors within the classroom. Second, as a student reaches the upper grades (4–6), he or she is ready to expand, explore, and apply those attributes, attitudes, and skills in a larger context, beyond the classroom in the larger society of the school. Finally, within the structure of the school, student eligibility for the many elective co-curricular activities and programs begins at the fourth-grade level.

Candidates for the Block "FW" must earn a minimum of 20 points in the Curricular category and at least some points in each of the other categories. Students who have met these initial criteria and have earned a specified total number of points receive the Exemplary Patriot Award at the end of each semester. Points are generated through participation and achievement in designated areas or activities in each category, or both. For example, a student will earn one point in the School Service and Leadership category for running for a student body office—even if not elected. If elected, the student will earn two points toward the award in this category.

Two additional categories are provided in which students may earn points: community involvement and attendance. Unlike in the five required categories, students are not required to earn points in these areas. Points earned in these categories apply to the total points for the award, but they cannot be used in lieu of points in the required categories.

The purpose of this award is to encourage planning, goal setting, and student participation in the programs and activities of the school. A student need not be a superstar to earn the award; however, he or she must participate actively and enthusiastically in the activities of the school, engage in the pursuit of excellence, and meet certain standards of achievement and performance. The Block "FW" is also an important form of recognition for individuals who exemplify the virtues that Fort Washington strives to foster in all of its students. The word *exemplary*, in fact, means worthy of serving as an example. Individuals earning this award receive a Block "FW" letter and a framed certificate presented at a special evening program in their honor.

It is a school goal that at least 25 percent of the students in each upper grade classroom earn this award. Teachers, therefore, are actively engaged in goal setting, monitoring, and encouraging the participation and progress of each student. A special handbook, *A Guide to Earning the Exemplary Patriot Award*, is distributed to each student, parent, and teacher. It describes the philosophy and rationale of the award as well as the details concerning the earning of points in each of the categories. As it has evolved, this handbook has become a significant statement of the mission and goals of the educational program at Fort Washington.

The award handbook serves as a "blueprint" for parents, teachers, and students in setting individual goals and planning each child's total school experience. Among the desirable features of the Exemplary Patriot Award is the element of choice. Students are not required to participate in all of the school's activities to earn the award. Many options, including choices from among alternatives and level of participation, are open to students in meeting the standards for the award. Although the award recipients reflect individuality and preferences in the manner they have chosen to achieve the award, they have in common perseverance, self-discipline, service to others, breadth of participation in school and community activities, and the accomplishments of personal goals.

Since its introduction in 1984, the number of students receiving the Exemplary Patriot Award has increased steadily. At the first award ceremony, 27 students were honored, representing only 17% of the fourth- through sixth-grade enrollment. During the 1988–89 school year, 112 Exemplary Patriot Awards were presented, representing 38% of the fourth- through sixth-grade enrollment. The significance of the increase in the number of recipients lies in the fact that more students planned their activities, set their goals, and rose to the standards for the award. Moreover, it provides some evidence that the desired "character qualities" are being developed in the school program.

Over the past 5 years the Exemplary Patriot Award has had a positive impact on the total school program in the following ways:

1. Many students who had been reluctant to participate or try new things have become much more active and involved.
2. The quality of student participation has improved as students began taking the responsibilities of their involvement more seriously.
3. The award is highly valued by students. Personal goals, participation, achievement, commitment, self-discipline, and perseverance,

the qualities required to earn the award, have become important to students.

4. The award has provided parents and teachers with a means to identify students who are either too heavily involved in school activities or not involved enough, resulting in the ability to intervene with appropriate guidance.

5. Parents, teachers, and students have begun to view the "school life" of a student as a whole, where full participation in a variety of activities and experiences is viewed as a positive contribution to the student's development, his or her class, and the entire school atmosphere.

Patriotic Classroom Award

The Patriotic Classroom Award is the third important component of the school's effort to promote and reinforce the desired qualities related to character. This award is based on a composite classroom score reflecting five areas:

1. Library responsibility (overdue books)
2. Playground behavior (number of citations issued for misconduct)
3. Campus and classroom housekeeping
4. Cafeteria behavior (classroom stars earned for proper conduct)
5. Money owed to the classroom revolving lunch-loan fund

The Patriotic Classroom Award, a banner displayed in the room, is presented to the top primary, upper grade, and special education class every other week. This award serves three purposes. First, it is an administrative vehicle to emphasize and monitor some key citizenship responsibilities in a positive manner. Second, it is a tool for teachers to communicate, instill, and reinforce the values and expectations of the school. Finally, because this is a class award, students learn that accepting their responsibilities as individuals has an impact on the success of the group of which they are members.

Teachers anxiously await the tabulation sheet for this award at the end of each 2-week period. Class discussions take place about the importance of maintaining the classroom and campus environment and about why the custodians, who rate each classroom once a week, may have rated the class down in the housekeeping category. The custodians have come to be regarded as part of the educational staff, and attention to the condition of the room at the end of the day is viewed as an indication of respect and concern for them. Classes talk about the ratings they received on their assigned school site clean-up areas from the elected Student Council Commissioner of Grounds and about how protecting property and helping the environment is every citizen's job. Children and teachers talk about why it is important to return materials to the library on time and can translate their discussions into action by monitoring their improvement from week to week. Good table manners are stressed in the cafeteria at lunchtime. Teachers and students talk about what good manners are and why they are important in civilized society as they review the results in that component of the award turned in by the cafeteria supervisors.

Classrooms that earn the award, of coure, are pleased with their accomplishment, proud to display the banner for the 2-week period, and have high hopes of retaining it. Classrooms that did not earn the award are able to identify the areas in need of improvement and set goals for the following week. There is always next week, and the concerted effort from a classroom bent on earning the award generally pays off. In the meantime, vital dialogue between students and teachers about personal responsibility, expected behaviors, and duties of citizenship has taken place throughout the school.

Program Results

The combination of the co-curricular program, the Exemplary Patriot Award, and the Patriot Classroom Award have been instrumental in creating an effective and positive school climate for students as well as staff members and parents. The result is an "organizational culture," a society in microcosm, that sends clear signals about its values and direction via the criteria for the two important award programs.

The impact of this approach to character development appears to substantiate the insights concerning excellence in education and quality school programs gained through recent and ongoing "effective schools research." The thrust of this body of research is to identify the qualities and characteristics that distinguish exceptionally effective schools from others. A number of principles have emerged from this research that serve to guide school improvement efforts and, in fact, form the substance of the California State Department of Education's quality criteria for school assessment.

To summarize briefly, the following are among the characteristics of highly effective schools.

1. A strong sense of school mission and commitment to clearly defined, measurable goals
2. High standards and expectations for student performance and behavior that are understood and accepted by teachers, students, and the community
3. A high level of participation by the staff, students, and parents in the activities of the school and decision making within the school
4. A well-planned student recognition structure that serves to communicate, encourage, and reinforce the attitudes and behaviors that are desired and valued by the school and community

There are a number of assessment criteria and indicators that might serve as a foundation for judging the effectiveness of the program from a more quantitative standpoint. Although it would be improper to attribute a direct cause-and-effect relationship between program and outcomes, marked improvement in several key outcome variables has been observed since the program was articulated in this fashion and implemented 5 years ago.

The following are among the more significant factors considered in assessing the reults of the program.

Academic

1. Typically, 93% to 95% of all students (K–6) score at or above the 50th percentile in reading, mathematics, and language on the Comprehensive Tests of Basic Skills (CTBS) administered at the end of each year.
2. For the past 3 years, Fort Washington's sixth-grade scores in all areas of the California Assessment Program (CAP) tests are in the 92nd to 98th percentile range among all schools in the state and in the top 10% to 15% of the statewide distribution of schools similar to Fort Washington (e.g., socioeconomic index and minority population). Similarly, third-grade scores are in the 79th to 94th percentile range among all schools and in the top 25% to 30% of the statewide distribution of schools with similar background factors. The areas included in this annual test are reading, mathematics, and written language.

3. Fort Washington has earned state recognition as a California Distinguished Elementary School (1986–87) and national recognition from the U.S. Department of Education for excellence in education (1984–85).

School Climate

1. For the past 5 years, Fort Washington has recorded virtually no school vandalism.
2. Fort Washington has consistently achieved top ratings on the district-sponsored clean-campus inspections and, indeed, earned an award from the Fresno County Board of Supervisors for the clean, well-kept condition of the schoolgrounds.
3. For the past 5 years, the rate of unexcused student absences has never exceeded 5% while the average daily attendance (ADA) normally exceeded 98%.
4. Approximately 60% of the fourth- through sixth-grade students participate in the school athletic program during any given season. This is an elective activity that includes both the interscholastic and intramural sports programs.
5. More than 200 fourth- through sixth-grade students (45%) participate in one of the two school choirs—an elective activity.
6. Typically, 30 to 35 students run for student body office each semester at election time. Including each candidate's campaign manager, 60 to 70 speeches are normally delivered at the student body campaign assemblies.
7. Typically, 34% to 37% of the third- through sixth-grade students receive honor roll recognition each quarter.
8. Typically, 70 to 90 fourth- through sixth-grade students (approximately 20%) participate in either the school or the Fresno County Science Fair each year—an elective activity.
9. As indicated earlier, Fort Washington experienced rapid growth during the past 5 years, with the K–6 enrollment expanding from approximately 450 to 898 students. Sustaining a positive, purposeful school climate during this period may be viewed as one of the beneficial outcomes of this approach.

Admittedly, Fort Washington is not a typical school as one views the total spectrum. There is the perception, of course, that good things are bound to occur in a middle-class suburban school with a relatively homogeneous student body and enlightened, supportive parents. An obvious question is, Can this approach to character development be implemented in a different school setting with the same degree of success?

Apparently, the answer to the question is yes. As indicated earlier, five of the elementary schools in CUSD and one of the two intermediate schools have implemented the principles and essential elements of the Fort Washington program. A brief account of one school's experience may serve to illustrate the general usefulness of this concept.

Nelson Elementary School implemented the Block "N" program in 1987. Nelson is far different from Fort Washington. It is, in fact, the district's most diverse school with respect to its cultural, racial, ethnic, and socioeconomic makeup. It is a large school with 770 students, 55% of whom are minority students (mostly Hispanic and South East Asian). Over 200 students (27%) are limited-English- or non-English-speaking. Fifty percent of the Nelson students come from low-income households (based on AFDC) and approximately 35% come from homes similar to those in the Fort Washington attendance area.

The Block "N" Award is the same in structure as the Block "FW," with some modifications and adjustments to fit the specific needs of the community and the activities at Nelson. During the first 2 years of implementation, Nelson's principal has reported virtually the same positive results relative to student achievement, participation, the sense of school mission, and improved student conduct as those experienced at Fort Washington. At the first award program in 1987, only 20 Nelson students received the Block "N" Award. At the most recent ceremony in 1989, more than 100 students received this award, many of whom were from the minority population at the school.

Conclusion

Developing the character of children has always been an important priority of our schools and is inherent in the often verbalized if vague goal, "to make every child a worthwhile member of society." The approach to character development at Fort Washington is neither new nor revolutionary. It is, in fact, predicated on some rather traditional notions. In the final analysis, it appears that the success of this concept at Fort Washington and other schools substantiates two simple truths well known to educators. The first is the power of high expectations. Students generally will rise to meet expectations if they have a clear grasp of what the expectations are and they are supported in their efforts. Second, things that are important to the adults in a child's life will be important to the child. Maintaining the staff's focus on the standards for the two awards and monitoring students' efforts to achieve them place high importance and value on desired attitudes and behaviors. The approach works.

References

Ryan, K. (1986). The new moral education. *Phi Delta Kappan, 68,* 228.
Wynne, E. A., & Walberg, H. J. (December 1985/January 1986). The complementary goals of character development and academic excellence. *Educational Leadership,* 15.

Focusing on Citizenship and Social Problem Solving

The chapters in Part IV do not share a unified conceptual perspective but rather speak to a variety of issues associated with the theme of the book. The topics range from law-related education through socializing young children in special education classrooms to peace education curricula and strategies.

Chapters 11 and 12, by Alita Letwin and Carolyn Pereira, describe the substantial efforts by two major nonprofit organizations to enhance civic education in the nation's schools. In Chapter 11, Letwin describes the work of the Center for Civic Education, established in 1981 by the State Bar of California to influence public school education. Students are taught, through small and large discussion groups, to consider the perspectives of all the characters in the presented dilemmas in terms of their needs, capacities, and deserts (i.e., the degree to which they may deserve something). Major concepts, such as responsibility and justice, are the vehicles through which students apply these categories.

Pereira of the Constitutional Rights Foundation describes, in Chapter 12, a law-related curriculum that focuses on participatory experiences for children that emphasize three aspects of citizenship—acting responsibly, making choices, and building community. Each lesson has been constructed to be easily adaptable to one of the major curricular areas normally taught in schools. Both formal and anecdotal evaluations of law-related programs such as these show them to have a positive impact on students' behavior and attitudes, and each program provides a series of well-designed activities that can be readily implemented in classrooms.

In Chapter 13, James Fox, Mary McEvoy, and Robert Day describe innovative research projects to teach social skills to children in special education programs. The focus of these programs is to teach these skills and increase peer interaction among withdrawn and handicapped children and their more socially advanced peers. Children with special needs thus get specific instruction, and their nonhandicapped peers get an excellent experience in tutoring. Both groups benefit.

The final chapter in this section addresses the continued need for peace education and conflict resolution strategies. As this book goes to press, the generally peaceful political revolutions in Eastern Europe during the final months of 1989 are close at hand. These exciting events notwithstanding, Robert Valett makes a thoughtful plea that increased attention to conflict resolution and cooperation between children in schools is our best hope in averting later disastrous disputes, whether they be between adults or between countries. In essence, the emphasis on cooperation, caring, and peaceful conflict resolution strategies is the binding theme for this section.

CHAPTER ELEVEN

Promoting Civic Understanding and Civic Skills Through Conceptually Based Curricula

ALITA ZURAV LETWIN

THE Center for Civic Education is a California nonprofit corporation engaged in research, development, and implementation of civic education programs for public and private schools at the elementary and secondary levels. The principal goals of these programs are to help students develop

1. An increased understanding of the institutions of our constitutional democracy and the fundamental principles and values upon which they are founded
2. The skills necessary to participate as effective and responsible citizens
3. The willingness to use democratic procedures for making decisions and managing conflicts

The center's major task is developing and disseminating new curricula in civic education. It offers a variety of materials and services, including K–12 multimedia instructional units; Spanish language materials for grades K–3; materials and programs on the United States Constitution and Bill of Rights for upper elementary, middle, and high school students; a series of policy-making exercises; teacher-training materials; and assistance in program development.

The center conducts its activities with the cooperation of the faculty of the University of California and other institutions of higher learning, school districts, bar and judges' associations, and other groups and agencies throughout the United States.

Philosophy of the Center

Although the Center for Civic Education was established in 1981 by the State Bar of California as a nonprofit corporation to administer its Law in a Free Society Project, its roots can be traced to 1964. At that time, the deans of the schools of law and education and the chair of the department of political science at the University of California at Los Angeles formed the Committee on Civic Education. This interdisciplinary group was devoted to developing and implementing more effective programs in civic education at the precollegiate and teacher-training levels.

The committee's concern stemmed from the apparent lack of understanding of and commitment to democratic values among the young and the shallow and didactic nature of most civics classes. Its members pointed to such prevalent educational practices as

- An overemphasis on memorizing facts about the formal structure and processes of our legal and political institutions at the expense of developing an understanding of and capacity to deal with the realities of those institutions effectively
- A lack of adequate attention to the development of participatory skills necessary to gather information and make decisions effectively
- A persistent gap between the knowledge of our legal and political institutions at university and professional levels and the treatment of those institutions in precollegiate education
- School governance that was either excessively authoritarian or, at the other extreme, lacked enforcement of standards of behavior under a "rule of law"

These curricular and organizational deficiencies hampered efforts to fulfill education's obligation to provide each citizen with the opportunities to gain the knowledge and skills required for full participation in society, including the enjoyment of its rights and benefits and the fulfillment of its responsibilities.

In order to remedy the situation, the UCLA committee developed a pilot program around a curriculum on due process of law (procedural justice) for upper elementary and intermediate grades. The principal methods advocated in the curriculum were a modified form of Socratic discussion and the role-playing of mock trials, moot courts, and other institutional forms of conflict management and decision making.

The program was first used at the University Elementary School at UCLA and then with approximately 600 Los Angeles public school students of widely varying achievement levels and socioeconomic and ethnic backgrounds. Among the findings when these programs were evaluated was that students were capable of dealing with the subject matter at a much higher level of understanding than anticipated, and that students in grades 4 through 6 could be taught to analyze, evaluate, and make decisions regarding the complex constitutional issues involved in procedural justice.

In addition, participating teachers and administrators who noted that their students gained a greater understanding of the constitutional principles involved in their lessons also observed that the increased understanding gained through a study of the curriculum led to improved behavior on the part of students, improved use of teachers' authority (teachers were more open to students' ideas and more concerned with making fair decisions, i.e., less authoritarian), and improved classroom governance.

Much of the work of the Center for Civic Education has been built upon the concerns of the UCLA committee, its experiences with these early curricula and programs, and the philosophy and approach to curriculum development established at that time. This underlying philosophical position includes a number of assumptions, hypotheses, and observations.

The rationale that underlies the center's curricula is that a constitutional democracy, more than any other form of government, presupposes and depends upon enlightened and responsible citizens. In the early years of our nation, while James Madison and Alexander Hamilton hoped that creating the right institutions would solve the problems of self-government, men like Thomas Jefferson and John Adams recognized that these institutions require the support of an enlightened people. The experience of the past 200 years confirms their beliefs that the operation of even the most carefully designed political institutions is ultimately dependent upon the character of the citizens and those who occupy public office in their behalf. As Jefferson argued, "I know of no safe depository of the ultimate powers of the society but the people themselves, and if we think them not enlightened enough to exercise their control with a wholesome discretion, the remedy is not to take it from them, but to inform their discretion" (cited in Wagoner, 1976, p. 20).

A fundamental hypothesis underlying the center's programs is that education—primarily elementary and secondary education—can do what Jefferson says is needed. It can increase a person's capacity and inclination to act knowledgeably, effectively, and responsibly. It follows that a principal role of educational institutions in a democracy is to foster enlightenment, that is, to increase students' capacity to make intelligent choices for themselves—to help students learn how to think rather than what to think.

This definition of the proper role of education in a democratic society is based on a number of assumptions:

- The alternative to such enlightenment, "indoctrination" in "correct" behavior, is an improper role for educational institutions to play in a free society and one that has had, in general, an effect opposite to that which its proponents have predicted.
- It is counterproductive to attempt to hide inequities in our society or political and legal systems from students and to attempt to instill in them a romanticized and unrealistic view of political and legal processes and institutions.
- One of the most effective ways of fostering the type of enlightenment discussed above is to provide students with the knowledge and skills needed to discuss social, legal, and political issues intelligently and with numerous opportunities to use this knowledge and these skills in classroom discussion and simulation activities.
- Of equal importance is the school environment itself. It must reflect respect for the dignity of human beings, legitimate use of authority, and fair procedures, including due process of law, equal opportunities for students to grow and develop, and open inquiry and debate.
- To be effective, a program for the development of such enlightenment must cover the K–12 spectrum. Lessons are most effective when they are introduced as early as possible and systematically reinforced throughout the educational process. Observations have shown that kindergarten and primary children can begin to acquire the desired knowledge and skills if the context in which they are taught is interesting and relates concretely to their experience.
- Interactive learning strategies can develop participation skills and an understanding of how institutions in our society work. Useful

strategies include cooperative group work and simulations of legislative debates, mock and appellate court trials, congressional hearings, arbitration sessions, and city council and other public meetings.
- To be usable, a civic education program should be articulated with and integrated into the existing social studies and humanities curriculum.

Methods and Substance

John Stuart Mill said that the clash of ideas may lead to the discovery of error, refinement of ideas, and the probability of truth being discovered. This is obviously not always true. For example, it may also lead to polarization and polemicism. However, under proper circumstances and with proper teacher guidance, it can serve these purposes.

Kohlberg's findings to some degree seem to corroborate Mill's hypothesis. They demonstrate that moral development is enhanced by the discussion or clash of ideas among persons who characteristically reason at different levels in their resolution of moral dilemmas. Further, Kohlberg has concluded that the intervention of teachers skilled in certain techniques of leading discussions can enhance the development of students' capacities to deal with moral issues on higher levels of reasoning—culminating perhaps in more principled modes of reasoning.

Experience in curriculum development and experimentation led the center to see the importance of these findings and to believe that the clash of ideas can be used to foster intellectual growth and to enhance the quality of debate on important legal and political as well as societal or moral issues. Its programs thus involve a structured intervention in the learning process that includes two general components:

1. A sound base of knowledge relevant to the types of issues to be discussed
2. The development of basic analytical, evaluative, and decision-making skills using the knowledge base in dealing with fundamental and pervasive issues of justice, authority, privacy, responsibility, and the like

When students became decision makers about such issues in the early pilot project, they used many of the same considerations and principles one observes in the reasoning of scholars in the fields of law, political science, and philosophy. The purpose of the center programs, however, is not to teach elementary students to sound like university professors or supreme court justices. What is important is that students are helped to examine fundamental and pervasive issues of fairness and morality. The center's approach, particularly at the elementary level, involves raising issues as they relate to the daily experiences of students. Issues were selected that were analogous to issues in the social, legal, and political realms. Considerations and principles were used in making decisions that were applicable to examining these broader issues as well.

For example, materials on the concept of procedural justice at the second- to third-grade level contain a story entitled "Missing Milk Money," in which several children are accused by their peers of stealing. The students are then asked to examine the fairness of the way characters in the story tried to find out things. They focus on the comprehensiveness of information gathering, on whether the accused were given a chance to tell their side, on the right to present witnesses, and on prejudice toward the accused. Students are then asked to decide what should be done in the situation and to identify similar problems in their own experience.

In materials on the same concept for grades 5 through 6, students read about the Star Chamber trial in 1637 of John Lilburne, an English Puritan accused of sending heretical and scandalous books from Holland to England. Student evaluation of the Star Chamber procedures includes the considerations listed above. In addition, they consider whether there was opportunity for public observation, effective presentation of all positions, a way of ensuring the reliability of information, notice to interested parties, a predictable set of procedures, opportunity for review and appeal, adequate protection of the rights to privacy and freedom, assurance of human dignity, and a procedure that was practical. Students are then asked to hypothesize about the effects of Star Chamber procedures on freedom of belief, expression, and other values.

The Law in a Free Society Project

In 1969, the State Bar of California asked the UCLA Committee on Civic Education for help in planning a comprehensive civic education curriculum and teacher-training program that it could use in cooperation with local bar associations and other groups. Based on the success of the committee's first upper elementary curriculum project on procedural justice, work began on devising a conceptual framework for an expanded K–12 curriculum. From a list of some 150 concepts considered by consultants, eight were chosen to be the core of the new Law in a Free Society curriculum. These were authority, justice, privacy, responsibility, property, diversity, freedom, and participation.

The concepts of authority and justice were seen as being the heart of political philosophy and therefore fundamental to the discourse of politics. Responsibility was chosen because a constitutional democracy places great emphasis on the idea of rights and the common welfare, with the implied correlation of civic virtue and responsibilities. It was felt, therefore, that a civic education program needed to reason about what rights and responsibilities are and how they should affect behavior. The remaining concepts were seen as expressing major values of a constitutional democracy.

The next few years were devoted to designing experimental curriculum modules, writing instructional materials, designing and implementing a model in-service program, and building a network of community resources to support the program.

Classroom Materials: Multimedia Instructional Units

Evaluations by teachers involved in these initial efforts indicated a strong desire for student materials that embodied both the conceptual content and the participatory teaching methodology to which they had been exposed in early Law in a Free Society in-service workshops. In 1974, therefore, the project began to develop multimedia instructional materials on its curriculum for use in grades K–12. These units are available on the concepts of authority, justice, privacy, and responsibility. Each concept has six instructional levels designed for grades K–1, 2–3, 4–5, 5–6, 7–9, and 10–12, progressing sequentially in scope and complexity of treatment. Each unit contains sound filmstrips or videotapes, 30 student books, and a teacher's edition with an evaluation component.

These materials emphasize focusing students' attention on the central ideas, principles, and values involved in these concepts. To do so, sets of considerations, which we call "intellectual tools," are introduced to help develop capacities of analysis, evaluation, and decision making.

Sample Lesson

The responsibility curriculum is divided into four units, each containing two to four lessons, that cover the following topical questions:

1. What is responsibility?
2. What might be some benefits and costs of carrying out responsibility?
3. How can one choose which responsibilities to carry out?
4. Who should be considered responsible?

The lesson in Figure 11.1 is taken from the student book, *Responsibility*, Level III, for grades 4 to 5. It serves as the evaluation exercise for the third unit. Students work individually or in small groups to answer the questions posed, followed by class discussion led by the teacher. There may also be a role-play of the situation or a debate on the different solutions presented. Teachers are asked to evaluate students' work in terms of the effective use of the intellectual tools contained in the questions, accurate statements of fact, and the reasoning on which positions are based.

The center does not provide "answers" for such exercises. Our interest is in increasing students' capacities to take informed and reflective positions on problems of responsibility in situations in which reasonable differences of opinion among well-meaning and thoughtful people are possible. Our standard for evaluating positions is the degree to which they are well grounded in fact, reasoned, and reflective.

The Development of the Concept of Justice—K–7

In our definition, "justice" is roughly analogous to "fairness." In class, students are exposed to and distinguish among various types of justice issues (i.e., distributive, corrective, and procedural). Each type of justice issues requires the use of different sets of "intellectual tools," or considerations that should be taken into account in decision making. Therefore the justice curriculum examines each type of justice in turn, devoting two or three lessons to each.

The first type of justice examined is *distributive justice*. After initial discussion of several issues presented in a filmstrip, students are introduced to the "intellectual tools" useful in dealing with distributive justice.

Figure 11.1 The Toy Airplane

Jamie and Luis were on their way home from school when suddenly Luis remembered that he had promised his mother he would buy some toothpaste at the drugstore.

"Come on, Jamie," Luis said, "it will only take a few minutes."

As they entered the store, Luis headed straight for the section where the toothpaste was kept. But a big display of plastic toys caught Jamie's attention, and he walked in that direction.

Luis looked and looked for the brand of toothpaste his mother wanted. At last he found it. He picked up the tube of toothpaste and set out to find Jamie. Jamie was crouched on the floor playing with a toy truck when Luis found him.

"Come on, Jamie," said Luis, "let's go."

"Okay, Luis," Jamie replied.

Just then, Luis thought that he saw Jamie quickly stuff a tiny plastic airplane into his pocket. "Jamie, did you take that airplane?"

"No," said Jamie.

"You did," said Luis, "I know, I saw you. You'd better put that back."

"No, I didn't," said Jamie, "and even if I did, what could you do about it?"

"I could tell the people who run the store," said Luis, "because I don't think people ought to steal things. Please put it back."

"Look, I told you I didn't take anything, so just forget about it, will you?" Jamie said angrily.

"I'm warning you, Jamie, if you don't put it back, I'll tell the lady at the cash register," Luis said.

"You wouldn't dare," Jamie snapped.

WHAT DO YOU THINK?

1. What are Luis' responsibilities in this story?
2. To whom is each responsibility owed?
3. What are the sources of each responsibility?
4. What rewards might he receive if he carries out each responsibility or penalties if he fails to carry it out?
5. What might be the results of his carrying out each responsibility? Which could be the benefits? Which could be the costs?
6. How urgent is it for Luis to carry out each responsibility?
7. How important is each responsibility compared to the other responsibilities?
8. How much time will it take him to carry out each responsibility?
9. Does he have the resources he needs to carry out each responsibility?
10. Are there other important interests or values he should think about?
11. What other ways could be used to carry out the responsibilities?
12. What should Luis do in this situation? Why?

"The Toy Airplane" from *Responsibility* Level III, Copyright Center for Civic Education, 1984. Reprinted with permission.

The intellectual tools students use in focusing on the problem have been developed from the time of the ancient Greeks. For our purposes, we have selected a principle used in dealing with issues of distributive justice and named it the *principle of similarity.* The principle of similarity means that justice requires that, in a particular situation, people who are the same or similar in certain relevant ways should be treated the same or equally. And, in the same situation, people who are different in those ways should be treated differently, or unequally.

The relevant ways in which people may be similar or different are in their *needs, capacities,* or *desert* (i.e., the degree to which they may deserve something). How this subject is treated at different grade levels is described in the examples given below.

Distributive Justice

Grades K-1

At this first level, we use problems closely related to students' experiences to introduce them to the principle of similarity and the three related ideas required to apply it. The principle is introduced implicitly.

The filmstrip/video and student books follow the activities of three bear families. In Figure 11.2, several problems of distributive justice develop that students are asked to identify and solve. The first involves a problem of the fairness of sharing something found by one of the bear children; the second presents a problem of the bears' receiving different responsibilities at different ages and different amounts of food proportionate to their sizes; the third examines a problem of taking turns; and the fourth raises a problem of who gets to play certain positions in a ball game.

The discussion of the situation portrayed in Figure 11.2 would be led by the teacher, working with small groups or with the entire class. It comes from the *Justice,* Level I, materials.

Grades 2-3

At the second- and third-grade levels, students' understanding of the use of the ideas of need, capacity, and desert in dealing with issues of distributive justice is reinforced and extended. The principle of similarity is still treated implicitly.

Figure 11.2 The Three Bear Families

Baby Bear had the smallest bowl.
"Why do I have the smallest bowl?" he said.
"Because you are the smallest bear." said his mother.
"Is that fair?" said Baby Bear.

- *Did Baby Bear need as much as the big bears? Why?*
- *Could he eat as much as the big bears? Why?*
- *Did he deserve as much as the big bears? Why?*
- *Do you think it is fair for Baby Bear to have a smaller bowl? Why?*
- *What problems have you seen like the one in this story?*

The excerpt from *Justice*, Level II, that follows in Figure 11.3 deals with two second-grade classes competing for a prize in a paper drive. After studying the situation, classes are divided into small groups to develop positions as to which class should be awarded the prize. Then, representatives of each group present their position to the entire class for discussion. Students might also role-play a student council meeting or a meeting with the school administrator in which both sides of the issue are dramatically presented.

Figure 11.3 The Paper Drive

The Adams Elementary School was having a paper drive. Students in each class were supposed to collect old newspapers in their neighborhoods. The school would then sell the papers. The money the school earned was to be used to buy books for the new school library.

There was a prize for classes that brought the most papers to school. The class at each grade level that brought the most papers would get a trip to the zoo. There were two second-grade classes at the school. One class was Mrs. Johnson's. The other class was Mr. Blue's. Each day students collected papers from their neighborhoods. Each class wanted to win the prize for its grade level.

Every student in Mrs. Johnson's class worked hard. By the end of the paper drive they had brought 700 pounds of papers to school.

Some students in Mr. Blue's class worked very hard. A few did not work hard. Bob was one of them. He did not do anything for the first three days of the paper drive. Mr. Blue and the students in Bob's class were upset with him. They told him to help the class just as the other students were doing.

Bob did not want to help. But he did not want his friends to be angry with him. One afternoon he asked people in his neighborhood for old newspapers. He was lucky. The first person he asked had a large stack of old papers in her garage. Bob's mother helped him bring the papers to school the next day. There were over 500 pounds of papers. These were added to those the other members of Mr. Blue's class had brought. At the end of the week, his class had gathered 1,000 pounds of papers. Mr. Blue's class won the trip to the zoo.

Some students in Mrs. Johnson's class said it was not fair for Mr. Blue's class to win the prize.

Before you decide what you think would be fair, look at the list of ideas. Answer the questions by each idea. Then answer the questions at the end of the list.

LIST OF IDEAS AND QUESTIONS

Question	*Your Answer*
1. What was being given?	A prize—a trip to the zoo
2. Who could get it?	Mrs. Johnson's class or Mr. Blue's class

3. Answer the questions after each of the three ideas you have just learned to use.
   a. NEED. Did one class *need* the trip more than the other? Why?
   b. ABILITY. Was one class more *able* to go on the trip than the other? Why?
   c. DESERT. Had one class *earned* the right to go on the trip more than the other? Why? Had some students *earned* the right to go on the trip more than others? Why?

Figure 11.3 *(continued)*

What Do You Think?
1. Which ideas—need, ability, or desert—should be used to solve this problem?
2. What reasons can you give why Mr. Blue's class should get to go on the trip?
3. What reasons can you give why Mrs. Johnson's class should get to go on the trip?
4. What might be another way to solve this problem?
5. What ideas besides fairness might be used to solve this problem?
6. What do you think should be done? Why?

"The Paper Drive" from *Justice* Level II, Copyright Law in a Free Society, 1979. Reprinted with permission.

Grades 4–5

The principle of similarity is introduced explicitly at this level, and students are asked to determine the similarities and differences among people in particular situations in terms of their needs, capacities, and desert. One lesson deals with the distribution of political rights in a school setting. Students are asked to develop alternative positions on whether fourth- through sixth-grade students and their teachers should have the right and the responsibility to suggest new school rules to the principal.

After developing positions, students may role-play a hearing before the school principal (or a person taking that role) by setting forth and explaining their positions. This is an issue upon which there is likely to be a range of reasonable differences of opinion among thoughtful people. A number of experiences with this exercise in classrooms has led to a closer relationship between students, teachers, and principals. In some instances this has led to actual student participation in the making of some school rules followed by a greater willingness to comply with the rules they have had a voice in making.

Grades 5–7

By fifth grade, students are asked to analyze a hypothetical medical care proposal being considered by Congress that would distribute medical care benefits to lower income citizens.

After adequate preparation, students take part in a simulated congressional hearing on the issue, thus learning the procedures used in such hearings and increasing their capacities to participate effectively in such settings. Students also look at the daily newspaper or recent magazines where it is likely that an issue related to the one in this excerpt will be covered. Students who have participated in this exercise should be capable of carefully analyzing and taking reasoned positions on such issues.

Spanish-Language Materials

Responding to the needs of Spanish-speaking students with limited English proficiency, the center has translated the Law in a Free Society materials for grades K–3 into Spanish. The materials are designed to be used by bilingual teachers so they can explain the objectives of the lessons and lead discussions of the issues in the students' own language.

How Effective Are These Programs?

In 1979 Law in a Free Society joined with a group of other law-related education projects in a program designed to discover effective ways to institutionalize this form of civic education. Supported by a grant from the Office of Juvenile Justice and Delinquency Prevention of the U.S. Department of Justice, the program included a 4-year study of the effectiveness of law-related education in preventing delinquency. The study involved the evaluation of elementary, middle, and secondary classes that used curricular materials of the projects involved.

The evaluators found that students who are exposed to properly implemented law-related education programs are less likely than others of the same age to engage in theft, to use violence against other students, to be involved in gang fights, to avoid payments for goods and services, to cheat on tests, to be truant, and to use marijuana. These students also showed improvement in many factors associated with law-abiding behavior, including maintaining a favorable attitude toward school and the police as well as avoiding delinquent peers. Students, in turn, felt that teachers, parents, and peers were less likely to view them in a negative manner.

As expected, exposure to law-related education resulted in significant gains in knowledge of the law, basic legal concepts, and the justice system. Beyond this, teachers in the study overwhelmingly reported that the curricular programs had favorable effects on the development of a number of general student skills and attitudes. These included participating competently in classroom activities, understanding a variety of views, and working cooperatively with students of different backgrounds. [For further information about the findings of this study and the methodology used in its completion, see Johnson, Hunter, & Turner (1984)].

In light of these findings and other initial successes supporting law-related education, the Office of Juvenile Justice and Delinquency Prevention has continued to support what is now entitled the Law-Related Education National Training and Dissemination Project. This project is currently working to institutionalize law-related education in 43 states.

As the center programs have developed, observations and anecdotal accounts from teachers, students, administrators, and parents have given further support to the more formalized research results. Overall, the wide variety of experiences the center has had in developing programs and materials has strengthened its belief in the learning experiences fostered by its curricula and programs. Students are making significant progress toward developing a rational commitment, freely given, to those principles, processes, and values essential to the preservation and improvement of our society.

References

Johnson, G., Hunter, R., & Turner, M. J. (1984). *Law-related education evaluation project: Final report, phase II, year 3*. Submitted by the Social Science Education Consortium, Center for ACT Research. Boulder, CO: National Institute for Juvenile Justice and Delinquency Prevention.

Wagoner, J. L. (1976). *Thomas Jefferson and the education of a new nation*. Bloomington, IN: Phi Delta Kappa Educational Foundation.

CHAPTER TWELVE

Educating for Citizenship in the Early Grades

CAROLYN PEREIRA

> Mary lives in an apartment building that has a big sign posted, "No pets allowed." Most of the people in the building don't have children. Mary would like to take care of some pets for friends who are going away for the summer. Her friends have a dog, a cat, a bird, four goldfish, and two gerbils. (Archer, Pereira, & Langan, p. 145)

SHOULD Mary offer to keep any of these animals for her friends? Would it make a difference if the animals in question were large or small, noisy or quiet, messy or neat? What if the animals were part of a school science experiment? Could she keep just one animal for just a few days for just one vacationing friend? If Mary were blind, could she keep a dog with her at all times?

How might a group of second or third graders respond to Mary's dilemma? What would they say to the questions it raises? How should a teacher integrate a discussion of Mary's problem into the curriculum and what might be the outcome?

Unfortunately, civic education and civic participation are too often neglected in U.S. schools, especially at the elementary level. School systems rarely list practice in civic responsibility as a high priority. It is, however, a central reason for the teaching of all subjects. President Kennedy's challenge, "Ask not what your country can do for you but what you can do for your country," reflected the primary rationale for public education in the United States—the creation of a constructive, participatory citizenry. As early as the Northwest Ordinance of 1787, education was seen as essential to our government. The ordinance allotted a certain portion of land in each township for education because "knowledge . . . (was) necessary to good government. . . ." (Gutek, 1970, p. 28). Mathematics, science, computer science, and language skills not only help the individual to survive but our nation as well.

Good citizenship in our democracy requires acting responsibly by being informed, making choices given limited and sometimes conflicting information, and taking part in building a healthy community. The creation of a constructive, participatory citizen poses a challenge for teachers and schools. What classroom experiences can be constructed for young people to help them gain the knowledge, skills, and attitudes necessary for "good citizenship"?

Curricula developed jointly by the Constitutional Rights Foundation, the Law-Related Education Program for the Schools of Maryland, and the National Institute for Citizen Education in the Law attempt to address these issues. The materials described in the following pages are designed to alert youngsters to the rights and responsibilities of citizenship and to give them opportunities to practice citizenship skills. Published in 1982, they are currently under revision. Arlene Gallagher, adjunct professor of education at Boston University, is assisting in the revision.

Experiences as a Method for Citizenship Education

Students retain the essence of experience longer than anything they are just told or read. Most people, when asked about where, when, what, and how they learned about what it means to be a citizen, recount an experience. No book, lecture, or audiovisual has as much power as watching a neighbor being evicted from her apartment or having a bicycle stolen or buying something that doesn't work. What are the rights and responsibilities of citizens and government in each instance? What is happening in the life of a child outside of school often provides that teachable moment. It is irresponsible as well as impossible to rely solely on the "what happened to you this week" approach. Classrooms, however, can be designed to provide simulated experiences. For example, young children role-playing animals, each with a different perspective on a proposed road through their territory, gives them the opportunity to experience a common problem in our democracy—the balancing of conflicting interests.

The lessons in the elementary curriculum *Educating for Citizenship*, therefore, are referred to as experiences. The experiences are highly participatory, based on the belief that students will become more active adult citizens if they have opportunities to partcipate in their school years under simulated conditions. In this way students can develop a broader perspective on local, regional, national, and world issues that concern all people. Techniques are intentionally varied to involve students with different interests and learning styles. These techniques include brainstorming, creative dramatics, gaming/role-playing/simulations, group discussion, picture analysis, case studies, and small groups.

The scope and sequence for *Educating for Citizenship* is based upon the Expanding Horizons (family, school, community, state, nation, world), the organizer most used in elementary grades. The organizer has been slightly modified to reflect the impact of the media upon children. For example, when focusing in on the family, comparisons are made to other families in the nation and the world. The materials are tailored to the current curriculum in order to encourage their use. Teachers are more likely to use materials that effectively teach some subject, such as language arts, or skill, such as writing, already included in the curriculum. The activities are designed not only to promote civic participation but also to enhance reading, writing, arithmetic, science, and critical-thinking skills. The resulting curriculum for elementary grades focuses on three aspects of citizenship: acting responsibly, making choices, and building community. Originally called responsibility, choices, and governance, they were renamed in order to reinforce the participatory nature of the lessons.

Acting Responsibly

Our democratic society assumes that the overwhelming majority of its citizens act responsibly. To act responsibly they must be aware of the societal rules and regulations that govern their lives and agree with underlying principles that help make those rules and regulations. Acting responsibly goes beyond taking care of oneself. Today's students need to understand that it is morally correct to be concerned about the welfare of others and that, more often than not, it is in their own best interest as well. A responsible action is an informed action based on good information, solid reasoning, and a concern for all those affected. In an increasingly interdependent society, each of us must realize our obligations and responsibilities, both to ourselves and to others. Personal responsibility demands personal integrity, which springs from the satisfaction of meeting personal and group goals that are compatible with democratic principles.

Thus an objective of a primary experience of acting responsibly is to get students to demonstrate an awareness that often people need to share responsibilities in order to solve problems. To help meet that objective, consider this story and the following activity.

> The city of Mixinwhich had a beautiful park. It was small but had many different kinds of trees and flowers. Everyone and everything loved the park.
>
> One summer day, a family stopped to have a picnic at the park. They finished their hot dogs and shakes and pushed the leftovers into a brown bag filled with leftovers from other lunches. The big brown bag broke. Smelly, sticky paper, candy bar wrappers, empty bottles, and cans flew everywhere. A pine tree caught some candy bar wrappers, a flower bed ended up with broken glass, and a couple of cans rolled into the duck pond. The family looked around and said, "Oh dear." They didn't have any more bags, and they couldn't find a garbage can anywhere. Finally, they climbed into their car and drove away.
>
> That evening, another family decided to have a picnic at the park. After eating, they stuffed their leftovers into a brown bag, but nobody wanted to carry the garbage home. Finally, they hid the brown bag underneath some bushes.
>
> The next day, three more families celebrated a birthday at the park. Everyone had a birthday cupcake. Almost everyone left a birthday cupcake wrapper stuffed in the flower bed, under a tree or bush, or in the pond. Each day that summer, someone left something in the park.
>
> One day a family came along. They didn't like the mess. They picked some of it up but couldn't get it all. By the end of the summer, the park was covered with paper, bottles, glass, and cans.

After reading and understanding this story, a class can brainstorm about what each family might have done differently, then evaluate each of the alternatives. Children may suggest that the first family return with large garbage bags, but in evaluating that alternative they might decide that the first family probably didn't think the park looked that bad or that they didn't have, or want to take, the time. This sets the stage for an action project of their own. Shifting the focus of the discussion to the students' own school, the teacher asks students to use their eyes to examine the schoolgrounds, the hallways, and their classroom for litter. Who caused the litter problem at the park in Mixinwhich? Who may have caused the litter problem at school? Why do people litter and damage nice things? Why should people take care of things in parks, schools, or anywhere? Brainstorming to prevent littering in their own school or classroom sets the stage for the school custodian to talk to the class about his or her responsibilities and daily problems with litter.

In order to brainstorm effectively a teacher must establish class guidelines, such as:

1. Say whatever comes to mind but wait until called upon.
2. Do not evaluate suggestions. The ideas will be evaluated later.
3. Build on ideas.
4. Do not threaten, intimidate, or put anyone down.

The custodian should be briefed before coming to the class or at the beginning of the class so that he or she can help evaluate ideas that the class has come up with for controlling litter. Resource people are too often viewed as a bother or a frill. Yet one of the most effective ways to transfer values is through positive adult role models. There are too few opportunities for young people to interact positively with adults so that both respect each other. Establishing a classroom atmosphere of mutual respect goes a long way in helping to build a mutual sense of responsibility. Needless to say, the teacher must clearly communicate what is expected of the resource person and structure the class so that there will be interaction between the adult and the students.

Throughout this experience students practice acting responsibly by thinking through solutions to the hypothetical problem involving litter in a park and then developing and implementing their own plan of action to deal with litter in their school. Students become more likely to notice litter and to feel empowered to do something about it. They think about what they can do to help themselves and others and how they can work with family, school, and government on personal or societal problems. Acting responsibly includes volunteering to be a part of the solution, not just voting for someone else to take care of the "problem." The lowest common denominator of good citizenship is informed involvement in problem solving. Acting responsibly also means making wise choices.

Making Choices

We live in a democratic society where individuals and groups are expected to make choices both in their personal and political lives. Students choose whether to do homework, listen in class, fight, vote in class elections, and so on. Making wise choices involves careful consideration of alternatives and consequences to the individual or groups as well as to society as a whole. It is important to complete homework, but it is also important to help in a family crisis. It is important to listen in class, but it may be impossible because of lack of sleep. It is important not to fight, but is defending oneself fighting? Needs and wants have a strong influence on the choices and decisions we make. The needs and wants of individuals and groups are similar in some ways. People need and want housing, food, education. However, needs and wants differ. This diversity bring richness to our lives, but it can also produce conflict. Rights come into conflict. Can an apartment dweller practice the tuba at home? Should we pay taxes on food in order to feed the homeless? What are the advantages and disadvantages of making everyone pass a literacy test before being able to vote? Similar choices and conflicts arise for students. When is noise allowed in a classroom? What can be done if someone does not have a lunch? Should a student be allowed to participate in an extra-curricular activity if he or she cannot read well?

In dealing with conflicting needs and interests, individuals and groups are faced with decisions about information and with personal choices about competing values. Decisions are even more difficult when they affect an entire community. What Lincoln said years ago about "pleasing all of the people" still holds true. The activities we've developed to help children make proper choices encourage them to strike a balance between satisfying their own needs and the needs of others. The ultimate goal is to make choices that build a sense of community in which all people's needs are considered and respected. The activities are designed to help children examine the variety of human needs, to recognize that people sometimes disagree about how to meet their needs, and to experience through practice some ways in which people can work out disagreements.

An intermediate experience from "Making Choices" helps children understand that disagreements often involve "rights in conflict," and that conflicts can be resolved in a variety of ways. The problem:

> Several neighbors have told the owner of their apartment
> building that he must either make the Hoopers get rid of their

dog or make the Hoopers move. The Hoopers are deaf. Their 2-year-old dog is trained to let the Hoopers know, by poking them with his nose, if anyone tries to enter their apartment. "The dog barks only when a stranger comes to the door or when there is a lot of noise in the hall," said Mr. Hooper. "My wife often takes the dog to work with her. The people at the office don't mind at all. He is quiet and well-behaved." Not all the neighbors agree.

However, one neighbor—who lives directly below the Hoopers—said that she had not heard the dog lately and that it had never bothered her. She also said she had noticed that, even though dogs are not allowed in the building, some people keep pets.

Should the Hoopers be allowed to keep their dog in the apartment?

This lesson fits into the language arts or social studies program, because it calls for oral communication skills and the construction and evaluation of logical statements. The lesson also serves as a pre-writing experience, asking students to draft an ending to the story as a final exercise.

The teacher divides the class into groups of three to four and assigns each student a role: attorney for the Hoopers, angry neighbor, a landlord, an observer (optional) to report the reasons given in the role-playing exercise to the rest of the class. If the class has little experience in role-playing, then generating options as a class, or meeting in groups of attorneys, neighbors, landlords, and observers to generate options, will strengthen the actual role-play.

Each group then acts out the situation as if in court, with the landlord serving as judge. First the neighbor speaks, then the lawyer. The landlord makes no decision until the class meets as a group. Then each landlord announces his or her decision and the reasons for it. If an observer is used, the observer should comment on the reasons for the landlord's decision, reporting on the strongest arguments given.

Not all the landlords will agree. How does the class explain this? Differences in the information, the way it was presented, and the previous experiences of individual "landlords" always surface as possible explanations. Are there other possible solutions to the problem? What proved to be the most difficult role to play? Why? Students have frequently tried to please all parties by suggesting making the apartment more soundproof, moving the Hoopers or the angry neighbor to another apartment, or putting a muzzle on the dog.

Other situations like this one can be constructed using controversies reported in the news. When studying state government, one might consider, for example, the various arguments to support the views of Indians who may have fishing rights, of vacationers who want to fish, and of the Department of Natural Resources (DNR), which is responsible for ensuring that fish do not become extinct. What should be a state government's final decision if its goal is to balance preservation of the environment with citizens' rights?

An activity particularly appropriate for the early primary grades, "Feathers, Feathers, Feathers," has children practice resolving a conflict between two individuals over a limited resource. The children are asked if they collect things or if they know someone who collects things. Items they mention are listed on the blackboard—stamps, baseball cards, glass figurines, post-cards, matchbooks, and so on.

The following prereading questions focus attention on the story.

Have you ever wanted something very badly?
Did you ever want something that someone else, like a brother, sister, or friend, also wanted?
What did you do if there was only one thing?

In the discussion children should be encouraged to talk about how important a collection is. People care a great deal about what they collect, and what might not mean much to one person might be very valuable to another. The following story is about a family of squirrels and their collection—feathers. The story may be read or told using puppet cutouts.

Feathers, feathers, feathers! They were all that little Sammy Squirrel could think of. Blue feathers, red feathers, green feathers! Big feathers, little feathers, middle-sized feathers!

Sammy's whole family loved feathers. Sammy's grandfather wore three big blue ones in a band around his head. Sammy's sister, Cindy, wore a purple one on her sweater. Sammy's mother kept a feather with both orange and black on it in a vase. Sammy's brother, Jeremiah, kept all types of beautiful feathers in a special treasure box under his bed.

Sammy loved looking at all those feathers and feeling how soft they were. But he was a little sad. Sammy did not have any feathers. He had looked but could not find a single feather.

"Do you think I'll ever find a feather of my own?" Sammy asked his mother. Sammy's mother gave him a great big hug and asked him if he would like to have one of her feathers. Sammy thought a minute. "No, it would never feel like my feather. I need to find one of my own."

The next morning Sammy decided to hunt really hard for a feather. He got up early. First he went to the swamp. His grandfather found feathers there all the time. He looked all through the tall grass and under the willow tree. No feather there.

He climbed up the hill by the sassafras plants. His sister, Cindy, had found her feathers there. No feather there.

He looked by the crystal blue lake. That's where his mother liked to go. He walked all the way around it, but no feathers there.

He went to the green meadow. His brother said that was a good place, but no feathers there.

Sammy sat down on a rock to rest. He put his head in his hands and began to cry. Suddenly he stopped and lifted his head. Out of the corner of his eye he saw something blue. No, it was green! No! It was blue and green and yellow. Sammy saw the most beautiful feather he had ever seen lying on the ground.

Just then, Sammy's brother, Jeremiah, scampered out of the trees. "Wow! What a beautiful feather!" he exclaimed. He started to scoop up the feather. "Wait!" screamed Sammy. "It's my feather. I was just going to pick it up!"

Sammy and Jeremiah looked at each other. They weren't sure what to do and sat down on a log to think. They put the feather between them for both of them to look at.

To begin the discussion check for understanding by reviewing the story's important parts. In order to resolve this conflict the children must be working with the same information. A case-study approach using the following questions will bring out the facts and issues related to this incident.

Facts:

What did the squirrels collect?
Who didn't have any feathers?
Who found the beautiful feather?

Who saw the feather first?
Who started to pick it up first?

Issues:

*What is the problem?
*What are some reasons why Sammy might think he should have the feather?
*What are some reasons why Jeremiah might think he should have it?

Half of the class will pretend to be Sammy and the other half Jeremiah. Pretending can be enhanced by having each child color a picture of a squirrel with the appropriate name underneath. Then each child can tape it to his or her chest or hang it around his or her neck with strings. If the students have not done role-playing before, discuss the idea of pretending. Ask the children to talk about times when they have pretended to be someone else. Suggest experiences such as playing house, family, robots, cowboys, or whatever roles are currently popular. Work with a few different pairs until most children grasp the idea. Being able to see the world from someone else's perspective can help build tolerance for diversity and is particularly useful in our pluralistic democratic society.

Before beginning the role-play, remind the children about the importance of listening to each other. Demonstrate this with one pair of students if necessary. Have the pair come to the front of the class and ask them each to say why they think they should have the feather. Then ask Sammy to repeat what Jeremiah said and ask Jeremiah to repeat what Sammy said. Listening is a skill that can help avoid unnecessary misunderstandings. Careful listening will also encourage better questions.

If the class has experience with role-playing, all of the children can pair up and tell their reasons to each other. Encourage them to try to come up with different reasons, not just a repeat of reasons already stated. They may need assistance in coming up with resolutions. Students should try to come up with ideas that are acceptable to both Sammy and Jeremiah. Add the following if they do not arise in discussion:

• Share the feather
• Own the feather on alternate days
• Give the feather to someone else—their mother or grandfather

- Hunt together for more feathers and then decide what to do with this one
- Leave the feather where it was for someone else to find
- Let Jeremiah get the feather and Sammy choose another one or two from his collection
- Ask another member of the family to make the decision
- Ask someone to be a "judge" similar to the one on TV's "People's Court" and let that person make the decision
- Flip a coin
- Play another game such as "Scissors, Paper, Rock" to decide

These solutions can be recorded on a chart and saved to refer to during other conflict resolution activities. Students may need help in making connections between similar situations when people's needs and wants conflict.

Experiences such as these are intended to build respect for the rights of others as well as for those of a single individual and help students understand that individuals and governing bodies often are confronted with difficult choices when two rights come into conflict. Agreeing on ways to resolve those conflicts is essential to building a strong community and nation.

Building Community

Building a sense of community or togetherness yet maintaining a respect for individual and cultural differences is a constant challenge to education and to the United States. All of us belong to a variety of groups or communities of people determined by both choice (clubs, unions, churches, etc.) and chance (families, gender, etc.). Conflict often arises both in groups where individuals may agree on the goal but disagree on the way to reach that goal and between groups with conflicting interests. Unless the conflict is resolved peaceably, the group, community, or nation will not survive. Procedures need to be established, understood, and accepted for resolving the conflict in order to maintain the group, community, or nation. For example, a team wants to buy their coach a present but cannot agree on how much is to be spent or what the gift should be. There must be consensus on how the decision will be made or the conflict will damage the team's spirit. As a nation we have agreed to resolve our conflicts between groups using the Constitution as a framework. Today our nation is divided on what to do about several issues.

Women's rights, drugs, defense, and taxation are only a few to which our system of government must respond.

In order to manage these conflicts and not destroy the group or community or nation, our society has developed formal governance procedures—legislatures, courts, executive offices. Although the team will not have to turn to either a lawmaking body or a court or a president to resolve its dilemma, it may, however, use one of these procedures to decide a course of action: vote, ask outsiders to decide, or let their captain decide. The procedures outlined in our Constitution will decide a course of action for the controversial legal issues facing our society today. Our Constitution provides the basis for our entire legal system. Building a strong community and nation depends on accepting and understanding the principles and procedures outlined in our Constitution.

One experience from *Educating for Citizenship*, intended for use in the intermediate grades, has as its objective to help students understand how representative government meets common needs and resolves problems. To develop that understanding, the students create their own formal mechanism—a law-making body, as did our nation's founders—and compare it with that of their own state or the national legislature.

This country's founders realized that it was too large and diverse to enable everyone to be involved in the day-to-day operations of the government. They created a republic, assuming that representatives could be chosen to reflect the will of the people and maintain the general welfare. The Constitution requires members of the House of Representatives to be 25 years old, citizens for 7 years, and reside in the state in which they are elected. It gives no other guidance on what qualifications representatives should have. It trusts the voters to make a wise choice. Neither does the Constitution clearly define the relationship between the representatives and the people they represent. They are to represent their constituency and the general welfare. What happens when there is a conflict? What should or can representatives do when they believe that a certain bill is good for the country but realize if they vote for it, they may not be reelected?

The teacher begins by explaining that every resident in a state cannot share in every decision made by a state government. Instead, the citizens elect representatives to make such decisions for them.

The class will be responsible for electing five to ten of its own members to serve as a representative body (or legislature) charged with making rules (or laws) to solve problems that confront the class as a whole. To ensure that this legislature represents all members of the class, the students are responsible for deciding which of the following criteria should determine a student's eligibility for election. Students may be chosen who

> Represent each table or row
> Are equally divided between girls and boys
> Have reached a certain age
> Possess a specified level of intelligence
> Have demonstrated an ability to deal with others effectively
> Represent special interests

After the class has listed the advantages and disadvantages of each criterion, it votes on the ones it will use and elects its legislature. To test the structure the class may role-play a lawmaking session. Serving as participants in a hearing, the remaining members of the class try to help this legislature make the decisions they think are best. Funding for day care, minimum wages for young people, rights of children in a divorce, and garbage recycling bills have all been used successfully. The representatives or teacher can draft a bill or series of bills and circulate them to everyone in the class. The class should be divided into groups of five to six representing potential interest groups. Each group should decide if it wants the bill to pass and why and select someone to represent its point of view at the hearing. Once the representatives have heard from all the interest groups, they discuss the bill in front of the class and vote to determine whether it passes. This presents an excellent opportunity to discuss whether the representatives voted the way the majority of the class felt. If they didn't, why not? Should representatives always vote the way their constituency wants? Are they always able to?

Finally, a state legislator or a representative of the League of Women Voters can talk with the class about how its legislative body compares with that of the state or how the state legislature is dealing with the issues selected for the class or both.

Additional lessons in this section are being designed to give students a historical perspective illustrating our "living democracy." How has our formal system of governance evolved over the years to respond to our pluralistic society and maintain core civic values in America's democratic system? The core values include a respect for the rights of individuals and groups and the acceptance of majority rule with respect for minority rights. Providing a historical as well as a contemporary perspective on how and why our legal system operates gives students an understanding that our system, although not perfect, has made progress toward a more just society. Both individuals and groups have made a difference and can still make a difference. This approach can combat disillusionment and apathy in later life. People are more likely to participate constructively in our public life by volunteering, voting, and running for public office if they feel a vested interest in their community and nation, understand how the legal system operates, and have the necessary skills.

If we want students to be constructive citizens, we must provide them with experiences to prepare them. The early grades will help make good citizenship a habit of the heart, not an unwelcome chore.

Evaluation

Educating for Citizenship was field-tested in more than 50 Maryland schools located in urban, suburban, and rural areas and revised based on teachers' evaluations. The teachers reported that students were enthusiastic and appeared to transfer some learning to other areas of their lives. However, no short-term evaluation can tell us whether the experiences have done the job.

The reports are only anecdotal because these curriculum materials do not include written tests for students. Many of the suggested activities are structured group experiences and do not lend themselves to traditional modes of evaluation. One teacher, for example, said that she was delighted with the cooperation and the enthusiasm of her students and with the final class product. Every member of her class had seemingly mastered the program objectives. Nonetheless, she was uncomfortable about giving every student an A. How could she have determined whether the stated goals and objectives had been achieved? The goals and objectives do not focus on the ability to memorize and recall information but rather on a set of experiences. It is, therefore, more appropriate to consider some of the other evaluation devices available, such as directed observations, rating scales, projective techniques, individual conferences, checklists, questionnaires, and work samples. Students can also be provided with self-evaluation checklists to engage them in the appraisal of their own progress. The evaluation is a part of the total instructional package and should promote a feeling of responsibility and self-direction.

Clearly, *Educating for Citizenship* cannot guarantee that every student will master every citizenship skill. Rather, students make progress on a continuum. They come to see that law does not have to be restrictive, punitive, and beyond people's control and understanding. They learn that people have the power to manage conflict in ways that are not destructive. They learn the perils of being self-centered and indifferent to others. Gradually, they acquire the knowledge, the skills, and the attitudes that a democracy demands of its citizens.

References

Archer, S. D., Pereira, C., & Langan, T. (1982). *Educating for Citizenship* (5 vols.). Rockville, MD: Aspen Systems Corporation.
Gutek, G. (1970). *An historical introduction to American education*. New York: Thomas Y. Crowell.

CHAPTER THIRTEEN

Developing
Social Competence
in Young Handicapped
and Withdrawn Children

JAMES J. FOX

MARY A. McEVOY

ROBERT DAY

SOCIALIZATION refers to a complex behavioral outcome, the child's "acquisition of behavior congruent with group norms and values" (Hess, 1970, p. 458). Socialization research has addressed a wide range of behavioral outcomes—moral judgment, cooperation, sharing, assertiveness, gender-related behaviors, and self-regulation—describing changes in these behaviors over time. Also, socialization may refer to the processes by which these behavioral outcomes are achieved (see, e.g., Mischel, 1970). Research on socialization processes has shown that other children can be and often are one of the most potent influences on development; although the specific ways in which children socialize each other are varied and often subtle, much of peer socialization is brought about through direct interaction (Hartup, 1983).

Preparation of this manuscript was supported in part by Grants #G008302979 and #G008630344 from the Office of Special Education and Rehabilitative Services, U.S. Department of Education, and in part by Grant #7-P01-15051 from the National Institute of Child Health and Human Development. The authors wish to thank Richard E. Shores for his comments on an earlier draft of this manuscript and Wilma Davis for her assistance to typing this manuscript.

This is the case for normally developing (Hatch, 1984; Hartup, 1983) and handicapped children alike (Strain, Cooke, & Apolloni, 1976; Widerstrom, 1983; Day, Fox, Shores, Lindeman, & Stowitschek, 1983).

Given the socializing function of interaction, it is not surprising that concern should be expressed for children who do not interact or who avoid social interaction. Indeed, concern for severely withdrawn persons is longstanding (see, e.g., Campbell, 1896) and well-founded. Social withdrawal appears to be durable and self-perpetuating; and, in the absence of active intervention, the withdrawn child may be at risk developmentally (Day et al., 1983; Odom & DeKlyen, in press). Simple physical integration, especially of handicapped children, does not appear to increase peer interaction reliably (Guralnick, 1978; Porter, Ramsey, Tremblay, Iaccobo, & Crawley, 1978).

The development and evaluation of procedures to teach effective social skills and increase peer interaction are relatively recent developments (see Day et al., 1983). Empirically validated curricula using systematic instruction to teach social competencies are even more fledgling (Stowitschek & Powell, 1981). Our overall purpose in this chapter is to summarize the research and development activities that we and our colleagues have conducted over the past 10 years at Peabody College, Vanderbilt University. The aim of these activities was twofold:

1. To develop procedures and materials that would allow teachers and other students to teach interaction skills to withdrawn and handicapped children
2. To increase interaction between these children and more socially advanced peers

Also, we will outline some of the basic procedural approaches to teaching social skills and promoting the social integration of children with and without exceptionalities. Finally, we will briefly note some of the more important issues facing researchers and practitioners alike with particular regard to social-emotional and moral development.

Overview of Social Interaction Training Approaches

Since 1964, research has shown that social withdrawal in normally developing and handicapped children is amenable to change through various interventions (Hops, 1982; McEvoy & Odom, 1987; Strain &

Fox, 1981). There are three general types of intervention approaches that can be discerned. The first consists of *arranging the environment* to facilitate interaction. Environmental arrangement interventions involve adjusting certain physical or social aspects of the classroom to provide a facilitative context for interaction. Research has shown that children's interactions can be affected by factors such as the type of toys or materials (Quilitch & Risley, 1973; Hendrickson, Strain, Shores, & Tremblay, 1981), the amount of space (Brown, Fox, & Brady, 1987; Speigel-McGill, Bambara, Shores, & Fox, 1984), and the availability of socially competent peers (Hecimovic, Fox, Shores, & Strain, 1985).

A second general tactic is *teacher-mediated instruction in social skills and management of interaction.* In this approach the classroom teacher directly teaches social skills to the withdrawn child and arranges interactions with more socially active peers using a variety of specific procedures. Specific tactics include verbal directions or suggestions to one child to interact with another (e.g., "Tommy, throw Suzie the ball"), modeling ("Tommy, watch how I throw Suzie the ball—now, you do it"), and contingent praise/reward for engaging in interactive behaviors ("Tommy, I like the way you threw the ball to Suzie").

In the third, the *peer-mediated approach,* the focus is on teaching nonhandicapped or less handicapped peers to initiate and maintain interactions with withdrawn children. As in the teacher-mediated approach, modeling, instructions, and contingent reward are used by the teacher, but the immediate focus of this direct teaching shifts from the withdrawn student to his or her peers. These peer "helpers" or "tutors" then become the intervention agent by modeling appropriate social interaction for or increasing their initiations to the withdrawn child.

All these general approaches and their specific tactics have been investigated, and each has received experimental confirmation of its effects on children's social skills and interactions. Yet, as Browning (1980) has aptly noted, the results of experimental procedures may not translate readily into effective practice. Much of our work and that of our colleagues has been devoted not only to careful experimental analyses of these interventions but also to the development of effective and practical social interaction curricula for handicapped withdrawn students. In the following sections we will briefly describe the social interaction training programs we have developed and illustrate their application.

The Social Competence Intervention Project

The *Social Competence Intervention Project* (SCIP), a 3-year, federally funded project, was begun in 1979 to generate effective practice from the findings of social interaction research. SCIP's major goal was to develop an empirically validated, social interaction instructional package for teachers to use with both handicapped and nonhandicapped young children. An initial observational study of nonhandicapped preschoolers identified specific social initiations that resulted in reciprocal social responding by peers (Tremblay, Strain, Hendrickson, & Shores, 1981). These were:

Sharing
Verbally organizing play (e.g., "Let's play house")
Assisting (helping another child to play or use a play material)
Affection
Rough and tumble play

Adult instructional behaviors found effective in teaching these initiations were:

1. Modeling
2. Prompting (descriptive instructions and physical guidance)
3. Contingent feedback in the form of behaviorally specific praise or rewards (Day, Powell, Stowitschek, & Dy-Lin, 1982; Hendrickson et al., 1981)

The *Social Competence Intervention Package for Preschool Youngsters* or SCIPPY (Day, Powell, & Stowitschek, 1980) was developed from these and other research findings. This interaction training package relies on a series of play situations in which socially active peers help the teacher increase the interaction of the withdrawn target child. The package contains:

1. A teacher's manual
2. Procedures for identifying and selecting those children in need of social skills training
3. Procedures for selecting peers and scripts for training them as "helpers"
4. Twenty activity cards (suggested situations) for teaching the social skills to the target child

5. Videotapes of the teaching procedures and of examples and nonexamples of the target social behaviors
6. Procedures for assessing progress
7. Trouble-shooting tips

Implementation of SCIPPY

There are several basic steps in implementing SCIPPY. First, using a combined ranking, rating scale and behavior checklist procedure, the teacher identifies several children who are most in need of social interaction training and places them in an appropriate skill level of the SCIPPY package. Next, the teacher arranges an area of the classroom in which to do instruction and selects an activity from the activity cards to provide a context in which to teach interaction skills. In the third step, he or she receives the script and procedures listed on that particular activity card and then brings the withdrawn child and a peer together in the activity area to begin actual instruction.

This instruction may take one of two forms to be decided by the teacher. On the one hand, the teacher may elect to use *SCIPPY*'s teacher-mediated procedures, the "direct-shaping" tactics. This choice would be influenced by several factors—lack of socially competent or cooperative peers, target children whose withdrawal skill deficits are very severe or who present serious behavior management problems.

To get a better grasp of the direct-shaping tactic consider the following example from the SCIPPY package. In Activity 6, "Balloons," the teacher might verbally prompt the withdrawn child, Suzie, to begin the session by inviting the peer to play ("Suzie, tell Tommy, 'Let's play balloons'"). If Suzie actually invites Tommy to play, the teacher would praise Suzie ("That's nice asking Suzie").

Once the children have gotten the balloons out, the teacher might again prompt Suzie to continue the interaction by saying, "Now, Suzie, hit the balloon to Tommy." Each such activity progresses in a natural sequence from invitation to getting the materials to cooperative play, and, finally, putting away the play materials.

On those occasions when the withdrawn child does not comply with a prompt or has difficulty engaging in the behavior, the teacher might model the desired behavior ("Suzie, hit the balloon to Tommy like this"; teacher hits the balloon to Tommy) and then prompt the desired behavior again ("Now, you do it").

Alternatively, the teacher might guide the withdrawn child physically through the behavior (teacher places his or her hands around

Suzie's hands and taps the balloon to Tommy) and again prompt her to perform this same behavior independently. As these interactions continue and the withdrawn child becomes more skillful at initiating and continuing interactions, the teacher would use increasingly less prompting and contingent praise, allowing the children's interactions to become more self-sustaining. Critical to the success of this latter process is that the teacher formally evaluate the children's social progress during each lesson.

Consequently, SCIPPY contains a short checksheet that the teacher uses simply to observe the children's independent interactions during the last 4 minutes of each daily, 12-minute lesson. These data are then summarized and used to make decisions about further teaching or fading of instruction.

The second instructional strategy of SCIPPY is that of training and using nonhandicapped or less handicapped peer helpers, essentially a peer-mediated approach. This approach was adapted and refined in a later extension of SCIPPY, the *Social Integration of Autistic Children Project*, which we describe presently.

Field testing of SCIPPY addressed three questions:

1. Would it increase teachers' use of the teaching procedures when compared to a general instruction to get the children to interact?
2. Would the package enable teachers to identify and teach the critical social skill targets?
3. If teachers used the package correctly, would students' peer interactions increase?

Nine teachers—three regular education preschool teachers, three teachers of preschool handicapped children, and three teachers of school-aged moderately and severely handicapped children—and 36 children composed the field test group. Each teacher selected one socially active child as a peer helper and three withdrawn children. Daily, direct observations of teacher and child behaviors were conducted throughout three successive phases—no intervention, general instruction, SCIPPY training. A multiple baseline across teachers was used as the evaluative design. The results showed that during SCIPPY:

Eight of nine teachers increased their use of the instructional tactics

They applied these procedures to teach the target behaviors

Children's rates of peer interaction were increased significantly
Most teachers chose to use the direct shaping tactics

Thus, when instructional materials specified desired student behaviors and provided systematic instructional procedures, teachers were
able to teach their students effective social skills (Day et al., 1984).

The Social Integration of Autistic Children Project

The SCIPPY field test showed that teachers could approach instruction of social behavior in a manner similar to that in other curricular
domains, by operationalizing instructional targets and by applying
direct teaching tactics. Subsequently, we pursued an extension of
SCIP's curricular approach to social development. The *Social Integration of Autistic Children Project/SIAC* was also a 3-year, federally
funded research and development project. Its overall purpose was to
extend the basic instructional philosophy and procedures of SCIP to
school-aged children with autism. Autism is a severe developmental
disorder, often characterized, among other things, by profound difficulties in or avoidance of social interaction (Kanner, 1943).

There were several reasons for this extension. Because of the
extent of impaired social relations characterizing this developmental
disorder, autism provided a stringent test of social interaction training procedures and materials. Prior studies had shown that under
controlled conditions, tactics similar to those used with less handicapped and socially withdrawn children could increase specific social
skills and overall interaction in autistic children (e.g., Ragland, Kerr, &
Strain, 1978; Romanczyk, Diament, Goren, Trunell, & Harris, 1975;
Strain, Kerr, & Ragland, 1979). Yet questions remained regarding the
effectiveness of these procedures in changing teacher and child behavior under naturalistic conditions, that is, actual classrooms. Too,
autistic and other severely handicapped students have often been
served in developmentally segregated settings with few or no opportunities to interact with nonhandicapped children. An intervention
package targeting students with autism also had to create opportunities for teaching social skills and to provide ongoing situations for
social *integration.*

Drawing upon SCIP and the first 2 years of development activities, the SIAC package was designed to include both the basic, direct
instructional procedures and the target social behaviors (sharing,
assisting, verbally organizing play) from SCIPPY. The multimedia
training format was also retained. The teacher's manual included

expanded sections on the development and organization of in-school integration activities, procedures for working with regular education personnel, and revised materials for selecting and training nonhandicapped student helpers (general information about autism and specific training scripts). The teacher-training workshop was increased from 3 to 4 hours and the child-child interaction training sessions 10 to 20 minutes, respectively. Finally, the teacher's role shifted from directly instructing the handicapped/withdrawn child during dyadic play sessions to training the nonhandicapped peers to act as "social skills tutors" for autistic children. Most of the instruction and feedback to peers was provided during the integration activities themselves rather than during separate training sessions, thus making this package potentially more efficient with teacher time and effort.

These integration activities are a critical part of *SIAC*, and a major goal of that package was to assist teachers in identifying and creating age-appropriate opportunities for teaching school-aged children with and without handicaps to interact positively with one another. For example, Shores et al. (1987) identified several steps through which a teacher should proceed in order to set up socially integrated activities. First, the teacher must decide *who will participate*. Whereas social integration of children with and without handicaps requires participation of the whole school, social interaction training requires the cooperation of at least one regular education teacher and his or her students.

Once a regular education teacher has indicated a willingness to participate, peers are selected for the integration activities. The regular education teacher recommends peers based on the following criteria:

1. A child who exhibits high rates of interaction
2. A child who is willing to participate
3. A child who has good school attendance and
4. A child who is generally cooperative with teacher requests and directions

After selecting peers, the special and regular education teachers decide *when the social interaction activities will be held*. The sessions last approximately 30 minutes and are conducted at least once a day. It is important that the sessions be scheduled at a time when the peers without handicaps are not involved in academic work. A portion of a lunch period, recess, or study period may be an appropriate time. It is critical that the special and regular education teachers work together to designate a mutually convenient time.

Once daily integrated play sessions have been scheduled, the teacher must determine *where the activities will take place.* Any of a variety of settings may be used, including the classroom, gym, playground, or auditorium. It is important to check on the availability of these areas since they will be used daily.

Finally, the special education teacher will need to *train the non-handicapped peers.* This does not need to be an elaborate training process. The teacher may simply discuss the individual differences between the children with and without handicaps, that is, likes and dislikes, types of handicapping conditions, and so on. In some instances the teachers may want to have the children without handicaps simulate several relevant handicaps—wearing a blindfold to simulate visual impairments, riding a wheelchair or using a walker to simulate physical impairments. Raab, Nordquist, Cunningham, and Bliem (1986) have developed and evaluated a curriculum for teaching nonhandicapped children about handicapping conditions. More intensive preparation of peers would include:

1. Discussing the nature and importance of their role—to help the handicapped child *initiate to them, to respond to these initiations and to help maintain ongoing interaction*
2. Describing and having peers rehearse specific instances of social initiations, responses, and interactions with one another and with the teacher
3. Practicing responses to even the most rudimentary initiation by the autistic student
4. Persisting in their own social bids, because initially many of the peers' initiations and responses may be ignored by the student with autism

This training and practice is accomplished both through didactic instruction and through role-playing between the nonhandicapped students and the teacher(s).

Although the basic instructional tactics remain the same, there are a number of critical differences in the implementation of *SIAC*. Whereas the primary focus of *SCIPPY* was to teach specific, effective social skills, *SIAC* sought not only to teach interaction skills but also to increase opportunities for interaction with nonhandicapped students, that is, social integration as well as social interaction. Second, rather than working with a single handicapped-nonhandicapped child dyad as in *SCIPPY*, the teacher worked with as many as six such dyads at a time in *SIAC*. The dyads were assigned to different stations, such as music or dancing, board games, and puppets, with each station being in a separate area of the room. A third, related difference was that the teacher, having already trained the peers, now circulated among the dyads, alternately observing and giving feedback and "on-the-spot" instruction (modeling, verbal prompts, physical guidance, and praise) to the peers and handicapped students. At the same time the teacher observed and evaluated whether or not instructional goals for that day were being met.

A final difference between *SIAC* and *SCIPPY* was that each day's session was preceded by a brief warm-up involving the teacher and the nonhandicapped students. At this time the teacher reviewed progress in and any problems with the previous day's activities, reinforced the peers for meeting their instructional objectives, and reminded them of their assignments for the current session.

Field testing of *SIAC* was conducted with 17 special education teachers in two metropolitan school districts (McEvoy, Shores, Wehby, Johnson, & Fox, in press). The results indicated that the classroom organizational procedures and peer-teaching tactics successfully increased the autistic children's interactions with nonhandicapped children during the integration activities. Furthermore, students of those teachers who most consistently applied the planning and instructional procedures experienced the greatest gains in social interaction and activity participation. Those teachers who least accurately implemented the procedures produced relatively little gain in interaction or activity participation for their students.

Group Affection Activities

One other approach for promoting interaction that has received increasing attention is *group affection activities*. Initially developed by Twardosz, Nordquist, Simon, and Botkin (1983) to increase the interactions of isolate children, the procedures have also been similarly effective with children with autism (McEvoy et al., 1988) and with mental retardation (Brown, Ragland, & Fox, 1988). These activities efficiently and naturalistically combine the environmental arrangement, teacher- and peer-mediated tactics previously described. Affection activities are conducted during regularly scheduled large- or small-group activities and consist of typical preschool games or songs to which an affection component has been added. For example, during the classes' "Good Morning" group activity the teacher would arrange to have a roughly equal number of children with and without handicaps seated alternately in a circle or semicircle. The popular children's rhyme "Farmer in the Dell" might be one of the activities during this group. However, instead of singing the song's typical lyrics ("the farmer takes a wife" or "the wife chooses a child"), the teacher may adapt the song to have the children sing "the farmer hugs the wife" or "the wife pats the child." Children, with and without handicaps, are encouraged through teacher prompting and praise to do such things as smile, say positive things to each other, or exchange other expressions of affection and positive social behavior. Although group affection activities have been primarily developed for use with young children and have yet to undergo large-scale field testing, experimental studies have shown increases in spontaneous child-child interaction during the affection activities themselves and also during freeplay times occurring later in the day (Brown et al., 1988; McEvoy et al., 1988; McEvoy, Niemeyer, & Fox, 1989; Twardosz et al., 1983).

Summary and Issues

Reviewing research on children's interactions, Hatch (1984) remarked that "teachers seem to recognize the importance of social development but do not quite know what to do about it" (p. 358) and, further, that "if educational practice is to be intentional and deliberate, it must be informed" (p. 359). We agree with such sentiments. SCIPPY, SIAC, group affection activities and other interaction training programs (see Gaylord-Ross & Haring, 1987; Gaylord-Ross, Haring, Breen, & Pitts-Conway, 1984; Walker et al., 1985) provide information and, more importantly, instructional tools with which educators can take effective action. Although much of what we have described comes from research with handicapped children, the same materials and procedures can be used with otherwise normally developing, socially withdrawn children. In fact, these procedures are derived from earlier studies with this type of child (e.g., Allen, Hart, Buell, Harris, & Wolf, 1964; Buell, Stoddard, Harris, & Baer, 1968). Several of our own studies (Fox, Shores, Lindeman, & Strain, 1986; Day et al., 1984; Hendrickson et al., 1981) and those of others (Twardosz et al., 1983) have also applied these social interaction training procedures to withdrawn but otherwise normally developing children. Regular education teachers involved in mainstreaming children with handicaps should find these interaction training procedures and materials help-ful if not necessary (Gunter, Fox, & Brady, 1984) as they cope with the process of integration.

Despite these advances, there is much we still do not know about children's social development. Most research has focused on the initial effects of teaching social behavior. Analyses of how improved social skills and interaction can be made to generalize to other situa-tions and to persist over time have begun in earnest only recently but show promising leads (Brady, Gunter, McEvoy, Fox, & White, 1984; Brady, Shores, McEvoy, Ellis, & Fox, 1987; Fox et al., 1986; Fox et al., 1984; McEvoy et al., 1988).

It also seems timely to re-assess the goals of social interaction training and research. That social skills can be taught and peer inter-action increased has been amply demonstrated, but to what end? Are those children who undergo such instruction at any reduced risk for later adjustment problems? Will social skills training and increased interaction with nonhandicapped students enhance handicapped children's socialization? Should training focus on developing friend-ships between withdrawn/handicapped children and other students as well as increasing their interaction? What are the immediate and long-term benefits (or costs) for nonnhandicapped children who par-ticipate in social interaction training of handicapped students?

Not surprisingly, most studies of social interaction training and field tests of training packages have restricted their evaluations to changes in targeted social skills and interactions. Yet, as we noted at the beginning of this chapter, social interaction has long been consid-ered important not only in its own right but also in terms of the context it provides for the acquisition and refinement of other skills. For example, a number of theorists of differing conceptual perspec-tives have suggested the central role that interaction and social pro-cesses play in moral reasoning and judgment (Abbott, 1981; Bandura & MacDonald, 1963; Hoffman, 1970; Kohlberg, 1964; Lefurgy & Wolo-shin, 1969; Piaget, 1965; Smith & Brett, 1980). Not only is there corre-lational evidence of a link between regular, successful peer interac-tion and the level of moral development in nonhandicapped children (Enright & Sutterfield, 1980), but some research also indicates that certain groups of children with behavioral handicaps, that is, con-duct-disordered/antisocial children and youth, exhibit deficits in moral reasoning (Kauffman, 1989). It would be important both theo-retically and practically to determine if social interaction training produces any positive side effects on participants' moral judgment and reasoning.

Resolution of these and other issues will require innovative and long-term research. However, the availability of systematic, effective social interaction curricula permits us to have deliberate, positive impact on children's social development and to further analyze peer socialization for our own and our children's benefit.

References

Abbott, A. M. (1981). Durkheim's theory of education: A case for mainstreaming. *Peabody Journal of Education, 58,* 235–241.

Allen, K. E., Hart, B., Buell, J., Harris, F. R., & Wolf, M. M. (1964). Effects of social reinforcement on isolate behavior of a nursery school child. *Child Development, 3,* 511–518.

Bandura, A., & MacDonald, F. J. (1963). Influence of social reinforcement and the behavior of models in shaping children's moral judgements. *Journal of Abnormal and Social Psychology, 67,* 274–281.

Brady, M. P., Gunter, P., McEvoy, M. A., Fox, J. J., & White, C. (1984). Generalization of an adolescent's social interaction behavior via multiple peers in a classroom setting. *Journal of the Association for Persons With Severe Handicaps, 9,* 278–286.

Brady, M. P., Shores, R. E., McEvoy, M. A., Ellis, D., & Fox, J. J. (1987). Increasing the social interactions of severely handicapped autistic children. *Journal of Autism and Developmental Disorders, 17,* 375–391.

Brown, W., Fox, J. J., & Brady, M. P. (1987). Effects of spatial density on 3- and 4-year-old children's socially directed behavior during freeplay: An investigation of a setting factor. *Education and Treatment of Children, 10,* 247–258.

Brown, W. H., Ragland, E. U., & Fox, J. J. (1988). Effects of group socialization procedures on the social interactions of preschool children. *Research in Developmental Disabilities, 9,* 359–376.

Browning, R. M. (1980). *Teaching the severely handicapped child.* Boston: Allyn and Bacon.

Buell, J., Stoddard, P., Harris, F. R., & Baer, D. (1968). Collateral social development accompanying reinforcement of outdoor play in a preschool child. *Journal of Applied Behavior Analysis, 1,* 167–173.

Campbell, H. (1896). Morbid shyness. *The British Medical Journal, 2,* 805–807.

Day, R. M., Fox, J. J., Shores, R. E., Lindeman, D. P., & Stowitschek, J. J. (1983). The Social Competence Intervention Project: Developing educational procedures for teaching social interaction skills to handicapped children. *Behavioral Disorders, 8,* 120–127.

Day, R. M., Lindeman, D. P., Powell, T. H., Fox, J. J., Stowitschek, J. J., & Shores, R. E. (1984). Empirically-derived teaching package for socially withdrawn handicapped and nonhandicapped children. *Teacher Education and Special Education, 7,* 46–55.

Day, R. M., Powell, T. H., & Stowitschek, J. J. (1980). *The Social Competence Intervention Package for Preschool Youngsters.* (Available from Dr. Sarah Rule, Department of Special Education, Utah State University, Logan, UT)

Day, R. M., Powell, T. H., Stowitschek, J. J., & Dy-Lin, E. B. (1982). An evaluation of the effects of a social interaction training package on handicapped preschool children. *Education and Training of the Mentally Retarded, 17,* 125–130.

Enright, R. D., & Sutterfield, S. J. (1980). An ecological validation of social cognitive development. *Child Development, 51,* 156–161.

Fox, J. J., Gunter, P., Brady, M. P., Bambara, L. M., Spiegel-McGill, P., & Shores, R. E. (1984). Using multiple peer exemplars to develop generalized social responding of an autistic girl. *Monograph in Behavioral Disorders: Severe Behavior Disorders of Children and Youth, 7,* 17–27.

Fox, J. J., Shores, R. E., Lindeman, D. P., & Strain, P. S. (1986). Maintaining social initiations of withdrawn handicapped and nonhandicapped preschoolers through a response-dependent fading tactic. *Journal of Abnormal Children Psychology, 14,* 387–396.

Gaylord-Ross, R. J., & Haring, T. G. (1987). Social interaction research for adolescents with severe handicaps. *Behavioral Disorders, 12,* 264–275.

Gaylord-Ross, R. J., Haring, T. G., Breen, C., & Pitts-Conway, V. (1984). The training and generalization of social interaction skills with autistic youth. *Journal of Applied Behavior Analysis, 17,* 29–247.

Gunter, P., Fox, J. J., & Brady, M. P. (1984). Social skills training of handicapped children in less restrictive environments: Research implications for classroom teachers. *The Pointer, 29,* 8–11.

Guralnick, M. (1978). Integrated preschools as educational and therapeutic environments: Concepts, design, and analysis. In M. Guralnick (Ed.), *Early intervention and the integration of handicapped children* (pp. 115–145). Baltimore: University Park Press.

Hartup, W. W. (1983). Peer relations. In P. Mussen (Ed.), *Handbook of child psychology* (pp. 361–456). New York: John Wiley & Sons.

Hatch, J. A. (1984). Forms and functions of child-child interaction in classroom settings: A review. *Childhood Education, 60,* 354–360.

Hecimovic, A., Fox, J. J., Shores, R. E., & Strain, P. S. (1985). An analysis of developmentally integrated and segregated free play settings and the generalization of newly-acquired social behaviors of socially withdrawn preschoolers. *Behavioral Assessment, 7,* 367–388.

Hendrickson, J. M., Strain, P. S., Shores, R. E., & Tremblay, A. (1981). Functional effects of peer social initiations on the interactions of behaviorally handicapped children. *Behavior Modification, 6,* 323–353.

Hess, R. D. (1970). Social class and ethnic influences on socialization. In P. Mussen (Ed.), *Carmichael's manual of child psychology* (3rd ed., pp. 457–557). New York: John Wiley & Sons.

Hoffman, M. (1970). Moral development. In P. Mussen (Ed.), *Carmichael's manual of child psychology:* Vol. 2 (3rd ed., pp. 3–72). New York: John Wiley & Sons.

Hops, H. (1982). Social skills training for socially withdrawn/isolate children. In P. Karoly & J. Steffen (Eds.), *Improving children's competence: Advances in child behavior analysis:* Vol. 1 (pp. 39–101). Lexington, MA: D.C. Heath.

Kanner, L. (1943). Autistic disturbances of affective contact. *The Nervous Child, 3,* 221–250.

Kauffman, J. M. (1989). *Characteristics of behavior disorders of children and youth* (4th ed.). Columbus, OH: Charles E. Merrill.

Kohlberg, L. (1964). Development of moral character and moral ideology. In M. L. Hoffman & L. W. Hoffman (Eds.), *Review of child development research:* Vol. 1 (pp. 383–432). New York: Russell Sage Foundation.

Lefurgy, W., & Woloshin, G. (1969). Immediate and long-term effects of experimentally induced social influence in the modification of adolescents' moral judgements. *Journal of Personality and Social Psychology, 12,* 104–110.

McEvoy, M. A., Niemeyer, J., & Fox, J. J. (1989). *Increasing children's social interactions through affection activities and correspondence training.* Unpublished manuscript, George Peabody College for Teachers, Vanderbilt University, Nashville, TN.

McEvoy, M. A., Nordquist, V. M., Twardosz, S., Heckaman, K. A., Wehby, J. H., & Denny, R. K. (1988). Promoting autistic children's peer interactions in an integrated early childhood setting using affection activities. *Journal of Applied Behavior Analysis, 21,* 193–200.

McEvoy, M. A., & Odom, S. L. (1987). Social interaction training for preschool children with behavioral disorders. *Behavioral Disorders, 12,* 242–251.

McEvoy, M. A., Shores, R. E., Wehby, J. H., Johnson, S., & Fox, J. J. (in press). Special education teachers' implementation of procedures to promote social interaction among children in integrated settings. *Education and Training of the Mentally Retarded.*

Mischel, W. (1970). Sex-typing and socialization. In P. Mussen (Ed.), *Carmichael's manual of child psychology:* Vol. 2 (3rd ed., pp. 3–72). New York: John Wiley & Sons.

Odom, S., & DeKlyen, M. (in press). Social withdrawal in childhood. In G. Adams (Ed.), *Behavior disorders: Theories and characteristics.* Englewood Cliffs, NJ: Prentice-Hall.

Piaget, J. (1965). *The moral judgement of the child.* New York: Free Press.

Porter, R., Ramsey, B., Tremblay, A., Iaccobo, M., & Crawley, S. (1978). Social interactions in heterogenous groups of retarded and normally developing children: An observational study. In G. Sackett (Ed.), *Observing behavior: Vol. 1. Theory, applications, and mental retardation* (pp. 311–328). Baltimore: University Park Press.

Quilitch, H., & Risley, T. (1973). The effects of play materials on social play. *Journal of Applied Behavior Analysis, 6,* 573–578.

Raab, M. M., Nordquist, V. M., Cunningham, J. L., & Bliem, C. D. (1986). Promoting peer regard of an autistic child in a mainstreamed preschool using pre-enrollment activities. *Child Study Journal, 16,* 265–284.

Ragland, E. U., Kerr, M. M., & Strain, P. S. (1978). Behavior of withdrawn autistic children: Effects of peer social initiations. *Behavior Modification, 2,* 565–578.

Romanczyk, R., Diament, C., Goren, E., Trunell, G., & Harris, S. (1975). Increasing isolate and social play in severely disturbed children: Intervention and post-intervention effectiveness. *Journal of Autism and Childhood Schizophrenia, 5,* 57–70.

Shores, R. E., McEvoy, M. A., Fox, J. J., Denny, R. K., Heckaman, K., & Wehby, J. H. (1987). *The social integration of severely handicapped children.* Nashville, TN: John F. Kennedy Center for Research on Education and Human Development, George Peabody College, Vanderbilt University.

Smith, J. C., & Brett, K. S. (1980). Moral development and social interaction: Implication for education. *Humanist Educator, 19,* 3–9.

Speigel-McGill, P., Bambara, L. M., Shores, R. E., & Fox, J. J. (1984). The effects of proximity on socially oriented behaviors of severely multiply handicapped children. *Education and Treatment of Children, 7,* 365–378.

Stowitschek, J. J., & Powell, T. H. (1981). Materials for teaching social skills to handicapped children: An analytic review. *Journal of Special Education Technology, 4,* 40–49.

Strain, P. S., Cooke, T. P., & Apolloni, T. (1976). *Teaching exceptional children: Assessing and modifying social behavior.* New York: Academic Press.

Strain, P. S., & Fox, J. J. (1981). Peers as behavior change agents for isolate classmates. In A. E. Kazdin & B. B. Lahey (Eds.), *Advances in child clinical psychology* (pp. 167–198). New York: Plenum Press.

Strain, P. S., Kerr, M. M., & Ragland, E. U. (1979). Effects of peer-mediated initiations and prompting reinforcement procedures on the social behavior of autistic children. *Journal of Autism and Developmental Disorders, 2,* 41–45.

Tremblay, A., Strain, P. S., Hendrickson, J. M., & Shores, R. E. (1981). Social interactions of normally developing preschool children: Using normative data for subject and target behavior selection. *Behavior Modification, 5,* 237–253.

Twardosz, S. L., Nordquist, V. M., Simon, R., & Botkin, D. (1983). The effect of group affection activities on the interaction of socially isolate children. *Analysis and Intervention in Developmental Disabilities, 3,* 311–338.

Walker, H. M., McConnell, S., Holmes, D., Todis, B., Walker, J., & Golden, N. (1985). *The Walker social skills curriculum: The ACCEPTS program.* Austin, TX: Pro-Ed.

Widerstrom, A. (1983). How important is play for handicapped children. *Childhood Education, 60,* 39–49.

CHAPTER FOURTEEN

Teaching Peace and Conflict Resolution

ROBERT E. VALETT

How can people learn to resolve their conflicts peacefully? How probable is it that humankind will destroy itself through nuclear confrontation or accident? How can diverse cultures learn to live together in mutually productive relationships? What are the essential components of effective peace and nuclear age education for citizens of the global community? These are some of the crucial questions of increasing concern to parents and educators in their attempts to help children learn how to cope with the emerging problems of the 21st century. The study of these questions and related issues is now being organized into a variety of peace and nuclear age curricula.

Although peace and nuclear education curricula are quite diverse, most emphasize the meaningful involvement of citizens in the peacemaking process. Peace is generally presented as a dynamic state of human tranquility and freedom from catastrophic disturbance, such as war with self and others, which is created by love and law with justice for all. Peace education begins with self-awareness and understanding and then proceeds to significant others in the family and global community.

Using a variety of materials with opposing and diverse viewpoints, students are encouraged to develop constructive critical-thinking skills such as clarifying goals, identifying problems, judging alternatives, and evaluating possible solutions to personal, social, and global conflict. Most peace and nuclear education programs also teach the importance of establishing good-will, empathy, fair treatment, and mutually beneficial projects (economic, cultural, scientific, etc.) with those who are perceived as possible adversaries.

The noted historian H. G. Wells (1944) stated that "human history becomes more and more a race between education and catastrophe" (p. 11). Wells called for educational institutions to teach a common conception of human history and destiny in order to develop universal peace and law—or humankind would be destroyed by the increasing power of modern weapons.

The Need for Peace Education

The need for peace education is increasingly apparent. The California Commission on Crime Control and Violence Prevention (1983) reported that the United States is now the most violent among all western industrialized democracies because certain aspects of our culture encourage violence. For example, research by Eron, Huesmann, Brice, Fischer, and Mermelstein (1983) indicates that from the ages of 5 to 18, children see approximately 20,000 murders and over 100,000 acts of violence on television. The commission concluded that violent behavior is learned and that we must begin to reduce the numerous models of violence in our society and teach alternative ways of solving personal and social problems.

Recently columnists such as Richard Reeves (1989) have questioned the sanity of America and have called for concerted action in dealing with crime and violence throughout the country. It is evident that we urgently need to improve our personal and social mores and ethical behavior; of course, this requires that somehow we learn to cope with our frustrations by nonviolent alternatives and peaceful conflict resolution strategies. One model for reducing violence has been developed by the Society for Prevention of Violence; it consists of a social skills training curricula for use in kindergarten through eighth grade with supplemental materials for parent education (Begun, 1989).

Considerable evidence exists that aggressive and destructive behavior can be changed through education. Studies have shown that we are strongly predisposed to violence under territorial pressure or economic scarcity. Wilson (1978) concluded that most wars have been the result of irrational ethnocentrism that failed to solve the underlying problems. It is clear that human aggression can be redirected through appropriate educational and cultural processes that emphasize rational problem-solving strategies. Wilson agrees with other scientists and educators who believe that peace can best be established through the creation of cross-cultural ties and mutually beneficial relationships.

Research has also provided direction for educational programs. Bandura (1963) and others have demonstrated that young children imitate both aggressive and nonaggressive models and have shown that aggressive responses to frustrating situations can be significantly reduced with positive models and training. Kreidler (1984) has discussed how aggression is learned through example, reward, and the perception of aggressors as successful people; and he has presented lessons and strategies for teaching peace and conflict resolution skills in the classroom. Schulman and Mekler (1985) have developed practical guidelines to teach such skills as fairness, love, empathy, cooperation, and constructive problem solving that will help to develop peace between people; for example, a series of lessons on fostering empathy includes activities in role-playing, self-control training, and guided imagery, whereby the child learns to identify with others and understand their feelings. In short, substantial evidence and resource material support the feasibility of peace education programs in home, school, and community situations.

In order to make rational decisions, an educated and politically involved citizenry is essential in a democratic system of government. Public ignorance and apathy are the primary obstacles to be overcome through education programs that strive to examine objectively the major peace and conflict issues confronting us. In order to create a more peaceful world we must learn to discern fact from fiction and truth from propaganda. This requires a careful study of the historical record and research on nuclear issues; it also demands that we teach students to analyze all of the available information critically.

Elementary students gradually acquire these skills from lessons that are appropriately designed on developmental age levels. Young pupils usually begin with a study of local neighborhood and community problems that are gradually extended to national and international issues on the upper elementary and secondary levels. A common example on the first-grade level is for pupils to study environmental concerns, such as litter and waste disposal, in their own classroom and school. Ultimately the critical examination of peace and nuclear age facts and issues should produce informed citizens capable of understanding and judging vital current affairs affecting their lives, such as regional-national-planetary pollution, atmospheric ozone depletion, nuclear waste disposal, and global famine; relevant education should also include the objective study of selected programs and cooperative ventures to prevent or minimize such disasters.

In addition to teaching students to evaluate information critically, peace education needs to consider the significance of human values and beliefs—such as the ideals of justice, freedom, love, and brotherhood—that have motivated people everywhere. The origin of prejudice, stereotyping, indoctrination, and bias must also be carefully examined. Students also need to learn peaceful conflict resolution strategies, including methods for reducing tension and for resolving interpersonal disputes. Eventually effective peace education must help humankind to develop an awareness and appreciation of the fact that we are all dependent upon our mutually cooperative ventures.

In most curricula these goals are emphasized in unit lessons on global education, peacemaking strategies, and conflict resolution skills like compromise, negotiation, and cooperative learning activities. One outstanding example is the use of varied active learning activities in the conflict managers program at the William De Avila Elementary School described by Graves (1988); through participation in role-playing and training in communication and problem-solving skills, pupils learn to become effective peer conflict managers, which reduces violence in school and also generalizes to home and family situations.

Public Awareness

Over the past 10 years the public has become increasingly aware of the need for peace and nuclear education. Numerous reports of children's nuclear anxieties, such as those by Beardslee and Mack (1982), Richter (1987), and Van Hoorn and French (1988), have appeared in the literature and popular press. Less well known, but equally important, are the results of studies of formal peace education programs in a variety of educational settings.

Children's nuclear fears and concerns are expressed through comments, stories, art work, nightmares, and formal polls. A summary of comments by different age groups, and their educational implications, has been presented by Valett (1983). For example, one child said, "When adults worry about nuclear war, it makes you feel scared." A young boy commented that he wanted to study the nuclear threat "because when we all get blown up, I'll know why it happened." An older child mentioned that "I think it is more terrifying *not* to talk about nuclear war—being left alone to deal with it is much more frightening." Regarding the need for peace education, an astute adolescent said, "What I've learned is that those who are uninformed about nuclear issues and unconcerned about the debate are more dangerous than the weapons themselves" (p. 6).

Most adults are unaware of the depth of children's concerns about the threat of nuclear war. However, recent reports in the popular media have been increasingly informative. Yudkin (1984) reviewed studies and examples of children's anxieties and discussed how parents and families might help them cope through such strategies as reassuring them by discussing their concerns and sharing what is being done to prevent nuclear destruction. For example, silence and avoidance of the issue of nuclear war tend to intensify children's despair and lead them to be suspicious of adults. Very young children need to be reassured and told that adults do care and are working to prevent nuclear destruction. Adolescents find the most reassurance in being told that parents also feel afraid, although not helpless. Another approach is to get children involved in projects such as corresponding with pen pals in the Soviet Union and other countries.

Children are also expressing their concerns on television programs, letters to the editor, school essays, and opinion polls. For example, the 1985 *Weekly Reader* "Goals for Our President" national survey of elementary pupils reported 40% believed that President Reagan's main task should be reducing the threat of nuclear war.

Surveys by Mack (1984) and others have shown that as many as 80% of adolescents are cynical and pessimistic regarding their chances of surviving a nuclear war, which they feel will occur in their lifetime. Mack suggested that educators begin to prepare reliable educational materials and programs that present knowledge about nuclear issues and enable the individual to distinguish "the threat which emanates from outside ourselves and the other danger which is our own continuing creation from within ourselves" (p. 268).

Adult surveys are also enlightening. Klineberg (1984) discussed the educational implications of a Louis Harris poll finding that 73% of the public are in favor of banning the production, storage, and use of nuclear weapons, and 86% want the United States and the U.S.S.R. to negotiate a nuclear arms reduction agreement; proposals made to realize these goals included creating educational programs in the schools that would emphasize conflict resolution; the effects of deterence, ignorance, and dehumanization of the enemy; and the search for superordinate international goals and mutually beneficial endeavors. In an Associated Press-NBC poll (1982) 84% of the adult respondents said that children should be taught in school the bad effects of nuclear war beginning in the elementary grades. Apparently adults feel that educational programs should provide factual information and knowledge about nuclear war, what is being done to prevent it, and how both children and adults may peacefully resolve interpersonal conflicts.

Educational Responses

Educators have gradually responded to public concerns. The National Educational Association (1984) passed a resolution urging its affiliates to develop age-appropriate learning materials that would show the effects of nuclear weapons and demonstrate strategies to achieve peace. The 1985 National Parent Teachers Association convention adopted a resolution on nuclear education for adults to enable parents and teachers to address more effectively children's fears concerning perceived nuclear dangers.

In a report to the California State Legislature on "Nuclear Age Education," the California State Department of Education (1986) found that 63% of public organizations and 87% of school district offices surveyed believed that the public schools should teach a planned nuclear age education program. The California State Department of Education has made a series of recommendations to the legislature based on their extensive survey. These recommendations call for the development of age-appropriate instructional materials that include critical thinking about nuclear age issues, conflict resolution strategies, and understanding decision-making processes in the modern world.

Numerous kinds of peace and nuclear education programs have been developed. These include private and public school curricula from preschool through graduate school. In addition, many community organizations (such as churches, parent-teacher groups, the League of Women Voters, and Beyond War) are experimenting with informal education projects. For instance, some community organizations have sponsored "visions of peace" contests that encourage children to create peace posters, exhibits, and essays. Other groups are cooperating in foreign exchanges of students and citizens. New interdisciplinary national organizations, such as the Nuclear Age Peace Foundation, promote and fund a wide variety of peace education programs and publications.

School boards in Cambridge, Massachusetts, and Milwaukee, Wisconsin, were among the first to start peace education programs. New York City, San Francisco, Berkeley, and Los Angeles were other relatively early pioneers in this field. Since then, many school districts have begun new programs or appointed community task forces to provide suitable guidelines to boards of education. For example, the Fresno Unified School District Board of Education (1986) appointed a 24-member Peace and Nuclear Age Education Committee consisting of citizens and curriculum specialists. After considerable deliberation, the committee recommended that a curriculum be developed to cover five major areas:

1. *Preservation of the Earth's Resources.* The intelligent use of resources to conserve them for future generations. The understanding and awareness of human beings' effects on the environment and the consequences of those decisions. The study of the causes and effects of world population problems. An understanding of the benefits derived from an exchange of ideas regarding priorities, technology, and distribution of resources.
2. *Global Perspectives in Education.* Global awareness, facts, and comparisons. Global connectedness and interdependence including trade relations, resources, religion, social, political, and economic interrelations between nations.
3. *Conflict Resolution Skills.* Personal- to global-level skills. Conflict definition, understanding causes, gathering information, examining facts and feelings, generating and choosing solutions, utilizing critical-thinking skills.
4. *Peacemaking Strategies.* Study of and participation in strategies resulting in a just and peaceful world, including cultural exchanges and networking; use of nonviolence and pacifism; religion; respect and empathy for human rights; economic, environmental, and scientific cooperation; force and deterrence; historical review of peacemakers.
5. *Understanding Nuclear Issues.* The awareness of nuclear age problems, including the development and control of nuclear power and weapons. The possible causes, prevention of, and alternatives to nuclear war. The physical and political effects of nuclear weapons, electrical power production, economics, and medical and industrial usage.

It is important to note that in accord with committee recommendations, the Fresno program consists of a curriculum guide for voluntary use by interested teachers and includes a strong staff development program, evaluations, and a balanced teaching effort that presents differing points of view on each topic. Also, the topics are to be integrated into existing K–12 curricula rather than introduced as new or separate courses. However, the Fresno program, like others throughout the country, has not been without controversy.

Community Responses

When the Fresno curriculum staff compiled 81 elementary lessons and 38 secondary-level lessons received from interested and experienced teachers into a first-draft teacher's resource guide for the Peace and Nuclear Age Curriculum, opposition forces in the community protested. The major complaints were that the newly proposed curriculum was not needed and would detract from teaching "basic skills"; the original advisory committee was being dominated by liberal "extremist groups"; and many of the lessons were inappropriate for specified grade levels or unbalanced in content. The board of education then reconstituted the advisory committee to include requested representation from the Chamber of Commerce, Concerned Women for America, the Valley Business Center, two representatives from Save American Values in Education, and two student representatives from district high schools. The new committee then began a public review and revision of all lesson materials with open discussion and input that actually became a model of grass-roots democracy in action with both majority and minority reports presented to the school board for final curriculum adoption.

Program Effectiveness

The effectiveness of peace education programs can be determined by research that measures the extent to which the program objectives have been accomplished. Reliable studies usually involve both control and experimental groups and attempt to determine the effects of specific peace education curricula on pupil attitudes, knowledge, and behavior. Examples of studies done on several different student populations are illustrative of current efforts in this regard.

Christie (1986) reported on the use of *Choices*, an educational unit developed by the National Education Association and the Union of Concerned Scientists (1986), with 1,518 sixth-, seventh-, and eighth-grade students. For several years now, *Choices* has been widely used with middle and junior high school students throughout the country. It has been the center of some controversy, however, with critics questioning its objectivity. This study attempted to focus on what effects this curriculum, presented in a special 7-month unit, would have on students' fears about nuclear war. The results indicated that pupils in the experimental peace education classes experienced a significant decline in their fears as a result of acquiring a sense of "empowerment" from their study of nuclear war and conflict resolution.

A similar study with 84 ninth-grade students was done by Zolik and Nair (1987). They used *Choices* and other materials in a nuclear education program conducted over a 6-week period. Findings suggested that adolescents who reported being afraid of nuclear war were not more generally anxious than children who did not report such fears. A result of discussing nuclear war and related issues was that students' fear became based on realistic factors and concerns; at the same time, pupils began to feel that something could be done to decrease the threat of war. Students were able to experience increased efficacy and empowerment, feeling they could help prevent nuclear war.

A general review of peace and conflict resolution programs in the public schools by Roderick (1987/1988) reported an increasing emphasis on teaching pupils negotiation skills. For example, all students in Chicago's 67 public high schools study dispute resolution in social studies classes; in the 6-week unit students learn through role-playing, discussion, and work sheets to deal with interpersonal and global problems. Evaluations conducted by the Chicago Board of Education's testing unit indicate that as a result of the program, student attitudes about how to cope with conflict have changed dramatically in positive ways.

In New York City's Community District 15, more than 75 elementary school teachers and thousands of their pupils are involved in the Model Peace Education Program, which includes units on cooperative learning, dealing appropriately with anger, dispute resolution techniques, preventing prejudice, peacemakers, and cultural exchange programs with the Soviet Union and other countries. Roderick states that over 300 schools around the country have now established some form of student mediation program. These programs have helped solve large numbers of disputes, dramatically reduced dropouts, and successfully provided students with alternatives to fighting and violence.

On the college level, Nelson, Slem, and Perner (1986) conducted a controlled study on the effects of classroom instruction about the nuclear arms race with 525 undergraduate psychology and physical science students. Attitudes about specific nuclear weapons issues were assessed before and after instruction. Students in experimental classes became significantly more favorable toward arms control, less favorable toward strategic defense, more positive in their perception of Soviet arms control intentions, less concerned about nuclear superiority, and slightly more concerned about nuclear war.

Studies have also been made of the effectiveness of peace education programs in foreign countries. For example, Japan has been making systematic attempts to teach peace education since shortly after World War II. The curricula used have continued to change and develop with time and experience. Hirao (1987) reports that the program promoted by the Hiroshima Institute for Peace Education is now the one most widely used. This extensive program teaches students about the inhumanities and agonies of warfare and how to recognize the causes of war through scientific analysis; it also outlines activities to inspire pupils to practice antiwar behavior. Repeated surveys show that students are becoming increasingly educated in these respects. However, although the Japanese have increased their knowledge and awareness of nuclear issues, they remain largely apathetic owing to feelings of helplessness. Hirao argues that peace education must be strengthened by including prescriptions for building a better future and by motivating students to become emotionally committed to positive participation in their own society as well as to global collaboration.

It is apparent that continued studies of peace education programs will help improve the curricula, methods, and materials used. However, even short-term instruction on nuclear issues can have a significant impact on students' attitudes and knowledge. Future research on newly developed programs carried out over an extensive period of time on different grade levels will be most informative.

Instructional Resources and Applications

The rapid development of numerous instructional materials for peace and nuclear education is bound to stimulate further innovative research on their use and effectiveness. Many organizations produce curriculum materials and programs. One outstanding example is the *Peace Education Resources* catalogue published by the American Friends Service Committee (1988).

The Consortium on Peace Research, Education and Development (1985) is the oldest international organization in the field and is comprised of institutions and educators who constantly produce and update reference materials. A number of universities, such as the University of Michigan, have developed special peace and conflict studies institutes or media centers that produce resource materials and directories. Some notable organizations that have focused on developing public school peace and nuclear education curriculum materials are the National Education Association, Educators for Social Responsibility, and the Union of Concerned Scientists. Educators for Social Responsibility (1984) has published several teaching guides widely used in grades K–12; they also coordinate regional and national curriculum development workshops and in-service training for teachers at all grade levels. However, most teachers and school districts are experimenting with many different materials. For instance, Marquand (1986) reported a survey showing that more than 70 kinds of peace curricula were in use at schools in the San Francisco Bay Area alone.

The School Initiatives Program developed by the Community Board Program, Inc. in San Francisco consists of workshops for teachers, videotapes, and curriculum guides dealing with conflict resolution on all levels. For example, the elementary school conflict manager program includes a manual for training students to become conflict managers by participating in six training sessions. Students are taught to understand the nature of conflicts and how they can be managed and resolved through role-playing, case discussion, and model practice activities. Detailed in-service training manuals and programs are also available for elementary school faculty. Schools using this conflict manager program report significant reductions in violent behavior and discipline problems. This curriculum also notes that conflicts over values are the hardest to deal with and emphasizes the importance of effective communication in conflict resolution.

One of the most widely used elementary school programs is Creative Conflict Solving for Kids by Fran Schmidt and Alice Friedman (1983). The program consists of a folder of individual lesson sheets with attractive cartoon figures that are highly appealing to children. Lessons include cooperative learning activities for such topics as personal conflicts, emotions, dealing with feelings and frustrations, values, fighting fair, communication skills, and strategies for resolving conflicts. The materials in this program are easily reproduced for individual pupil use.

Students on all age levels are also studying the effects of cooperative business ventures with other societies. Recently Bazhenov (1989) reported on the results of joint business ventures between the Soviet Union and other countries. The United States has long been involved in assisting the Soviet Union in various industrial development projects. But it has been only since Mikhail Gorbachev established the policy of perestroika that restructuring of the economic system has stimulated many mutually cooperative business arrangements. There are now more than 105 joint ventures under way. Exchanges between chambers of commerce and research groups have been most productive. The Western Siberian Soviet-American consortium involves Combustion Engineering and McDermott International of the United States and Mitsubishi and Mitsui of Japan. Soviet officials predict that the super consortium is likely to become the biggest U.S.-U.S.S.R. joint venture. Other future possibilities include cooperative medical, space, and scientific projects that will undoubtedly lead to extended communications and understanding.

Citizen diplomacy is another example of successful peace education; a book by Warner and Shuman (1987) details a number of successful approaches undertaken by nine individuals including physician Bernard Lown, industrialist Armand Hammer, and author Norman Cousins and explains how other interested citizens can join in similar projects. International friendship has long been the purpose of pen pals; in Moscow, School No. 5, at 6 Kutuzovsky Prospekt, is one of many Soviet schools exchanging letters with American students on a regular basis. Over the last few years numerous Soviet and American groups and individuals have exchanged visits to further communications. Traditional student exchanges have now been superseded by special-interest groups of all kinds with widespread media coverage. Videotaped reports and direct telecommunications between Soviet and American schools have improved communications significantly.

Some notable examples are the early trips of Samantha Smith and the more recent ESR-Soviet Institute (1988) at Hampshire College, which involved 18 Soviet and 23 American teachers in developing a curriculum on "teaching for new ways of thinking." In 1989 the Soviet Academy of Pedagogical Sciences and Educators for Social Responsibility co-sponsored "Teaching Critical Thinking: A U.S.-Soviet Institute" in Leningrad. Other organizations, such as the Center for U.S.-U.S.S.R. Initiatives, offered 31 special citizen diplomacy travel experiences to the Soviet Union in 1989 and continue to expand their program.

The National Education Association has promoted multicultural/global education as a way of helping every student perceive the cultural diversity of U.S. citizenry so that children of many races may develop pride in their own cultural legacy, awaken to the ideas embodied in the cultures of their neighbors, and develop an appreciation of the common humanity shared by all people. Kinghorn and Shaw (1986) have written a working manual for global education under the auspices of the Charles E. Kettering Foundation. Typical global education topics include ecology, pollution, distribution of resources, cultural values and aspiration, world population, intercultural projects and transnational communication, global economic and multinational business development, human rights, international law, and multicultural conflict resolution strategies.

Good resources for effective peace education must also include a positive and supportive instructional environment. Critical environmental factors include recognition of the importance of peace and conflict studies as well as encouragement and assistance from school boards, administrators, parents, and concerned citizens. Only with such support can teachers begin to teach the issues involved effectively.

Within the classroom the teacher's knowledge, positive attitude, and instructional methods help create the kind of interpersonal environment whereby peace education is learned and practiced. For example, research by Johnson and Johnson (1986) on the use of cooperative learning strategies in the schools has shown that such methods tend to improve personal and social abilities, reduce interpersonal conflicts, and improve academic performance. Such an instructional environment becomes a model laboratory for students to practice basic peace and conflict resolution skills, which, it is hoped, they can then generalize to their neighborhood and the global community.

Moral and Ethical Implications

President George Bush hopes to be known as the "education president" who helped to create a kinder and gentler America. With such renewed commitment to moral and ethical values, the American education system is challenged to develop more constructive instructional programs. However, a truly effective moral education must move beyond parochial concerns and also teach students to understand and care for the global community of which we are a part. These changes will require a major shift in the thinking of educators, parents, and policymakers.

In his later years, Albert Einstein (1950) wrote that the unleashed power of the atom changed everything except our ways of thinking and we thus drift toward unparalleled catastrophe (pp. 204–206). Einstein proposed that to avoid such catastrophe schools begin to give priority to developing independent thinking and judgment in their pupils, a program that would include the critical study of global and international issues. Undoubtedly the time has come for students on all levels to be taught critical-thinking skills and moral and ethical values as an intrinsic part of their education. It is hoped that through developing their critical-thinking faculties, children will become more able to examine the moral and ethical effects of their own behavior as well as that of others.

Essentially, we need to teach students to understand and manage their own behavior better. Without ethical and moral guidelines, self-evaluation and social responsibility are demeaned. Without a multi-cultural global orientation, our perception of the real world is distorted and our sense of affiliation with all humankind is stunted. But when confrontation and destructive encounters are replaced with negotiated interests and mutually beneficial cooperative ventures, the seeds of a just and meaningful peace have been well planted.

We must also educate our children to treat themselves and others with good intentions, without harm, and in fair and just ways. And as Moyer (1985) has stated, we need to learn to confront the enemy within our own minds that may lead us to personal or collective destruction. Accordingly, this kind of moral and ethical education invariably results in exploring and refining affective-emotional commitments and human values. Newly emerging values, ideas, and feelings gradually begin to appear in the interpersonal behavior of children and are commonly observed in their academic products: stories, poems, essays, music, and dramatic productions. A notable example is found in the highly emotional stories, writings, and drawings of young immigrants who vividly attempt to describe their flight from oppression and their visions of new opportunities and challenges awaiting them. One of the most expressive forms of ethical feelings and aspirations is poetry, which is an intrinsic part of all effective peace education programs. In this respect we need to learn that from a planetary perspective we are one.

As we become constructively critical citizens of our global community, we must teach people to acquire the essential knowledge and skills necessary to appreciate and preserve our uniquely beautiful planet. In this sense, peace education is an essential component of any contemporary moral or ethical system for guiding human behavior

References

American Friends Service Committee. (1988). *Peace education resources.* Philadelphia, PA: Author.

Associated Press-NBC Poll. (1982, May 17). 75% see nuclear arms are leading to war. *Fresno Bee,* p. B3.

Bandura, A. (1963). The role of imitation in personality development. *Young Children, 18* (3), 207–215.

Bazhenov, G. (1989, January). First results of joint ventures. *Soviet Life,* pp. 22–23.

Beardslee, W., & Mack, J. (1982). The impacts on children and adolescents of nuclear developments. In *Psychosocial Aspects of Nuclear Developments* (pp. 64–93). Washington, DC: American Psychiatric Association.

Begun, S. (1989). Why children worry. *Society for Prevention of Violence Newsletter, 13* (2), 1.

California State Department of Education. (1986). *Nuclear age education* (AB 3848). Sacramento: Author.

Christie, D. (1986). *The psychological impact of an educational unit about conflict and nuclear war on adolescents.* Final report, Ohio Department of Mental Health (Grant No. OSURF718265). Columbus: Ohio State University, Department of Psychology.

California Commission on Crime Control and Violence Prevention. (1983). *Ounces of prevention: Teaching an understanding of the causes of violence.* Sacramento: Author.

Consortium on Peace Research, Education and Development. (1985). *Membership resources list.* Urbana, IL: Author.

Educators for Social Responsibility. (1984). *Perspectives.* 23 Garden Street, Cambridge, MA 02138.

ESR. (1988). Learning together—an ESR-Soviet institute. *Forum, 7* (1), 1–2.

Einstein, A. (1950). *Out of my later years.* New York: Philosophical Library.

Eron, L., Huesmann, L., Brice, P., Fischer, P., & Mermelstein, R. (1983). Age trends in the development of aggression, sex typing and related television habits. *Developmental Psychology, 19,* 71–77.

Fresno Unified School District Board of Education Minutes. (1986, March 20). *Peace and Nuclear Education Committee Recommendation.* Fresno Unified School District, Fresno, CA.

Graves, N. (1988). Cooperation in education. *International Association for the Study of Cooperation in Education, 9* (5), 15–17.

Hirao, K. (1987). Peace education: A search for strategy. *Peace and Change, 12* (3/4), 59–67.

Johnson, D., & Johnson, R. (1986). *Circles of learning: Cooperation in the classroom.* Edina, MN: Interaction Books.

Kinghorn, J., & Shaw, W. (1986). *The handbook for global education.* Dayton, OH: Charles E. Kettering Foundation.

Klineberg, O. (1984). Public opinion and nuclear war. *American Psychologist,* *39* (11), 1245–1253.

Kreidler, W. (1984). *Creative conflict resolution.* Glenview, IL: Scott, Foresman.

Mack, J. (1984). Resistance to knowing in the nuclear age. *Harvard Education Review, 54* (3), 260–269.

Marquand, R. (1986, January 31). More courses on nuclear issues. *The Christian Science Monitor,* p. B6.

Moyer, R. (1985, January). The enemy within. *Psychology Today,* pp. 30–37.

National Education Association (1984). *Today's Education* (Annual Resolution H-28). Washington, DC: Author.

Nelson, L., Slem, C., & Perner, L. (1986, July 2). *Effects of classroom instruction about the nuclear arms race.* Paper presented at the Ninth Annual Meeting of the International Society of Political Psychology, Amsterdam, The Netherlands.

Nuclear Age Peace Foundation, 1187 Coast Village Road, Suite 123, Santa Barbara, CA 93108.

Reeves, R. (1989, January 16). Is America going crazy? *Fresno Bee,* p. B11.

Richter, H. (1987, August/September). Dealing with nuclear anxiety in children. *Peace Magazine,* pp. 7–8.

Roderick, T. (1987/1988, December/January). Johnny can learn to negotiate. *Educational Leadership,* pp. 87–90.

Schmidt, F., & Friedman, A. (1983). *Creative conflict solving for kids.* Miami Beach, FL: Grace Contrino Abrams Peace Education Foundation.

Schulman, M., & Mekler, E. (1985). *Bringing up a moral child.* Reading, MA: Addison-Wesley.

The Community Board Program, Inc. (1987). *Conflict resolution: A secondary school curriculum.* San Francisco: Community Boards.

Twain, M. (1962). The damned human race. In *Letters from the earth* (pp. 166–184). New York: Harper and Row.

Union of Concerned Scientists. (1983). *Choices: A unit on conflict and nuclear war.* Washington, DC: National Education Association.

Van Hoorn, J., & French, P. (1988). Different age groups' similar outlook on nuclear war. *American Psychologist, 43* (9), 746–747.

Valett, R. (1983). *100+ peace strategies for conflict resolution and the prevention of nuclear war.* Fresno, CA: Panorama West.

Warner, G., & Shuman, M. (1987). *Citizen diplomats.* New York: Continuum.

Wells, H. G. (1944). *CruxAnsata.* London: Agora.

Wilson, E. (1978). *On human nature.* Cambridge, MA: Harvard University Press.

Yudkin, M. (1984, April). When kids think the unthinkable. *Psychology Today,* pp. 18–24.

Zolik, E., & Nair, D. (1987, May 30). *Evaluation of a nuclear war psychoeducational program for adolescents.* Paper presented at the International Physicians for the Prevention of Nuclear War Conference, Moscow.

PART V

Epilogue

CHAPTER FIFTEEN

Synthesis and Evaluation in Moral and Character Education

JACQUES S. BENNINGA

PHILOSOPHY and psychology. These two fields provide the basis for much of what has been discussed in this book and, indeed, for the whole of moral and character education in the 20th century. The interaction of these two disciplines is nowhere better exemplified than in the life of the philosopher John Dewey, recognized as the father of progressive education in the United States. Dewey was, in fact, simultaneously chairman of the philosophy, psychology, and pedagogy department at the University of Chicago at the end of the 19th century. It was because of this administrative opportunity that the philosopher Dewey first wrote about education, thereby dramatically affecting teaching practices in the century to come. Just so, many of the educators contributing to this book rely on examples from philosophy and psychology to justify their various positions.

For much of the past 50 years, philosophy has directed educational practice, vacillating regularly between progressive and traditional approaches (Ravitch, 1985). This trend is clearly reflected in the first three sections of this book. The progressives, then and now, speak of "teaching the whole child" and "making the school program fit the needs of the child." They advocate learning through experience, cooperative planning, and theme-oriented instruction (known as the integrated curriculum). They reject traditional educational approaches for their reliance on externally imposed, authoritarian methods and argue instead for a curriculum focused on issues of social responsibility, emanating from the relevant problems of class-room and school life (Tanner & Tanner, 1975).

Thus the chapters in Part II of this book describe programs in which children are given the opportunity to address social problems arising as part of their daily lives through such classroom activities as working cooperatively on academic tasks, publicly discussing personal problems affecting the group, and participating in creating classroom rules and procedures. They are also involved in helping set schoolwide procedures through an active student council, with their teachers modeling the related problem-solving processes they wish their students to emulate.

The traditional approach to moral or character education, on the other hand, has its roots in the philosophical rationales commonly known as perennialism and essentialism. In contrast to progressive practices, practices that spring from these philosophical positions call for education to pursue the perennial truths found in the great works of our heritage and in the fundamental academic disciplines. As Robert Maynard Hutchins stated, "The ideal education is not an *ad hoc* education, not an education directed to immediate needs. . . . It is an education calculated to develop the mind" (Tanner & Tanner, 1975, p. 68). These educators see children's minds as containers to be filled and stretched to the utmost of each mind's capacity with a combination of well-developed curricular offerings. To them, the elementary school years are the time to develop the skills and habits necessary for future learning and participation in life. Because young children do not really know what they want, reason advocates of this position, they should be strongly encouraged to participate in and conform to activities and standards that will serve them well in the future.

The chapters in Part III address these conceptual issues, describing classrooms and schools in which central values, emphasizing good academic and social conduct, are defined for children by adults. Consequently the schools reflect community values and offer incentives for attendance, academic achievement, citizenship, and successful participation in curricular and co-curricular activities. In these classrooms and schools, teachers make their positions on values evident to both students and parents and provide good role models for their students by adhering to the standards and policies established by the school as reflected in community values.

Thus the first approach contends that children develop good moral *attitudes* by participating in the processes of shared classroom/school decision making and group problem solving, whereas the second argues that children develop good moral *habits* by participating in more structured, preplanned activities. The first approach holds that the motivation for this attitude enhancement must come from inside the student, the second that the motivation must be external to the student.

Psychology and the Contribution of Piaget

In the early 1960s a dramatic new element was brought to this debate between competing philosophies. Psychology as applied to education had come of age. Jean Piaget, who for more than 30 years had been researching and writing about the development over time of children's thought processes, was finally introduced to his American audience. His impact on the debate has been most significant in the realm of moral and character development.

Although Piaget did not write specifically about educational methodology, he did describe children's thinking about a range of experiences and issues as qualitatively different from that of adults. His well-known conservation and classification experiments clearly demonstrate this fact, and his observations receive regular confirmation in many households when, at dinner, children receive the same amount of milk in different-sized glasses. Arguments about who got more inevitably occur.

Piaget's experiments related to qualitative differences in thinking were applied to social understandings as well. In one of his more famous moral dilemmas, young children were presented with the following problems and then asked if the children involved were equally guilty or if one was naughtier than the other. In either case, the children were asked to explain their reasoning.

> 1. A little boy who is called John is in his room. He is called to dinner. He goes into the dining room. But behind the door there was a chair, and on the chair there was a tray with fifteen cups on it. John couldn't have known that there was all this behind the door. He goes in, the door knocks against the tray, bang go the fifteen cups and they all get broken.
> 2. Once there was a little boy whose name was Henry. One day when his mother was out he tried to get some jam out of the cupboard. He climbed up on to a chair and stretched out his arm. But the jam was too high up and he couldn't reach it and have any. But while he was trying to get it he knocked over a cup. The cup fell down and broke. (Piaget, 1965, p. 122)

Through children's answers to problems such as these, Piaget identified two major stages of moral development: heteronomous and autonomous. The first of these stages is defined by children's belief in rules as unchangeable and emanating from outside themselves and their belief in the justification of external control and arbitrary punishment; the second, more mature stage is defined by their belief in subjectivity and intentionality in making moral decisions (Piaget, 1965). This line of research formed the basis for the more complex and refined work of Lawrence Kohlberg (see Chapter 3).

Advocates of moral education have relied on these developmental theories to provide the basis for pedagogical programs, arguing that an understanding of how individuals develop over time has direct bearing on the processes implemented in those programs. The advocates of character education, on the other hand, have not relied on these findings, arguing that the purposes of moral education are well established historically and in need only of consistent implementation.

Concurrently Larry Nucci in Chapter 2 reviews the argument for a distinction between these two notions of morality and convention, inferring that as children develop, they form increasingly more mature conceptions of each. He concludes that individuals at all points in their development may generate reasoning in response to Kohlbergian moral dilemmas that emphasize either justice or human welfare (moral thinking) or rules and authority (conventional thinking). In addition, if one reviews Kohlberg's own stage theory (see, e.g., Reimer, Paolitto, & Hersh, 1983), the first three of these stages are dominated by children's notions of right and wrong based on what others might do to them or think of them in response. Thus, when presented with dilemmas clearly constructed to elicit moral responses and themes, children of elementary and middle school age are likely to respond with conventional justifications.

An Emerging Synthesis

Though the underlying rationales may vary, the methods to enhance children's moral behaviors begin at this point to overlap. Thomas Lickona (1976) argues that children's judgments are very much subject to direct and indirect social influence, and so does Edward Wynne (Chapter 8). The two educators differ as to the control orientation necessary to bring about moral behavior, with Lickona arguing from the developmental perspective in Chapter 4 for teacher-student joint problem-resolution strategies and Wynne arguing for a more externally controlled environment. Larry Nucci, as has been noted, provides the intermediate perspective that although moral and social judgments are actually distinct entities, their separate existence does not preclude their coordination when resolving social problems.

This intermediate perspective has been explored in recent research comparing the effects on children's social development in elementary schools with disparate instructional systems and control orientations (Benninga & Tracz, 1988; Tracz & Benninga, 1989). Two schools were studied, and students in those schools were followed and assessed each year from the second through the fifth grades. One school's program stressed cooperative activities, intrinsic motivation, and student autonomy (Watson, Solomon, Battistich, Schaps, & Solomon, 1989), whereas the second school's program focused on student achievement of measurable goals and standards coupled with an external reward system for positive student activity. Students' social development was monitored in each of these 4 years through a series of individual, small-group, and large-group assessments (for a description of these measurements, see Solomon, Watson, Delucchi, Schaps, & Battistich, 1988; Stone, Solomon, Tauber, & Watson, 1989; Deer, Solomon, Watson, & Solomon, 1988).

After 4 years, results of this study indicated that teachers in each of these schools conducted their classrooms in ways consistent with their intentions; that is, the teachers in the intrinsic school used more cooperative activities and more programs designed to develop students' social understanding, whereas faculty in the external school used more points, rewards, and competitive structures. Teachers in the external school reported that their school was more businesslike, creative, and innovative; it also had more involved and supportive parents, a more supportive and accessible principal, a more traditional academic focus, a more pleasant atmosphere, and better relations between teachers and students. Students in this externally oriented school also scored higher on measures of self-esteem in the third and fourth grades than did students in the school emphasizing cooperative activities and intrinsic motivation. Students in the latter school, on the other hand, tended to be more helpful and supportive, and their teachers placed greater stress on positive interpersonal behavior. Despite these differences in the two approaches to educating children, the effects on students were not so well defined. In most cases, students did not differ significantly on measures related to resolving individual or group social problems. Both groups equaled the control group on measures of concern for others, liking for school, and many of the behaviors observed in the small-group tasks (Benninga et al., 1990).

Thus, although differences were evident in the manner in which classroom instruction was delivered and in the ways in which these programs were perceived by the teachers in them, students performed well in both school programs. Slavin (1987), in an attempt to reconcile these two points of view as related to cooperative learning research, has suggested that regardless of whether a school program emphasizes the developmental or the motivational perspective (e.g., the character education approach), both must emphasize active involvement of the learners in the school program, and students in both programs must come to realize that the learning and achievement of their classmates are important to their own. According to Slavin (1987), the position taken by the developmentalists to dismiss the importance of extrinsic incentives is not supportable. Group rewards and other incentives are central features of effective programs.

Thus effective programs in moral education must focus on concern for justice and human welfare as well as on the sound rules and organizational structures underlying social conventions and regulations. A common ground can now be established.

In reading the chapters by Sadowsky, Weintraub, Martin-Reynolds and Reynolds, and Sparks in Parts II and III, one finds that activities that enhance both the moral attitudes and character (or behavior) of students are possible through a variety of educational approaches. Though there are differences in the *why* of moral or character education, and these are clearly articulated by the authors of the first two chapters in Parts II and III, the differences begin to fade when the various ideas are put into practice, as illustrated in the last two chapters in each of those sections.

Despite how the various school programs described here differ in locus of control and in philosophical and psychological rationales for moral or character education, they adhere to similar practices. Thus whether children are expected to develop moral understandings through cooperative activities or through conforming to a set program, and whether the rewards for such understandings or behaviors are expected to come from within themselves or are presented externally, each approach to the common goal suggests similar activities for children. Teamwork, cooperation, concern for others, and academic excellence are recurring themes throughout each program described. This is also the case for the programs described in Part IV.

Evaluating Moral and Character Education Programs

How then can we know if what is being done in schools is consistent and effective? Education is, after all, an applied field. It is the job of the educator to take the best of our collective knowledge and apply it to the real world of children. Unless a school is able to translate its philosophy into practice, the philosophy is nonfunctional and may be counterproductive to its intended purposes. Philosophy gives meaning and direction to a school's actions, and in its absence, teachers and students are left to the whim of whatever is fashionable at the moment. Thus philosophy and its companion, psychology, take on added significance as they are used to justify classroom and school practices. School programs that are clear about their purposes, regardless of their approach, are most likely to offer their students that balance of experiences necessary to moral and character development.

At the same time, individuals (and schools), as argued by Slavin (1987), must be motivated to engage in such elaborated explanations and need to take their work seriously. Without some sort of recognition for their efforts, many may find these tasks burdensome. Carelessly implemented programs can result. But school faculties who can anticipate public affirmation and recognition are encouraged to devote extra time and energy to ensuring quality programs for their students. The ripple effect of such recognition can inspire efforts in other schools.

For the past 3 years, a group of educators in the Central Valley of California have organized a voluntary evaluation of moral education programs in elementary and middle schools. Known as the Values and Character Recognition Program, it was inspired by the For Character Program described by Wynne in Chapter 8 and locally sponsored by representatives of two large school districts, the University's School of Education and Human Development and the Fresno/Clovis chapter of Phi Delta Kappa.

Each year individual schools in each district are sent an application form asking them to document how they address a series of open-ended questions related to the enhancement of moral and character education. Participation is voluntary. The questions are generic, and no bias is intended; rather, the selection committee evaluates the consistency of responses and the quality of activities provided for the students in each school.

Responses in five broad areas are called for, and it is expected that each of the schools returning the application will demonstrate through its responses, and at the time of the follow-up site visit, evidence of performance in each area. The five areas include

1. School planning
2. Instructional activities
3. School goals, standards, and procedures
4. Opportunities for student involvement
5. Student recognition

Exemplary schools are awarded plaques each year at a local educational conference.

The questions posed and the types of responses given by the award-winning schools are indicative of the high quality of involvement of many elementary schools serving students at all socioeconomic levels. The selection committee expects differences in approaches, but the questions are important regardless of the community served by the school. The specific questions, with selected responses at the elementary level, are included below to give readers a sense of the variety of ongoing activities consistent with sound moral and character education.

Area 1: School Planning

Statement. The planning process is an essential ingredient in schools that are effective in meeting students' educational needs and providing meaningful activities for student participation. Plans should be based on a clear understanding of the kind of student the school desires to develop. The planning process should involve the community, parents, teachers, administrators, and students. Such planning provides direction to school efforts and indicates an organized approach to character and values education.

Question. Describe the kind of student your school wants to develop and provide evidence of planning and organization of your school's programs and/or activities as they relate to character and values education.

Responses from Elementary School Example 1. "To promote greater achievement through high expectations, a comprehensive educational program will be provided for all students with emphasis on basic skills instruction, the development of critical thinking skills, and development of a physically fit child.

"To promote a balanced educational program by providing students the opportunity of participating in a variety of enrichment activities and extra-curricular programs thereby ensuring experiences which develop respect, trust, and dignity for self and for others while teaching students to become responsible citizens.

"To provide a stimulating, effective educational program for all students by focusing on hands-on experiences, inquiry, activities and projects, and reading through content areas.

"This statement was derived through a collaborative approach of staff, key school planners and suggestions of parents who are representative community members of our School Site Council (SSC).

"After reaching consensus about our mission statement, it was printed and is displayed prominently in all classrooms, throughout our school—cafeteria, office, library, etc.—and is included in our Parent Handbook so that all students, staff and parents are aware of and can work together toward the goals stated therein."

Responses from Elementary School Example 2.   "Provide an environment that gives each child a sense of belonging, a feeling of pride in his background and his accomplishments and an understanding and appreciation for one's own and others' cultural and ethnic differences and likenesses.

"Provide a balanced and varied curriculum and experiences that enrich, enhance and extend over to all life situations.

"Expect mastery of skills and curriculum at all levels, giving each individual student the opportunity and time to achieve and progress at his or her own developmental rate and level.

"The entire student body, staff and many parents are involved in monthly programs that highlight the District 'Value of the Month.'"

Area 2: Instructional Activities

Statement.   School's that are effective in providing meaningful character and values education programs conduct classroom instruction and activities that relate to character and value development.

Question.   Cite specific activities that offer evidence that instruction in the area of character and values education is part of the school/classroom curriculum.

Responses

- Every teacher in the first through sixth grades uses a form of sociometric grouping for enhancing learning, motivation, and classroom discipline.
- Each teacher frequently rewards appropriate desired behavior and outstanding individual effort.
- A school Personal Responsibility Award has been established to recognize students' conduct, completion of assignments, promptness, attendance, and return of library books.
- A Refusal Skills, Say No, program for substance abuse is in place.
- A co-curricular program, including school sports, oral interpretation, chorus, spelling team, and history day competition, has been developed.
- Family, friendship, and feeling units are offered in all classes to promote healthy relationships.
- School Spirit Day is held and special T-shirts are worn.
- A school food drive is held during Thanksgiving season.
- A "Citizen of the Week" is announced in every classroom.
- Real-life classroom issues are discussed to develop better social understanding and improve reasoning about fairness.
- A Staff supervised intramural sports program has been established during lunch.
- Cross-age tutoring programs are in place.
- Pen pal programs between students in the same school and between students in middle school and their elementary feeder schools have been developed.
- Student mediators assist fellow students in positive conflict resolution strategies.

Area 3: School Goals, Standards, and Procedures

Statement. In schools that effectively implement value and character programs for students, rules of conduct, disciplinary procedures, standards, and expectations for all students are clearly understood.

Questions

1. What means are used to communicate school rules, school plans, and student expectancies to teachers, parents, and students?

2. Describe how teachers, parents, and students are involved in the development of school rules, school plans, and school expectancies for students.
3. How does your school evaluate the effectiveness of school rules, school plans, and school expectancies?
4. How does your school demonstrate to students, parents, and teachers its emphasis on values and desirable character qualities?

Responses

- The student-parent handbook, distributed at the beginning of the school year, is the basis for communicating the school's philosophy, rules, plans, procedures, and expectations.
- A regular newsletter is mailed home by the school.
- A newsletter is mailed home by the teacher.
- A special literature section has been established for parents in the school library.
- All communication to parents is in parents' dominant language.
- Home visits are made regularly by the teacher and principal.
- The student council and PTA suggest changes in rules and activities around the school.
- Parent input is given high priority, with suggestions followed and changes made whenever possible.
- There is frequent and open communication between principal, teachers, and parents about all school matters.
- An end-of-year survey is mailed to all parents to obtain parental rating and feedback about the school and about their child's educational experiences during the past year.
- A written plan is developed by the teacher for each child below grade level and is discussed with that child's parents.
- Bulletin boards with positive messages are posted around the school.
- Bulletin boards in the library, office, and cafeteria display student work.
- Special emphasis is given to helping students understand tolerance, patience, and acceptance as they work with mainstreamed students in their classes.
- A local convalescent hospital has "adopted" a school, and each week a different class walks to the hospital to entertain or just visit the residents.
- Well-planned reward assemblies are held regularly.

Area 4: Opportunities for Meaningful Student Involvement

Statement. In effective schools, the development of desirable character qualities includes opportunities for students to contribute in meaningful ways to the school and to others.

Questions

1. From the following list of activities provided at many elementary schools, please estimate the percentage of students that participate at your school.
   Academic competitions
   Instrumental music
   Choir
   School spirit activities
   Classroom/campus cleanup
   Class monitors, messengers, crossing guards, assistants, etc.
   Dramatic presentations
   Interscholastic sports
   Intramural sports
   School newspaper
   Cross-age or peer tutoring
   Well-organized academic group projects
   Community service
   Other (e.g., school clubs, school service organizations, etc.)
2. Describe how students are involved in the government of your school, how the members are chosen. What are the functions and responsibilities of the student government?

Responses. All schools that returned the application had a student council. In all cases, the elected officers were to be chosen from the fifth or sixth grades, with some schools opening the slate to fourth graders as well. Other grades elect class representatives. Although all councils discuss school problems with the principals, some councils do such things as operate a student store, coordinate food and shoe drives, and coordinate the Adopt-A-Class program within the school.

Area 5: Student Recognition

Statement. Students are motivated by recognition for achievement and participation in school activities. In turn, these recognitions encourage other students to become involved.

Questions

1. Describe the opportunities for students to earn awards and recognition as individuals or as members of groups or teams.
2. What methods are used in your school for recognizing students at the classroom and school level?

Responses

- Monthly Good Citizen luncheons are held.
- Cultural assemblies are held so that students (Hmong and Cambodian) can share their backgrounds with others.
- Morning announcements recognize specific good deeds and achievements.
- Well-planned assemblies are held monthly to recognize student achievement for academics, sports, and citizenship.
- Honor roll students and their parents are invited to breakfast each semester.
- Music students are given busts of famous composers.
- A party is given for students who consistently complete their homework well.
- A banquet is held each semester honoring students who perform well in all areas.
- Teachers send notes home, make phone calls, or give certificates for hamburgers, bumper stickers, and so on, to deserving students.

An evaluation of this sort serves several purposes. Although it is concrete in the questions posed, it allows for flexible responses. Each of the five areas requiring responses can be consistent with the purposes of either moral or character education, and schools favoring one approach over the other need not be constrained by the questions. Yet each question needs a full answer, and the sum of all answers should define the school program's direction. In the evaluation of moral education programs, expected goals must be stated together with evidence of activities in place to address those goals (Cline & Feldmesser, 1983), and the questionnaire described here fulfills both criteria.

A Word About Reliability and Validity

The evaluation outlined above should not be confused with controlled research. The idea behind such an evaluation is to recognize exemplary schools where practices and emphases have been planned to enhance the moral thinking and behavior of their students. It is not specifically designed to compare schools but rather to encourage all schools to participate in well-designed activities for students. The expectation is that any school, regardless of the population served or its philosophical orientation, can offer well-planned programs that enable students to participate fully and become active in the school community.

Still, it is necessary that the application clearly reflect a stable, dependable program that has been closely monitored. For this reason, the application form requests that relevant school documents be attached. A typical school may include as documentation its student/parent handbook, past copies of its school/classroom newspapers, photographs or announcements of special programs and activities, or other evidence that the school administration and students have, over time, given careful attention to its programs. This is one way to ensure program reliability without undue intrusion.

The question of validity seeks to determine if the program does what it says it does. To ensure validation, a team of four reviewers screens all applications and chooses finalists, after which separate teams of validators make site visits to each of these schools to obtain firsthand confirmation that the written data are operational.

Although there is some room for error in these approaches to ensuring the reliability and validity of the individual school program, the staff of the recognized schools and the review teams generally agree that the schools have been fairly evaluated and that they have been given ample opportunity to explain their programs and activities. Schools receiving the award are proud of their accomplishments and serve as models for other schools in their district.

Conclusion

It has not been the purpose of this book to make recommendations as to moral or character programs in elementary schools. Rather, we have sought to present clearly articulated positions with equally clear examples of the two dominant approaches and to present curricular options provided by major nonprofit organizations and for special populations of children. Finally, we offer an option for rewarding schools for their hard work, no matter what their philosophic orientation.

By examining these full descriptions, school personnel in charge of planning programs for children will be in a better position to choose and implement *consistently* and thereby offer more meaningful programs for their students. I hope this book will prove useful toward that end.

References

Benninga, J., & Tracz, S. (1988). *The effects of a competitive program on the prosocial attitudes and behaviors of elementary school children.* Paper presented to the American Educational Research Association, New Orleans.

Benninga, J., Tracz, S., Sparks, R., Solomon, D., Battistich, V., Delucchi, K., Sandoval, R., & Stanley, B. (1990). *Effects of two contrasting school programs on children's social development.* Working paper, California State University, Fresno.

Cline, F. C., & Feldmesser, R. A. (1983). *Program evaluation in moral education.* Princeton, NJ: Educational Testing Service.

Deer, J., Solomon, J., Watson, M., & Solomon, D. (1988). Assessment of children's motives, attitudes, values and perceptions. *Moral Education Forum, 13,* 18–34, 37.

Lickona, T. (1976). Research on Piaget's theory of moral development. In T. Lickona (Ed.), *Moral development and behavior: Theory, research and social issues* (pp. 219–240). New York: Holt, Rinehart & Winston.

Piaget, J. (1965). *The moral judgment of the child.* New York: Free Press.

Ravitch, D. (1985). American education: Has the pendulum swung once too often? In D. Ravitch (Ed.), *The schools we deserve: Reflections on the educational crises of our time* (pp. 80–89). New York: Basic Books.

Reimer, J., Paolitto, D. R., & Hersh, R. (1983). *Promoting moral growth: From Piaget to Kohlberg.* New York: Longman.

Slavin, R. E. (1987). Developmental and motivational perspectives on cooperative learning: A reconciliation. *Child Development, 58,* 1161–1167.

Solomon, D., Watson, M., Delucchi, K., Schaps, E., & Battistich, V. (1988). Enhancing children's prosocial behavior in the classroom. *American Educational Research Journal, 25,* 527–554.

Stone, C., Solomon, J., Tauber, M., & Watson, M. (1989). Procedures for assessing children's social behavior: Four-person tasks. *Moral Education Forum, 14,* 1–11.

Tanner, D., & Tanner, L. (1975). *Curriculum development: Theory into practice.* New York: MacMillan.

Tracz, S., & Benninga, J. (1989). *Effects of the accountability model on the prosocial attitudes and behaviors of elementary school children.* Paper presented to the American Educational Research Association, San Francisco.

Watson, M., Solomon, D., Battistich, V., Schaps, E., & Solomon, J. (1989). The child development project: Combining traditional and developmental approaches to values education. In L. Nucci (Ed.), *Moral development and character education: A dialogue* (pp. 51–92). Berkeley, CA: Mc-Cutchan.

About the Authors

William J. Bennett, U.S. secretary of education during the Reagan administration, is currently director of the United States Office of Drug Policy. He received his Ph.D. in political philosophy from the University of Texas and his law degree from Harvard University.

Jacques S. Benninga is professor of education at California State University, Fresno, and chair of the Department of Literacy and Early Education. He also serves as coordinator of the university's Liberal Studies program. He has written extensively on children's social and moral development and education. He received his Ph.D. from George Peabody College of Vanderbilt University in Nashville, Tennessee.

Robert M. Day is superintendent of the Kansas Neurological Institute in Topeka. Until assuming this position he was clinical director of the Parsons State Hospital in Parsons, Kansas. He received his Ph.D. in special education from Peabody College of Vanderbilt University in Nashville, Tennessee.

James Fox is associate professor, Department of Human Development and Learning, East Tennessee State University, Johnson City. He was previously Assistant Professor of Special Education and a Kennedy Center Research Scientist at Peabody College of Vanderbilt University in Nashville, Tennessee. He received his Ph.D. in psychology from the University of Tennessee.

Robert W. Howard is director of Community of Caring and Prevention/Intervention for the Sacramento Unified School District. He has done much work on democratic schooling and shared decision-making governance and has taught at Harvard, Northeastern, and Dartmouth. He received his Ed.D. from Harvard University.

Alita Zurav Letwin is director of educational services of the Center for Civic Education's Law in a Free Society Project. She is a specialist in staff and curriculum development at the elementary, secondary, and university levels and is writer and editor of instructional materials for the project. She received her M.S. degree from the Bank Street College of Education in New York.

Thomas Lickona is professor of education at the State University of New York at Cortland. His publications include *Moral Development and Behavior, Raising Good Children, Teaching Respect and Responsibility*, and many articles and book chapters related to children's moral development and education. He received his Ph.D. in psychology at the State University of New York at Albany.

JoAnne Martin-Reynolds is a professor in the Department of Educational Curriculum and Instruction at Bowling Green State University in Bowling Green, Ohio. She has published and presented extensively in the areas of supervision, rural education, and character development and serves as associate editor of *American Secondary Education*. She received her Ph.D. from Bowling Green State University.

Mary A. McEvoy is a research assistant professor of special education and a Kennedy Center research scientist at Peabody College of Vanderbilt University. She received her Ph.D. in child development and family relations from the University of Tennessee, Knoxville.

Larry Nucci is associate professor and chair of the Committee on Educational Psychology at the University of Illinois, Chicago. His publications include many articles on children's moral and conventional thinking and the book *Moral Development and Character Education: A Dialogue*. He received his Ph.D. in psychology from the University of California, Santa Cruz.

Carolyn Pereira is executive director of the Constitutional Rights Foundation-Chicago Project. She is the author of several texts and articles, which include *Educating for Citizenship, Citizens on Assignment, Drugs, the Constitution, and Public Policy*, and *From the School Newsroom to the Courtroom*. She has been active in service organizations in Chicago and was awarded the 1983 Liberty Bell Award by the Chicago Bar Association. Her M.A. in political science and education is from Northwestern University.

Bill Reynolds is a professor in the Department of Educational Administration and Supervision at Bowling Green State University in Bowling Green, Ohio. A former elementary and secondary teacher and administrator, Dr. Reynolds has published widely in the areas of administration, personnel development, rural education, and character development. He received his Ed.D from the University of Kansas, Lawrence.

Ethel Sadowsky is principal of the Heath School in Brookline, Massachusetts. Before coming to Heath, she was a teacher of English, co-chairperson of the English department, assistant to the headmaster, and housemaster at Brookline High School. She received her Ed.D from Harvard University.

Richard K. Sparks, Jr., is currently principal of Valley Oak Elementary School in Clovis, California. For 16 years he served as principal of Fort Washington Elementary School in Clovis, where his school was a 1985–86 recipient of the National Recognition Award presented by the United States Department of Education. He received his Ed.D from the University of the Pacific in Stockton, California.

Robert E. Valett is professor of education and human development, California State University, Fresno. He is the author of numerous books and articles related to education and child development and is locally active as a member of the Fresno Unified School District's advisory committee on Peace and Nuclear Age Education and its advisory committee on Moral and Civic Education. He received his Ed.D from the University of California at Los Angeles.

Robert Weintraub is currently assistant headmaster at Brookline High School in Brookline, Massachusetts. He was formerly principal at both the Runkle Elementary School in Brookline and City Magnet School in Lowell. He received his Ed.D from Harvard University.

Edward A. Wynne is professor, College of Education, University of Illinois at Chicago. He is a sociologist and essentially concerned with how young people move toward wholesome adulthood. This necessarily has led to his focus on schools as transmitters of moral values, because such values are a critical component of vital adult life. He has written or co-authored eight books and about 75 articles and book chapters. He received his Ed.D from the University of California, Berkeley.

Index